SECRETS OF
ORIGAMI
The Japanese art of Paper Folding

SECRETS OF

ORIGAMI

The Japanese art of Paper Folding

ROBERT HARBIN
illustrated by the author
photographs by
Kingsley Mitchell
and Robert Harbin

OCTOPUS BOOKS LIMITED
LONDON NEW YORK SYDNEY HONG KONG

Dedication

To all those paper folders who have given so generously of their creations to make this book possible.

To A. E. Bestall who, for so many years, has done so much to promote Origami in the Rupert Annuals, published by the Daily Express, London.

To the late Ligia Montoya, of Argentina, who for years did so much for the art, and who gave so liberally of her creations to all who asked her.

To Samuel Randlett and his late wife, Jean, who helped so unselfishly to make this book a success.

Since original preparation of this material Vicente Solorzano has died, and Adolfo Cerceda has moved to France.

Originally published by
Oldbourne Book Company
under the title
Secrets of Origami Old and New

This edition published by
Octopus Books Limited
30 Bouverie Street, London E C 4

This edition © Octopus Books Ltd, 1971
SBN 7064 0005 4

Printed in Czechoslovakia by Svoboda, Prague

Contents

INTRODUCTION

As with other books by Robert Harbin, my first reaction has been to wonder, "Why has this one never been written before?"

He tells of a pastime that was the delight of our childhood and has retained its attraction through life, a pastime that has been too long ignored in this country as a serious subject for publication. Neglect of this gentle craft is the more curious because, almost alone among one's earliest hobbies, it satisfies the natural urge for creating something out of nothing—or nearly nothing.

Most of us can remember the time when a page from a school exercise book seemed more worthily applied in making a paper dart, a boat, a bird's-head snapper or an airplane than as a vehicle for essays or algebra! Later, when we learned how to make a true square, the repertoire expanded quickly to include water-bombs, frogs, flapping birds and, if one was lucky, the Chinese Junk itself whose last manipulation, a double-pull that suddenly transforms a most unlikely shape into a graceful ship with sails ready for hoisting, is one of the thrills of the game.

Why has the matter generally stopped at that point? The reason may be that essential folds are so easily forgotten and that references in print have been mostly confined to odd pages in books of indoor amusements showing only the simplest figures.

Fortunately for us, among those who did not forget their early keenness was the South African, Robert Harbin, a much-travelled entertainer and magician. Being sure that his special interest was shared by many more than would normally admit it, he has pursued his quest with endless pertinacity in his journeyings, gradually discovering how universal is the practice of this fragile and innocent form of art, and how much more highly it is regarded in some other countries than in England.

With his accumulated knowledge gained from international specialists and with the results of his own experiments he produced his first considerable book *Paper Magic* (Oldbourne Press) containing enough material to keep one busy for months. Now, after one smaller book, comes this volume, fully illustrated by himself, which is in some degree a sequel to *Paper Magic*. While it contains many old favourites, its importance lies in the wealth of new models. He has "dipped the flag" to certain experts in different countries, giving the inventions of each a separate section.

Some of the work is necessarily not very easy, but all is eminently possible and the fact that Robert Harbin himself is a member of the Inner Magic Circle must not lead one to suppose that superhuman skill is needed. Many results may evolve from one early set of folds, just as a chess opening leads to a great variety of subsequent play; so he has started by describing certain Basic Folds that are well worth mastering before one savours the ensuing ingenuities. In his search for the sources of the craft he has traced its origin to Japan whence comes so much art of the most delicate perfection, and where paper-folding is termed ORIGAMI.

For myself as a less dedicated paper-folder it was a lucky day when I met Robert Harbin and had my interest re-lit by the warmth of his enthusiasm. I had intermittently, over a space of years occupied spare moments with the hobby and had even hit on certain curiosities afterwards published in *Rupert Annuals*, but he revealed how much more can be done with proper organisation and how widespread is the appeal of this intriguing pursuit.

The models in this book have sufficient variety of ease and complexity to recommend Origami to everyone as a fresh, amusing and sometimes exasperating pastime. For those who are experimenting for the first time with paper of different shapes and colours might I hazard a word of advice? You will probably produce happy and unexpected effects that seem new to you. When you do, be sure to keep a specimen or jot down a diagram. The procedures are so very easy to forget; as I once found to my sorrow.

Years ago I remember whiling away the time, during a long ride on the front seat of a 406 bus, by fiddling with two bus tickets interlocked by their slots. Suddenly I found I had made quite a reasonable spitfire. Making another I carried on and it turned into a little dog apparently baying at the moon. When it was placed on the shelf in front a small boy in the next seat called out, "Puppy Dog!" The quite ridiculous pleasure I derived from the spontaneous recognition of the invention by the eyes of a child made me determine to use it in another *Rupert Annual*. It had seemed so simple. Unfortunately, six months later, when I needed it, I found myself unable to make the thing. One necessary fold somewhere had eluded memory—and still eludes it.

The usefulness of Origami in schools, for training in manual dexterity, needs no emphasising. The concentration it calls for has still greater value in certain forms of occupational therapy. Apart from these, is it to be left as a pastime appealing only to children? There is certainly nothing in this book that will *not* interest a child. Equally it must appeal to the child in all of us. It is a joy just for its own sake, rewarding the neat-fingered with its engaging and quietly humorous results. And its possibilities are apparently inexhaustible.

ALFRED BESTALL

AUTHOR'S PREFACE

Origami experts are generally very jealous of their secrets. There are some folders who are extremely loth to part with details of construction of their favourite models under any circumstances whatsoever. For this reason, I am particularly happy to be able to reveal in this book many of the secrets of the great folders.

Thanks to names and addresses supplied to me by Mr. Gershon Legman, when I was compiling *Paper Magic*, I have been able to collect some really wonderful material, most of which you will find explained in this book.

Origami is of Japanese origin. The word, Origami, means paper folding, and the art is closely linked with traditional festivals, the giving of gifts, and the craft of doll making. If you wish to learn more of the history and application of paper folding, you would be well advised to obtain a copy of *The Art of Origami*, by Samuel Randlett. In Mr. Randlett's book you will find all you want to know about Origami.

At the time of writing, Mr. Randlett is compiling another fine work on contemporary folders (see Bibliography, Page 246) and we have taken great pains to ensure that there is no duplication, in this book and Mr. Randlett's, of the models explained.

The art of paper folding has spread from Japan to Spain and America, and in a small way to the Continent of Europe. It is from Spain and America that most of the material contained in this book has emanated.

At this moment a tremendous work on the subject has just been completed by Dr. Vicente Solórzano Sagredo, now living in Spain (see Bibliography). The book is an epitome of his life's work, so there is today a wealth of material ready for the enthusiast to turn to.

I am happy to think that *Paper Magic*, published in 1956, has played quite an important part in the sudden interest in the art, especially as far as the Western World is concerned. In that book, I tried to isolate various procedures, and generally to arrange methods in some sort of order. More lately, however, I have corresponded at great length with other Origami teachers, and between us we have adopted more or less the same formula when endeavouring to explain and illustrate the models.

I have tried to make each page of this book an adventure and a fresh experience. Some figures are explained in greater detail than others, and you will find the simpler procedures at the beginning. The more difficult ones are grouped in sections, so that you can get used to the particular style used by the creator of the figures in that group.

Whenever there has been a little space left over I have managed to slip in a traditional Japanese fold, or something else of equal interest.

You may well appreciate that few artists would be prepared to illustrate a work of this kind because of the thousands of hours' work involved. For this reason, I have been obliged to make the drawings myself, which has been no mean task. In each one I have done my best to show as clearly as possible the modus operandi. And at all times I have tried to make the finished article as attractive as possible in order to tempt you to fold.

ROBERT HARBIN

London, 1964

READ THIS CAREFULLY

Use good, thin, strong paper. If you can obtain a supply of Japanese Origami paper, so much the better. If not, there are a multitude of other papers which are suitable when cut to size. Various qualities of wrapping papers, brown paper, note paper and decorative paper give a wide choice for experiment. For the larger models, a good quality metallic paper can be used.

The paper you use must be cut accurately, otherwise the models will go wrong almost immediately. Your folds, too, must be done with precision, otherwise your models will go awry just as quickly as if the paper had been wrongly cut. The careful cutting and folding of your paper applies to whatever shape you are using—squares or rectangles.

Standard Japanese Origami papers measure 17·5 cms. square, 14·5 cms. square, and 12 cms. square. Most Japanese papers are coloured on one side only.

Do not try to make difficult models at the start. Begin at the beginning and familiarise yourself with the symbols, the various procedures, and the Bases, and then tackle the simpler models to be found in the earlier sections of the book.

The photographs—mainly they are of the models folded by the creators themselves—have been "loosened up" a little, so that you can easily see the correct result. These photographs should convince you that even the most difficult model is by no means impossible.

I have tried to include as much information as possible, so that you may be spared the irritation of having to search elsewhere. It is for this reason that many classical folds have been repeated.

This book does not pretend to cover the whole art, which would be impossible as the pastime is limitless. It does, however, offer you hours of entertainment—as well as first-rate mental and physical therapy—and opens up a creative world which is infinite.

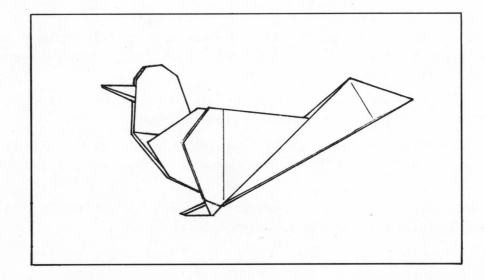

THE SYMBOLS
AND HOW TO USE THEM

The symbols on the opposite page are based on Akira Yoshizawa's code of lines and arrows, plus one or two others which I have added in the hope that the student will benefit.

When a *Valley Fold* is indicated by a series of dashes, make a concave crease (as the little diagram opposite shows). If, on the other hand, a *Mountain Fold* is indicated, by a series of dots and dashes (two dots in the West, and one dot in Japan), make a convex fold; in other words, fold under, and not in front. To fold under, you would of course turn the paper over, and then turn it back again.

Be sure to study the symbols on a diagram, because this will make all the difference to the ease with which you understand the procedures. Be sure, also, to note the difference between the arrows, because each one indicates a different job to do.

You will notice that various procedures have standard notations, or markings. After a while, you will recognise these markings, and will automatically make the necessary folds without having to refer to the instructions. On Page 16 you will see the standard notation for a *Rabbit's Ear*, and on Page 17 the notation for a *Petal Fold*. As soon as you know and recognise the different folds required you will be able to proceed without further help.

It has always been found difficult to indicate that after one flap in a model has been folded in a certain way, other similar flaps behind or at the side are to be treated in the same way. For this reason, I have devised a little arrow with a bar or bars across its stem (see opposite page), which indicates that the same fold must be repeated on similar flaps—the number of flaps is shown by the number of cross-bars. The Lily (Page 48) is a good example of the use of this arrow, which can, of course, be used in front or behind.

The symbols are designed so that they can be understood internationally, regardless of the language problem, and, what is more, a thorough understanding of the symbols should enable the student to ignore the instructions.

Do not be confused by the *Turn Over* symbol; just turn the model over in the direction of the arrow, and adjust it so that it lines up with the next diagram.

Japanese illustrators simply make a *Valley Fold* symbol and expect you to know what to do. You will notice, however, that I give the symbol, plus an arrow or arrows, so that you are doubly informed.

Finally, I cannot stress too much the importance of making yourself familiar with these simple symbols. You will find that they tell the whole story.

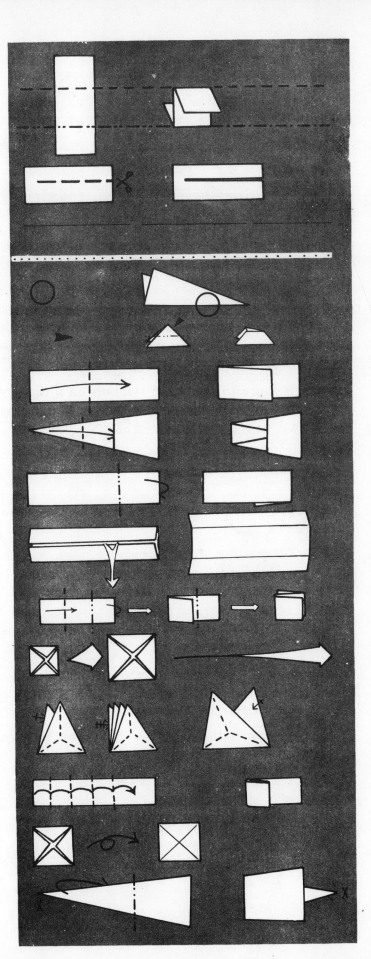

lley Fold (series of dashes).

untain Fold (series of dots and dashes; two dots the West, and one dot in Japan).

t along here (long heavy dashes and a scissor nbol).

ease (a thin line).

ray view, future, or past position.

ld here.

sh in, or sink, where the black arrow indicates.

ld in front in this direction.

ld into, or under.

ld behind in this direction.

en out after folding (the next diagram will show w much).

llow through, from fold to fold (used for ad- ional folds).

larged view of model.

peat same fold or folds with similar flaps, as any times as there are cross-bars.

ld over and over.

urn model over in direction of this arrow.

atch this spot, or spots.

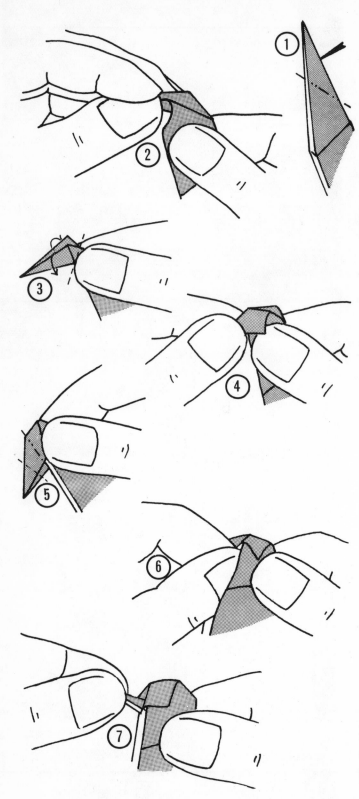

BE SURE TO STUDY THESE PAGES ON FOLDING

If you are folding for the first time you ma~~y~~ wonder just how to hold the models. The eigh~~t~~ drawings on the left show how a bird's head ~~is~~ formed.

1. You are required to reverse fold this poin~~t.~~

2. If you are right-handed grip with the rig~~ht~~ hand and work with the left. Here the poin~~t~~ is pulled down between the right finger an~~d~~ thumb.

3. This is the result. Now you are required t~~o~~ fold the head flaps back and front.

4. The left thumb and fingers do this. Rig~~ht~~ fingers and thumb move up and press th~~e~~ fold flat . . .

5. . . . like this. Now you are required to fol~~d~~ the beak.

6. The left thumb and fingers grip the tip an~~d~~ push into and out of the head . . .

7. . . . like this. The right thumb and finge~~rs~~ press the head flat.

8. Here is the completed head.

For some reason the left hand which you do n~~ot~~ normally use (the opposite if you a left-hande~~d)~~ seems able to do the difficult little folds while th~~e~~ right thumb and fingers do the holding.

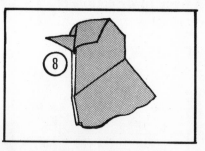

The finished head.

everse Folds

Here are various examples of Reverse Folds Study
e notations, or markings.

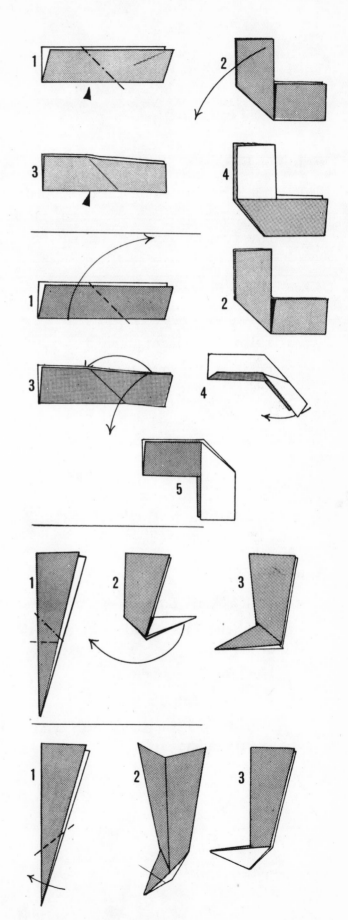

ush-In type of Reverse Fold

1. Crease along the marked line.
2. Unfold.
3. Push in, or Reverse Fold.
4. Reverse Fold completed.

aside-Out type of Reverse Fold

1. Crease along the marked line.
2. Unfold.
3. Turn arrowed flaps inside-out.
4. Fold half done.
5. Fold completed.

everse Folds combined to make a Foot

1. Reverse Fold along the Mountain symbol.
2. Completed, now Reverse Fold along the
   Valley symbol (Fig. 1).
3. Foot completed.

ingle Reverse Fold make a Foot

1. Reverse Fold (inside-out).
2. Half done.
3. Foot completed (the other way up, it is a
   Head).

15

Crimp

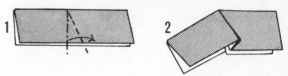

1. Two Reverse Folds are indicated. Crease along marked lines, and fold.

2. Fold completed.

Rabbit's Ear

A Rabbit's Ear procedure can be applied to any flap of paper.

1. The standard markings for a Rabbit's Ear.

2. Valley Fold.

3. Valley Fold made; unfold.

4. Valley Fold again.

5. Valley Fold made; unfold.

6. Fold the flap into the creases made, and fold the point over to the left.

7. Half done.

8. Rabbit's Ear completed.

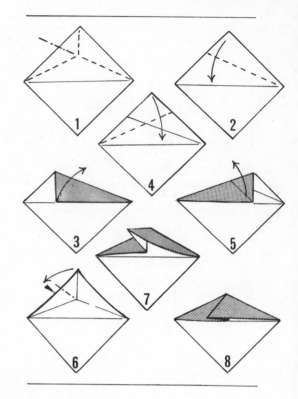

Squash Fold

Start with a Water Bomb Base (*Page* 20).

1. Make the Valley Fold indicated at the base of the flap.

2. Hold the flap upright, and squash it.

3. Squashing half done.

4. Squash Fold completed, with centre crease exactly in line.

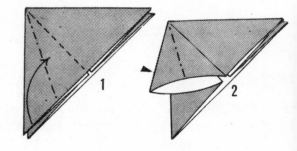

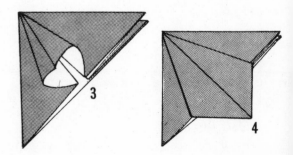

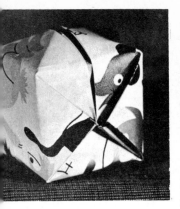

Water Bomb. (Above)
ditional Japanese.

2. New and Traditional Decorations. (Above)

3. Bookcase. Traditional Japanese. (Left)

New and Traditional
Designs

4. Dragonfly. Traditional Japanese. (Below)

6. *Seal.* *(Right)*

5. *Bird in Flight.* *(Below)*

7. *Harbin's Macaw.* *(Right)*

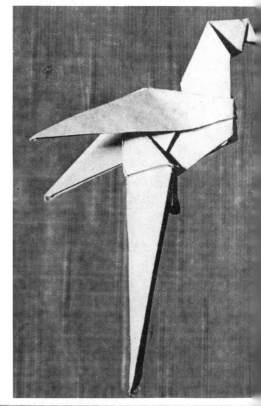

Designs by Robert Harbin

8. *Card-Table.* *(Below)*

9. *Harbin's Bat.* *(Below)*

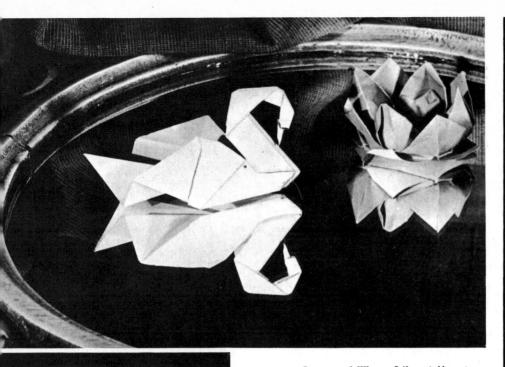

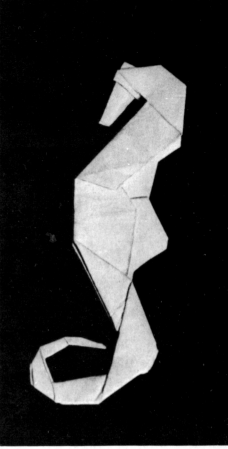

10. *Swan and Water-Lily.* *(Above)*

12. *Sea-Horse.* *(Right)*

11. *Montoya's Macaw.* *(Left)*

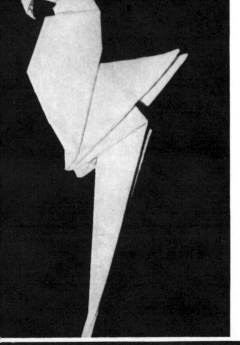

Designs by Ligia Montoya

14. *Pigeon.* *(Below)*

13. *Pelican.* *(Below)*

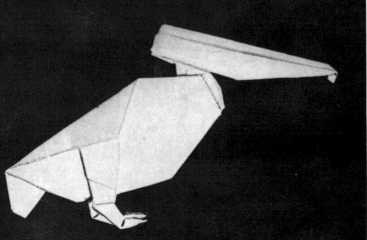

15. *The Creche. Ligia Montoya.*

16. *Group of Tropical Birds.*
Ligia Montoya. (Left)

17. *Japanese Vase. John Nordquist. (Below)*

Designs by Ligia Montoya,

John Nordquist and Jack Skillman

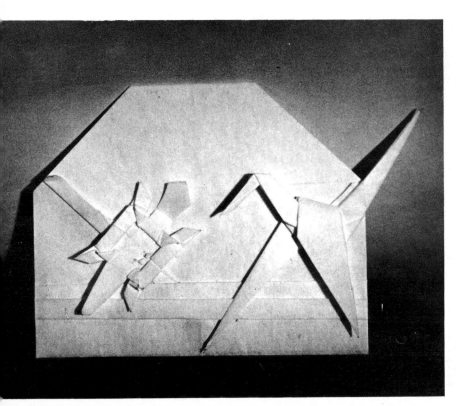

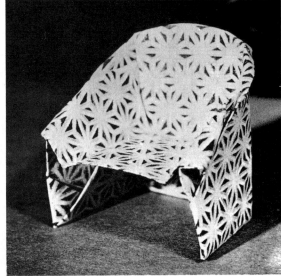

Helmet with Tortoise and Crane. John Nordquist.

18. *Armchair. Jack L. Skillman*

20. *Moor on Horseback.*

21. *Adolfo's Peacock.*

Designs by

Adolfo Cerceda

22. *Adolfo's Angel.*

23. *Adolfo's Pig. (Below)*

Hiawatha. (Above)

25. Fisherman in a Boat. (Above)

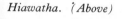

Designs by

Neal Elias

26. *Sitting Scottie Dog and Reclining Scottie Dog. (Left)*

Goat. (Below)

28. Stork with Baby. (Below)

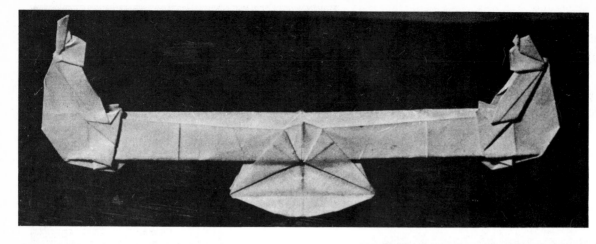

29. See-Saw. (Left)

34. Hippopotam
(Rig

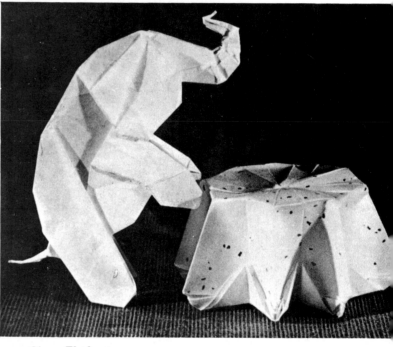

31. Circus Elephant

30. Circus Pony. (Left)

32. Rohm's Pig. (Below)

Designs by Fred Rohm

35. *Performing Seal.* (Right)

Santa Claus.

t's Magic.
(Right)

37. *Vera Cruz.* (Below)

38. *Neale's Elephant.*

39. *Giraffe. (Right)*

40. *Flamingo.*

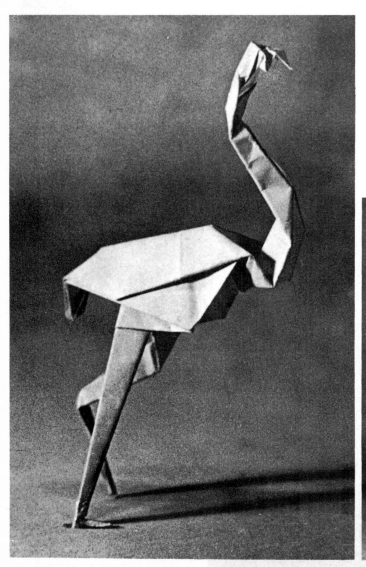

Designs

41. *Matador and Bull. (Below)*

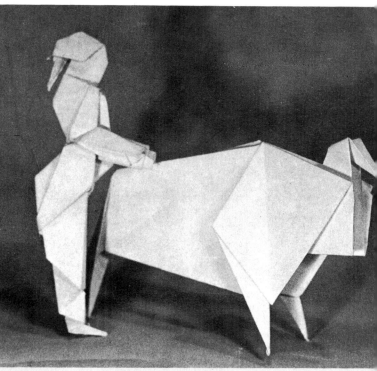

43. *Parakeet in Flight.* *(Right)*

...orilla. *(Below)*

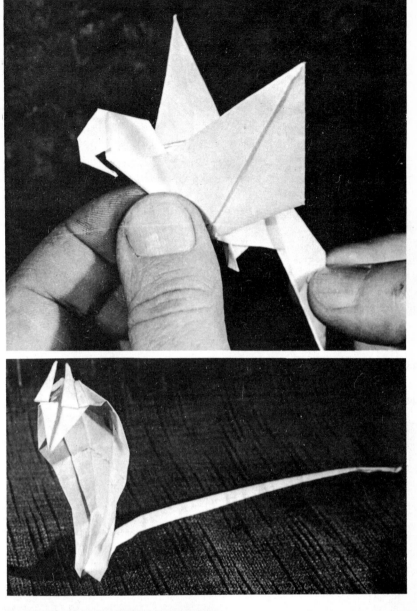

...bert Neale

44. *Neale's Cobra.* *(Above)*

45. *Neale's Humming Bird.*
(Left)

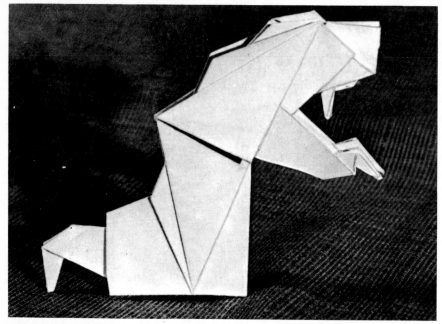

46. *Moor at Prayer. Traditional Spanish.*

47. *Rhoads's Llama.* *(Above)*

Designs by George Rhoads and Others

50. *Sleeping Bat. George Rhoads.* *(Below)*

48. *Husky Dog. Alan Cohen and Samuel Randlett.*

49. *Rhoads's Bat.* *(Below)*

Petal Fold (1)

Begin with a Squash Fold (*see previous page*).

1. Make Valley Fold creases along the Mountain Fold marks, and unfold. Lift flap upwards.

2. Flap half up, and sides now Valley Folding inwards.

3. Procedure completed. Press flat.

Petal Fold (2)

Here is another form of the Petal Fold, with typical markings. You will come into contact with this version often.

4. First make Valley Fold creases on the Valley Fold lines, then lift the straight edge flap upwards.

5. Here the Petal Fold is completed.

When the Frog Base (*Page* 19) is being developed into a Frog, or a Lily, or something similar, you will have to make four Petal Folds like the above. The first Petal Fold method could be applied, but it would leave the small triangular flap (*shown in Fig.* 5) in a down position, and not up, as it is in this case.

BASES (1)

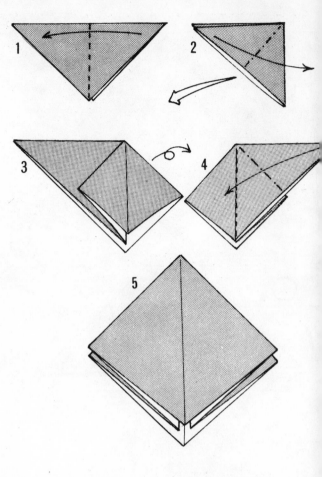

Preliminary Fold

Mr. Samuel Randlett and I have agreed that this should be called a Preliminary Fold, rather than a Base, because two Bases are made from it—the Bird Base and the Frog Base.

1. Fold a square in half diagonally. Make the Valley Fold as indicated.

2. Now Squash-fold the flap marked.

3. After Squash-folding, turn the model over.

4. Squash-fold the flap indicated.

5. Preliminary Fold completed.

Note: In *Paper Magic*, by Robert Harbin, the Bases were given numbers. This system has been dropped in this volume, as names are easier to remember.

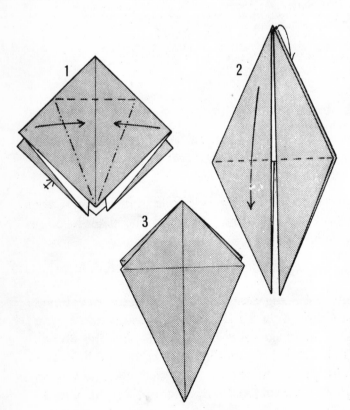

Bird Base

The most important of all Bases. In Japan, Spain, and America, the Bird Base is the beginning —and, indeed, the inspiration—for most of the famous models.

1. Begin with the Preliminary Fold, open end downwards. Study the markings, which indicate a Petal Fold, and make the folds in front and behind.

2. Petal Folds completed. Now Valley-fold the top flaps downwards in front and behind.

3. Here is the completed Bird Base. See it in use on page 24.

You will find that the second position of the Bird Base is the one most used when beginning a model, and it is the position automatically arrived at when the Bird Base is made.

You will find throughout the book that constant reference is made to this second position.

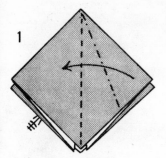

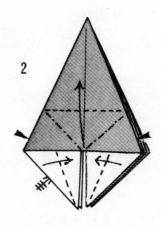

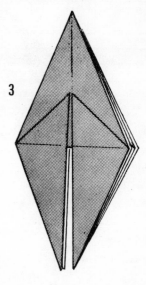

Frog Base

Begin with the Preliminary Fold (*Page* 18), open end downwards.

1. Squash-fold the flap indicated, and repeat with the other three similar flaps. This is indicated by the Repeat-fold symbol.

2. Petal-fold the open side and repeat with the three similar sides. You will find these sides by opening the flaps like leaves of a book.

3. Frog Base completed. When it is finished, be sure that you have four flaps on each side of the centre line.

Blintz Fold

(A Preliminary Fold)

When the four corners of a piece of paper are folded to the centre, we say the paper has been Blintzed, or Blintz-folded. This is an Americanism, which stems from the method of folding the dough for a Blintz—a famous type of bun.

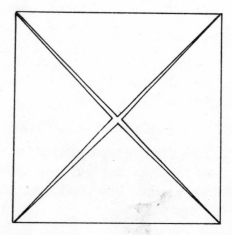

B A S E S (3)

Diamond Base

1. Begin with a square of paper with two sides folded to the middle. Make the two Valley Folds.

2. Diamond Base completed.

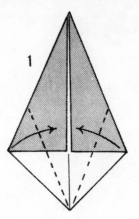

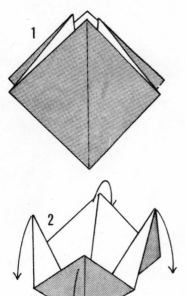

Water Bomb Base

This is the best-known Base, because of the Water Bomb associated with it (*see Page* 50).

1. Start with the Preliminary Fold shown on the previous page. Turn this fold inside out.

2. Almost inside out.

3. Inside out. This is the Water Bomb Base, which can be produced in several other ways, as will be shown later.

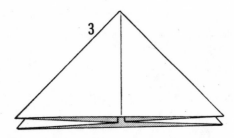

Fish Base

1. Start with a Diamond Base. Pull up and out the two flaps indicated, making two Rabbits' Ears.

2. Fish Base completed in its first form.

3. Fish Base in its second form, with top flap of Fig. 2 folded back and behind.

Another method for producing Fig. 2 can be seen on Page 93.

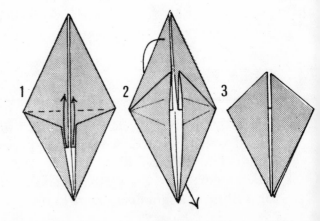

20

SINKING

When you are required to "Sink a corner", you will find that the procedure is indicated by a Mountain Fold and the Push Arrow.

In this example, the top of a Bird Base has to be sunk.

1. Crease along the marked line by Valley-folding and Mountain-folding.

2. The creases made, grip the model at the "Hold" points indicated, and pull slightly.

3. Release, and pull on two other corners, and so on until the top flattens. Now gently push the top in and refold.

4. Here you see the process completed, and the point sunk.

5. Here is another example of Sinking a corner. Crease as you did in the first case, and then pull the obtuse corner into shape. In this case, there will be only three points to pull on, but the result is the same. Flatten out and sink.

6. Operation Sink completed, and you are ready for the next instructions.

Many of the wonderful models illustrated in this book require you to Sink corners. Do not confuse the instructions with corners that merely have to be folded in; these will have the Mountain Fold or Valley Fold symbols, without the black "Push" symbols. Please watch carefully for these variations.

AN EXERCISE IN FOLDING

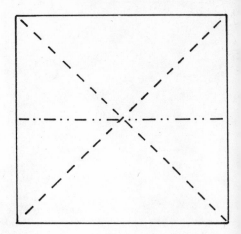

Water Bomb Base

Here you have a square notated in such a manner that you should know you are required to make a Water Bomb Base. You can either do this by following the instructions for the Water Bomb Base on Page 20, or you can do the following:

Valley-fold creases along the diagonals marked. Turn paper over, and crease along the middle (Mountain Fold).

Turn paper over again, and bring the corners together, and the Water Bomb Base will practically fall into place.

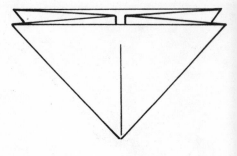

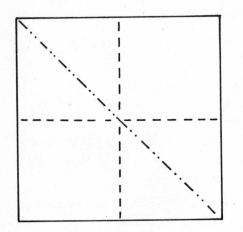

Preliminary Fold

One again, you can arrive at this either by following the instructions (Preliminary Fold, *Page* 18), or you can do the following:

Valley-fold across the middle both ways. Side must meet side exactly.

Turn over, and make a diagonal Mountain Fold.

Turn over again, bringing the corners together, and once again, the paper will fall into place.

When you are making creases, make them well, by rubbing the thumb nail along the crease. Good creases help you to make perfect models.

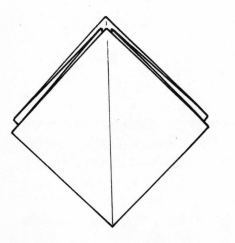

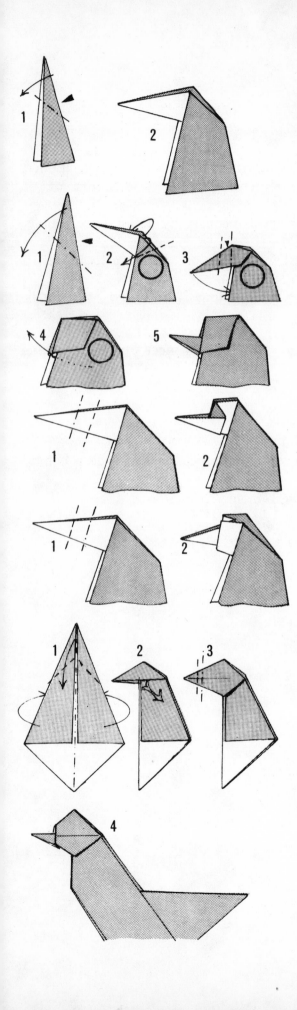

FOLDS IN COMMON USE

Simple Bird Head

    1. Note the markings, and fold accordingly.

    2. The completed head (Reverse Fold, *Page* 14).

Bird Head (*after Akira Yoshizawa*)

    1. Reverse-fold.

    2. Reverse-fold again.

    3. Crease, and then make a deep Crimp. In other words, Reverse-fold in and out. Grip the neck, and work with the left thumb and finger.

    4 and 5. The Figures show what happens.

Bird Head (*Akira Yoshizawa and others*)

    1. Reverse-fold twice outside.

    2. The head completed.

Bird Head (*the opposite of the above*)

    1 and 2. Reverse-fold twice *inside*.

Advanced Bird Head (*Yoshizawa and others*)

    1. For practice purposes, start with the square of paper, sides folded to the diagonal. Make a Rabbit's Ear, and Mountain-fold the model in half.

    2. Folds completed. Now open out the head, and pull down the little flaps underneath to form a diamond shape.

    3. The head opened out. Make the beak with two inside Reverse Folds.

    4. The head completed.

By altering the length of the Reverse Folds, you can alter the character of the head to resemble different birds. Many examples are given in this book.

BASES (4)

Blintz Bird Base

This is arrived at by folding a Bird Base on to a Blintzed square of paper. This can be applied to any of the basic folds. The purpose of the Blintzing is to make advanced models with lots of legs, or decorations with many points.

The Blintz principle seems to have been originated simultaneously by about four people, so I will not try to pinpoint its conception.

The best model made from this Base is Rhoad's Elephant, details of which are to appear in Mr. Randlett's book (*see Bibliography*).

A piece of paper with one coloured side should be used; the colour is indicated by a tint in the diagrams.

1. Fold the four corners of the square to the centre, so that they meet where the creases cross. Turn the model over.
2. Valley-fold.
3. Squash-fold the flap indicated.
4. Squash Fold completed.
5. Squash-fold the flap indicated.
6. Squash Fold completed. Petal-fold the top flap, and repeat with the flap behind (*see arrow*).
7. Carefully open out the model and pull out the Blintzed flaps.
8. Half done.
9. Almost completed.
10. Completed. Now Mountain-fold the model.
    Finally—the Blintz Bird Base.

Please note that although you are now able to produce this most useful base which gives you many points to work with, it is only partially used in this book.

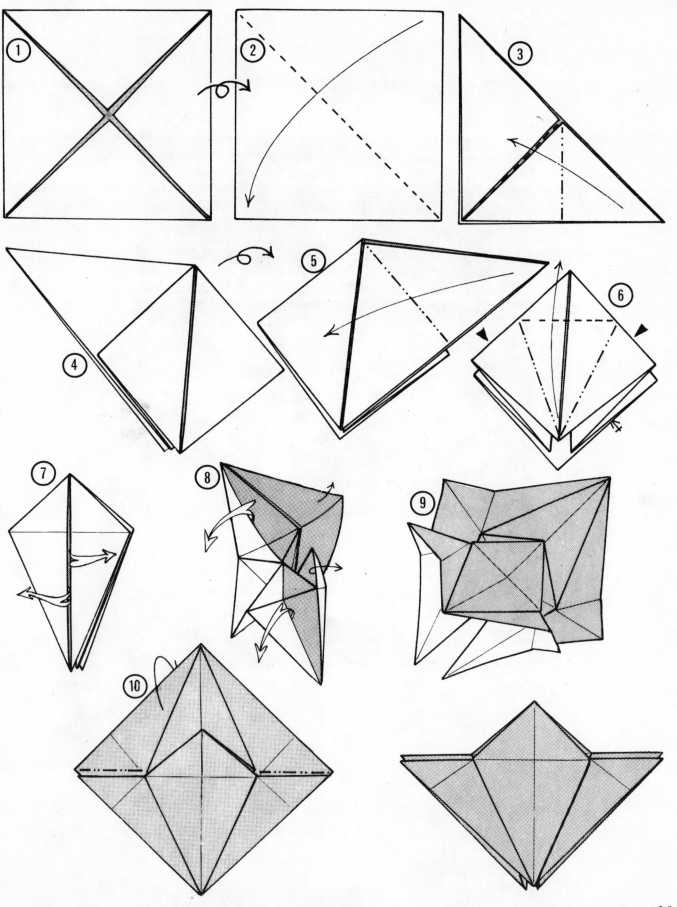

When you have thoroughly mastered the foregoing procedures and folds in general use you can now proceed to bring to life some of the wonderful models which will be laid before you from now on. Take care to do the simpler ones at first and when just a little expert try those more difficult.

ORIGAMI

NEW AND
OLD
DESIGNS

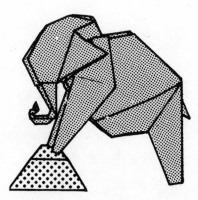

THE MULTIFORM

Origin: *Japan*. Traditional.

The name "Multiform" was first applied in *Paper Magic*, and has now become the general term. The basis is the Envelope, or Blintz Fold. Use a square of paper which has been creased diagonally and across the middle.

1. Fold corner flaps to the centre.
2. Turn over.
3. Valley-fold the corner flaps to the centre.
4. Enlarged view. Turn the model over.
5. Valley-fold the interior. Mountain-fold the corners.
6. Folding half done.
7. The SALT CELLAR (a famous model) completed.
8. Begin with Fold 5. Valley-fold corner flaps to centre.
9. Open up to 10.
10. Press corners together, and the model will fall into shape.
11. The shape. Mountain-fold the model in half.
12. THE CATAMARAN.
13. Begin with Fold 11. Valley-fold the two flaps indicated.
14. THE WINDMILL. Mountain-fold upper half. Arrowed flap moves right.
15. SEAT or VASE. Valley-fold flap indicated to the left.
16. Sideways view—BOAT WITH SAIL. Reverse-fold the head.
17. THE HOBBY-HORSE. This is a favourite model on the continent.
18. Begin with Fold 11. Pull the inside flaps out, and Mountain-fold the model.
19. Valley-fold the flaps indicated to the centre. Repeat behind.
20. Valley-fold the front flap downwards. Repeat behind.
21. Open up the model.
22. THE CONTAINER.
23. Squash the box.
24. Half done.
25. Completed. Mountain-fold the two flaps indicated.
26. Mountain-fold the model in half.
27. Hold at the points indicated, and pull in the direction of the arrows.
28. Open up the arrowed flaps.
29. Finally, the famous CHINESE JUNK.

SHELL DECORATION

Origin: *Spanish*.

1. Begin with Fold 2 above. Carefully pleat four flaps.
2. Completed. Turn over.
3. Valley-fold the corner flaps to the centre, where a drop of gum is waiting.

Finally, THE SHELL DECORATION. A number of these can be pasted on articles to be decorated.

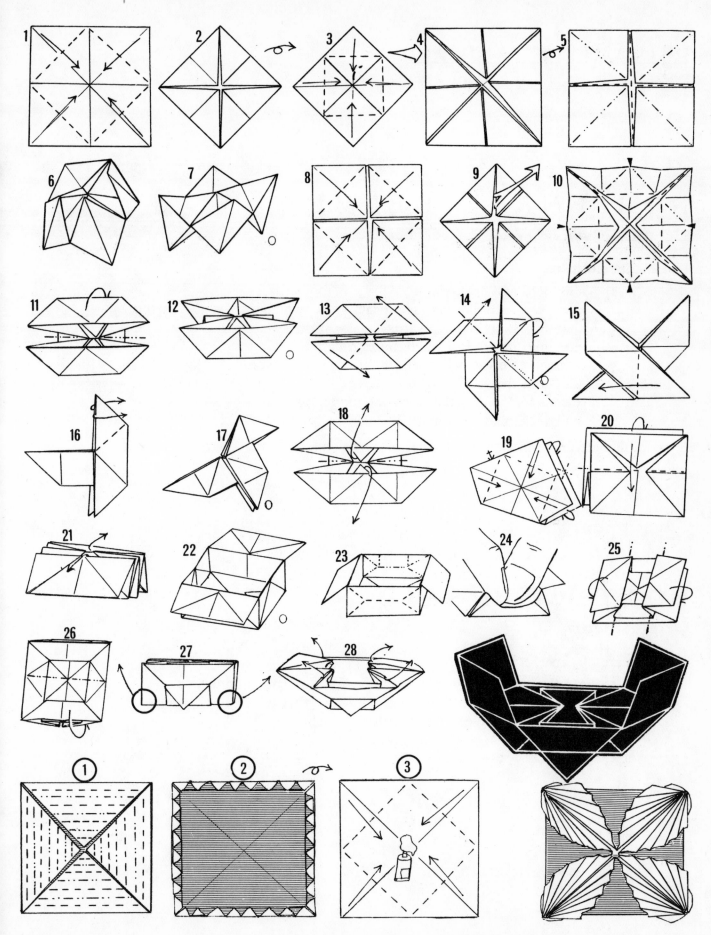

NORSEMAN'S HELMET

Origin: *Spain.* Dr. Vicente Solórzano.

Use a square of paper.

1. Valley-fold and crease well.
2. Valley-fold both flaps to meet exactly the two corners at the bottom.
3. Valley-fold both flaps upwards.
4. Valley-fold upwards a single bottom flap.
5. Mountain-fold the edges, and turn the model over.
6. Valley-fold the single flap upwards.
7. Previous fold completed, turn the model over.
   Finally, the model completed.

A wearable hat can be made from a sheet of paper about 50 cm. square.

BOAT WITH SAIL

Origin: *Japan.*

Use a square of paper.

1. Fold the square diagonally. Reverse-fold the corner indicated.
2. Mountain-fold the bottom of the boat, so that it will stand firmly.
   Finally, the completed boat with sail.

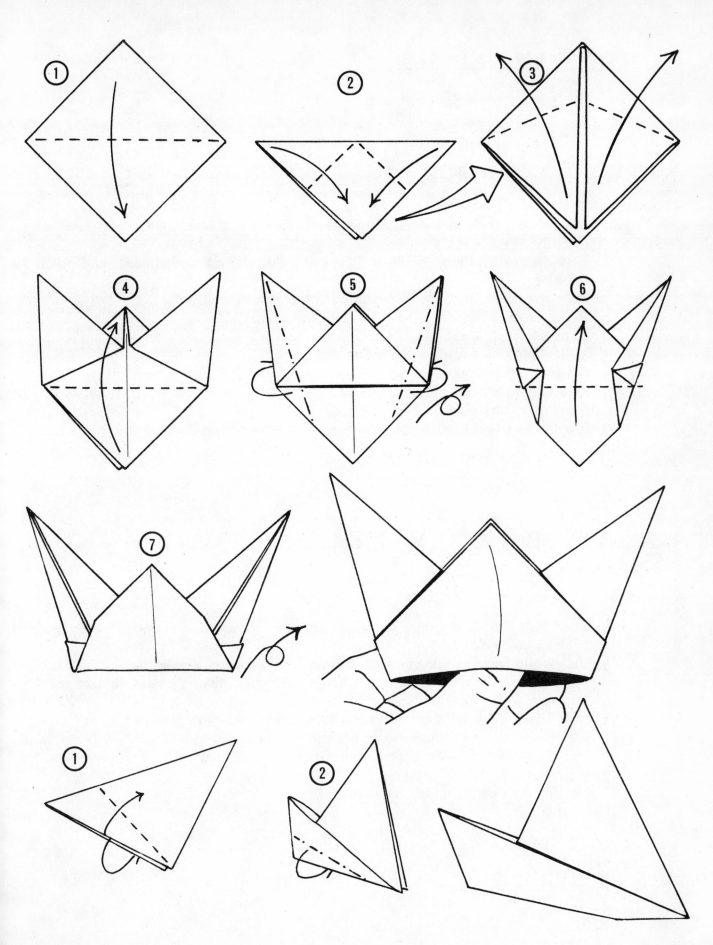

NOVELTY PURSE

Origin: *Japan. Akira Yoshijawa.*

Use a square of paper coloured on one side.

1. Begin with Fish Base, position 2 (*Page* 20). Pull down arrowed edges and watch the markings.
2. Half-way down, with tip of model moving down as well.
3. Right down. Valley-fold the three flaps upwards.
4. Repeat folds 1, 2 and 3 with the flap marked.
5. Valley-fold downwards a single flap only.
6. Squash-fold both pointed flaps.
7. One flap squashed. Valley-fold small triangle to the right. Repeat folds with the similar flap on the left.
   Finally, the completed purse, which is most attractive in two colours.

FANCY BOX ON LEGS

Origin: *Japan.*

Use a square of paper, coloured or plain.

8. Start with Bird Base (*Page* 18,) separate points upwards. Valley-fold flaps upwards in front and behind.
9. Valley-fold front flap downwards. Repeat with the three similar flaps.
10. Flaps folded down back and front. Open up hidden flaps by book-folding the flaps sideways. Valley-fold the flaps.
11. Now Valley-fold the obtuse corners. Repeat with six other corners.
12. All obtuse corners folded down. Mountain-fold under the legs. With finger inside and thumb on top, press edge flat with right hand Repeat with three other legs.
13. Finger inside, thumb on top.
    Finally, the opened-up box on legs.

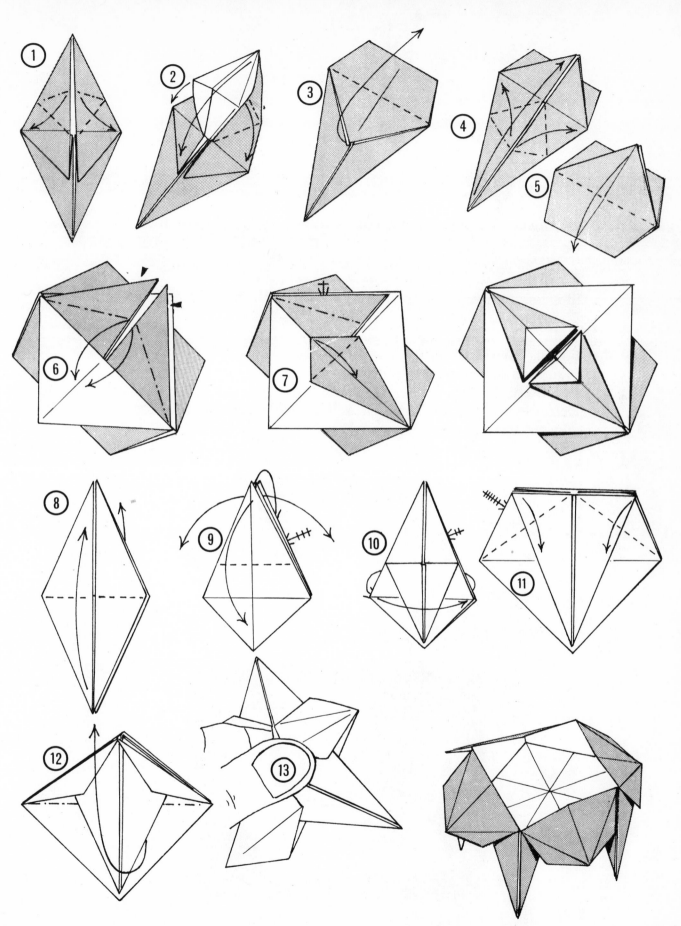

FANCY BOX

Origin: *Box, Japan; Pleating, Argentine.*

Use a square of paper, which must be coloured on one side.

1. Blintz the square. (Four corners Valley-folded to centre.)
2. Blintzing complete, turn the model over.
3. Blintz corners again. (Four corners Valley-folded.)
4. Valley-fold the four flaps or corners as indicated, outwards.
5. Folding completed, turn the model over.
6. Pleat carefully each of the four single-thickness flaps. Valley-fold and Mountain-fold alternately.
7. Here you see two flaps completed, with one flap on the way and one flap still to be folded.
8. With all flaps complete, place fingers of the left hand into each corner, one by one, and open the model up.
9. With thumb and forefinger of right hand press the corners together.
   Finally, the finished model.

This easy model makes a splendid container for sweets and gifts.

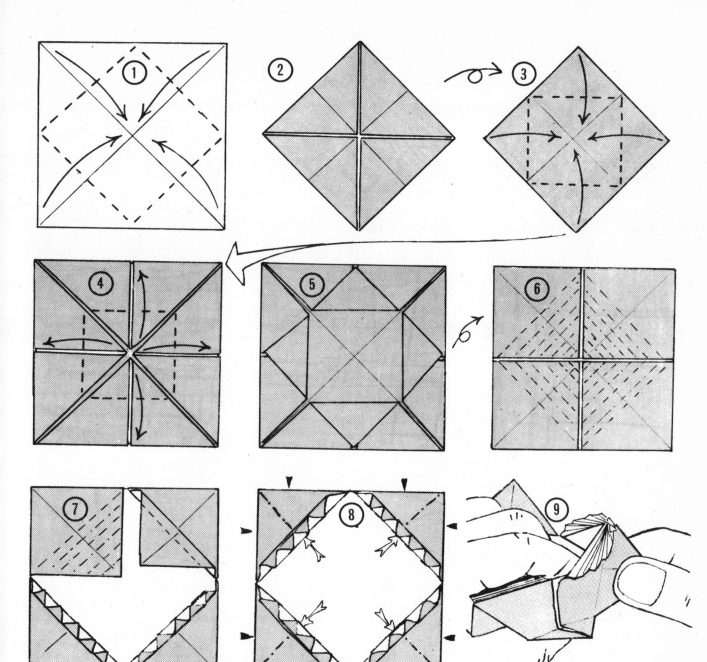

The Japanese make a similar box but the flaps in
Fig. 6 (above) are folded over and over and not
pleated.

SQUASHED BIRD BASE PATTERNS

Origin: Universal. Many folders.

Use a square of paper. Fold a Bird Base position 3 (*Page* 18).

1. Valley-fold all four flaps upwards.
2. Valley-fold the corner flaps to the centre in front and repeat behind.
3. Hold in the same way as Persimmon (*Page* 42).
4. Open out and flatten.
5. The squashed Bird Base completed.

This fold is the source of any number of stars. Six possibilities are shown on the left and right and it is left to you to work them out. Second from the bottom on the left was worked out by Adolfo Cerceda and also by Samuel Randlett. The position 5 is turned over and can be seen on the left.

Try squash folding the four inside flaps on the left and start from there. You will be surprised how many stars you will be able to form.

Here no explanation is given as to how the results may be arrived at; so from time to time see whether you can solve these folding problems, and in doing so produce many other results not drawn here.

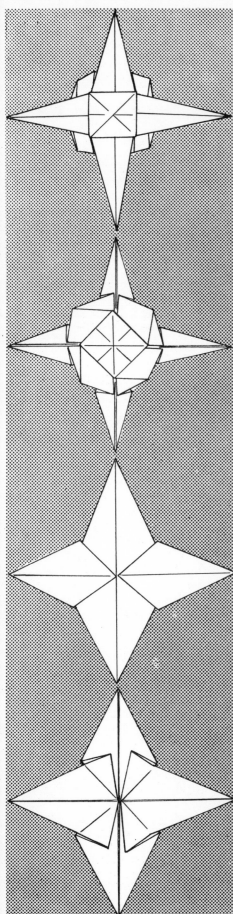

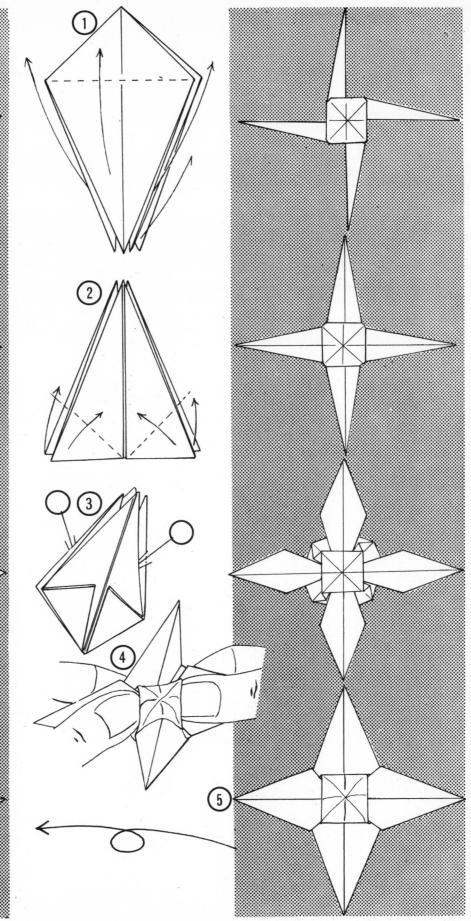

1

2

3

4

5

JAPANESE PURSE

Origin: *Japan*. Discovered by John M. Nordquist.

Use a square of paper, coloured on one side.

1. Make the middle creases. Pencil lines where the Valley Fold symbols are shown.
2. Valley-fold each corner to make good sharp creases.
3. All creases made, Valley-fold the corner indicated.
4. Valley-fold the arrowed corner over to the spot X at the base of the crease.
5. With the finger, hold at the spot shown, and Valley-fold the arrowed corner along the prepared crease.
6. Operation complete. Now crease heavily each corner.
7. All corners creased, gently push the corners together.
8. All corners together, and forming a kind of swastika, Sink all obtuse angle corners. Finally, the purse complete. If the paper is fairly stiff and the purse is opened out, it will spring back into shape.

CICADA

Origin: *Japan*.

Use a square of paper, green on one side.

1. Valley-fold across the diagonal. Make the two folds shown.
2. Valley-fold the flaps downwards.
3. Valley-fold a single top flap downwards.
4. Valley-fold the next top flap downwards.
5. Mountain-fold both sides.
6. Mountain-fold the two corners of the head. Turn model over.
   Finally, the Cicada ready to sing!

This is a very popular model and there are many variations of it.

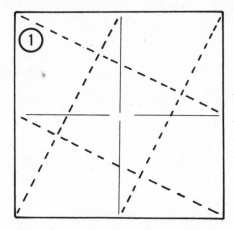

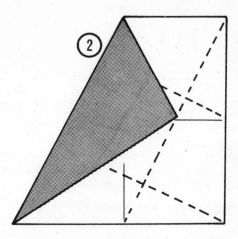

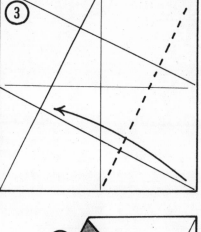

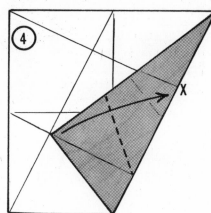

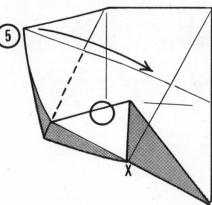

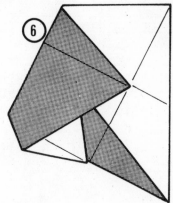

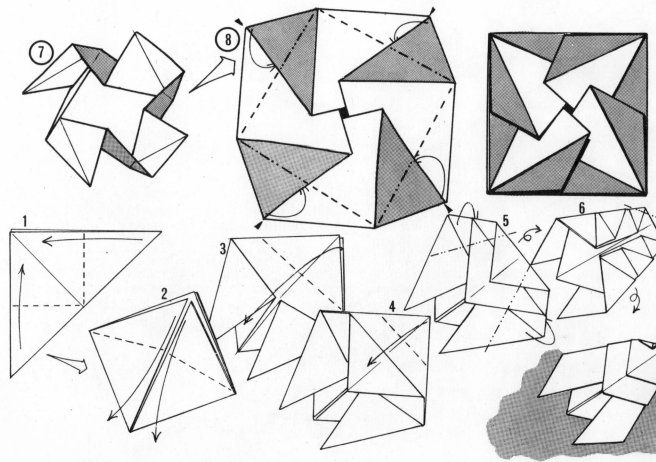

39

INSIDE-OUT BOAT

Origin: *Japan*. Collected by Lillian Oppenheimer.

Use a square of paper, of any colour. It must be strong.

1. Valley-fold the square across the middle.
2. Valley-fold again.
3. Twist the model into position.
4. Valley-fold the top flap only, downwards.
5. Valley-fold the bottom flap (all layers) upwards.
6. This is the result. Turn the model over.
7. Valley-fold top flap downwards (all three layers).
8. Valley-fold bottom flap upwards (all layers).
9. Carefully Mountain-fold the edges. Do not tear the paper. It is helpful to crease first.
10. Turn the boat inside-out, very carefully.
    Finally, the sturdy little boat is complete.

LILLIAN

OPPENHEIMER

Lillian Oppenheimer heads the Origami Centre in New York, and publishes the Origamian. This charming lady devotes her time to the art, teaches others, helps to answer mountains of correspondence, and has a large library of Origami books and papers.

Mrs. Oppenheimer, with her late husband, has travelled widely, and has met many of the world's best paper-folders.

She may be found at The Origami Centre, 71 West 11th Street, New York 11, N.Y., U.S.A. Telephone SPring 7–4825.

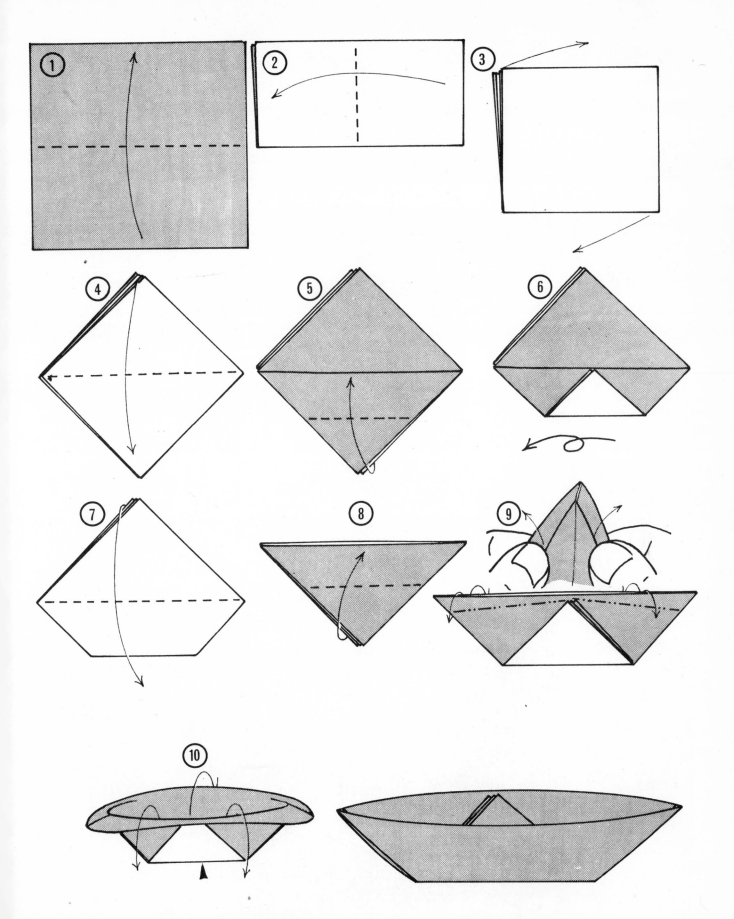

PERSIMMON
Origin: *Japan*.

Use a square of paper light green in colour.

1. Fold a Frog Base to position 2 (*Page* 19) and place it this way up. Book-fold flaps back and front to reveal plain surface.
2. Valley-fold single flap upwards.
3. Half done—note the gussets being formed automatically.
4. Gussets flattened down. Treat all three similar faces in the same way. Do the back one first, and the other two will fold easily.
5. Valley-fold the corner flaps back and front.
6. Grip the model by finger and thumb of both hands—left front flap in left hand and right back flap in right hand.
7. Bend the model so that the centre spreads. Now grip the other two flaps and do the same with them. Keep this up until the Persimmon is formed.
   Finally, the finished model.

TEAPOT
Origin: *Spain*. N. Montero—see Bibliography.

8. Begin with the Bird Base, and Sink the blunt end (*see Page* 21). Valley-fold the front flap downwards.
9. Reverse-fold the two points.
10. Valley-fold the top flap of the spout on the left. Mountain-fold inwards the handle on the right.
11. Open out the top of the pot, and tuck the point into itself. Valley-fold the spout inwards. Reverse-fold the handle upwards. Valley-fold the bottom flap upwards.
12. Valley-fold edges of the spout inwards, then Valley-fold bottom flap of spout upwards. At the top, you see the point tucked in. Reverse-fold the handle again.
13. Spout ready, handle ready. Now Valley-fold bottom flap and tuck arrowed point into pocket. Follow the arrow.
    Finally, the finished teapot.

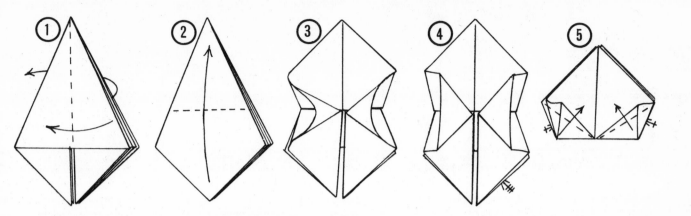

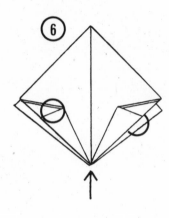

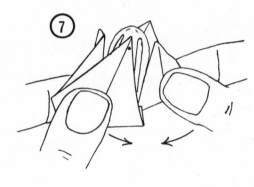

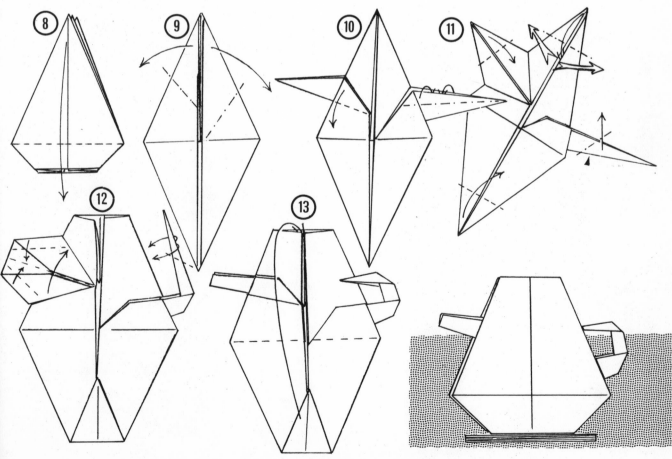

FLAPPING BIRD

Origin: *Japan*. Traditional.

Use a square of paper.

1. Begin with the Bird Base, position 2 (*Page* 18). Reverse-fold the head on the left and the tail on the right.
2. Holding points are shown, to be used while the tail end is being Reverse-folded.
3. Reverse-fold the head end.
4. Form the head with a Reverse Fold. Valley-fold one wing downwards exactly along the marked line.
5. Turn model over.
6. Valley-fold the second wing so that wing-tip meets wing-tip. Finally, hold the bird at the points indicated and pull the tail backwards and forwards. The wings will flap, and you will have made the famous Japanese flying bird after which the Bird Base is named.

A K I R A   Y O S H I Z A W A

*Akira Yoshizawa model
"Swivel Monkey"*

Akira Yoshizawa is undoubtedly the world's greatest paper-folder, and his imitators are many. Certainly, most paper-folders base their creations on principles or procedures originated by this remarkable man.

At his home in Tokyo, Akira Yoshizawa folds continuously, and has created some thousands of almost unbelievable figures. Many of his creations are to be found in Japanese magazines, as well as in the three books he has published.

44

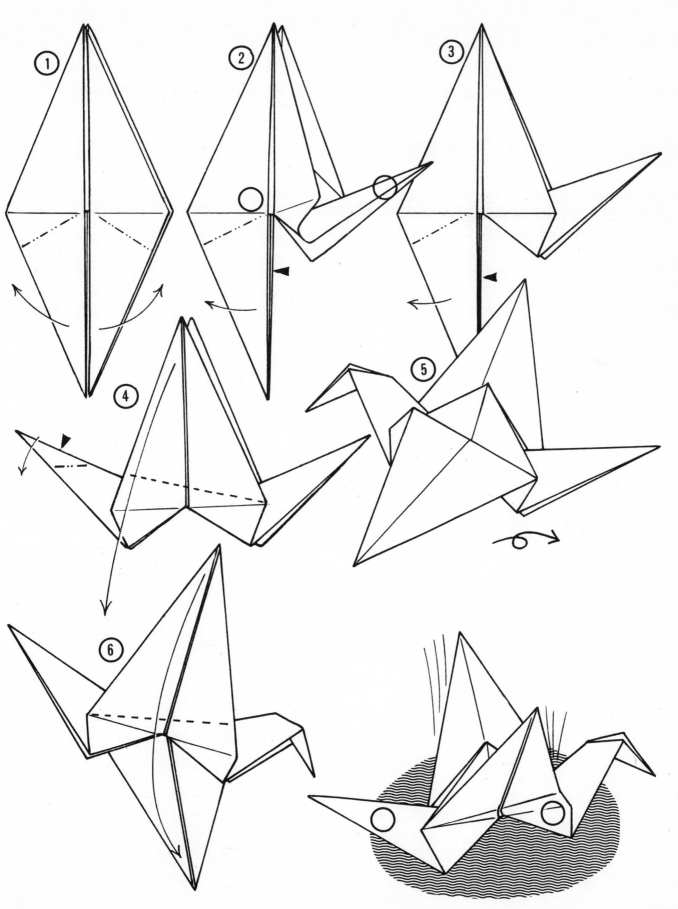

JUMPING FROG

Origin: *Japan*. Traditional.

Use a square of green paper.

1. Begin with the Frog Base. Book-fold front and back so that a smooth face shows.
2. With smooth face showing back and front, Valley-fold side back and front, and on the other two similar faces.
3. Book-fold flaps back and front to take up original position.
4. This is the original position. Reverse-fold the two points, which will be the fore-legs of the frog.
5. Turn the model over.
6. Reverse-fold the two points, which will become the frog's back legs.
7. Reverse-fold all four legs.
8. Reverse-fold legs again.
   Finally, the Jumping Frog. If the paper is of a crisp quality and you stroke the Frog's hindquarters, he will jump as the finger slips off.

OCTOPUS

Origin: *Japan*.

Use a square of brown paper.

9. Begin with Fold 3 above. Pull the four points outwards and flatten them on the table.
10. Cut each point along its middle. This will give you eight "tentacles"
    Finally, blow up the body and adjust the Octopus.

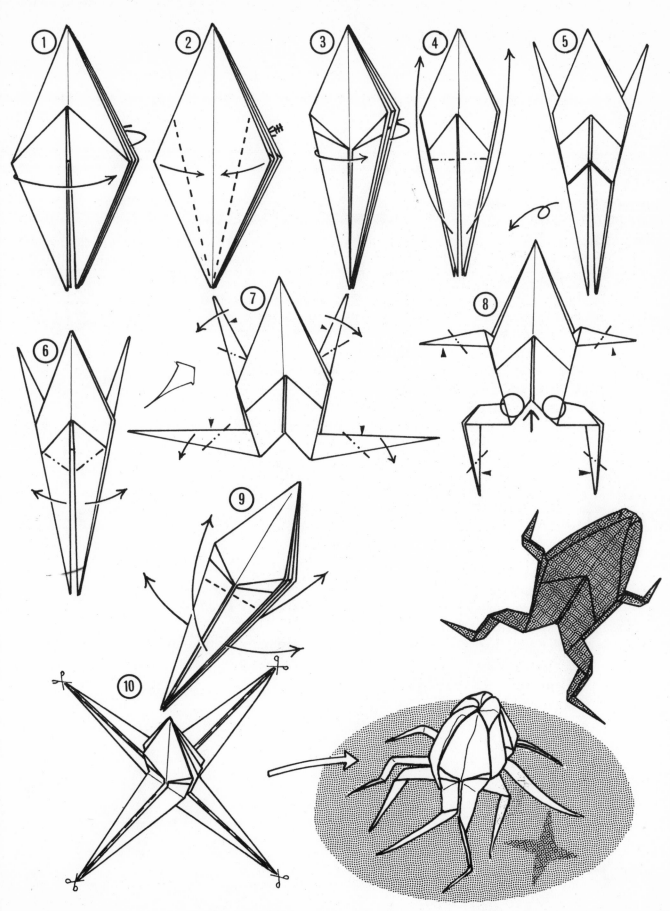

LILY

Origin: *Japan.* Traditional.

Use a square of paper.

1. Begin with Frog Base (*Page* 19). Valley-fold flap upwards and repeat with three similar flaps.
2. Book-fold front and back flaps.
3. Valley-fold side flaps to centre line.
4. Fold completed, repeat with the three similar sides.
5. Valley-fold petals downwards.
6. One petal down. Curl all four petals with a pencil.
   Finally, the completed Lily.

PARTY HAT

Use a square of paper.

1. Fold the paper diagonally. Mountain-fold the two corner flaps behind.
2. Enlarged view. Valley-fold the two side flaps to centre line.
3. Enlarged view. Valley-fold arrowed flap upwards. Turn over.
4. Valley-fold both flaps upwards.
5. Valley-fold two middle flaps outwards. Mountain- and Valley-fold the bottom flap to form front.
   Finally, the completed Party Hat.

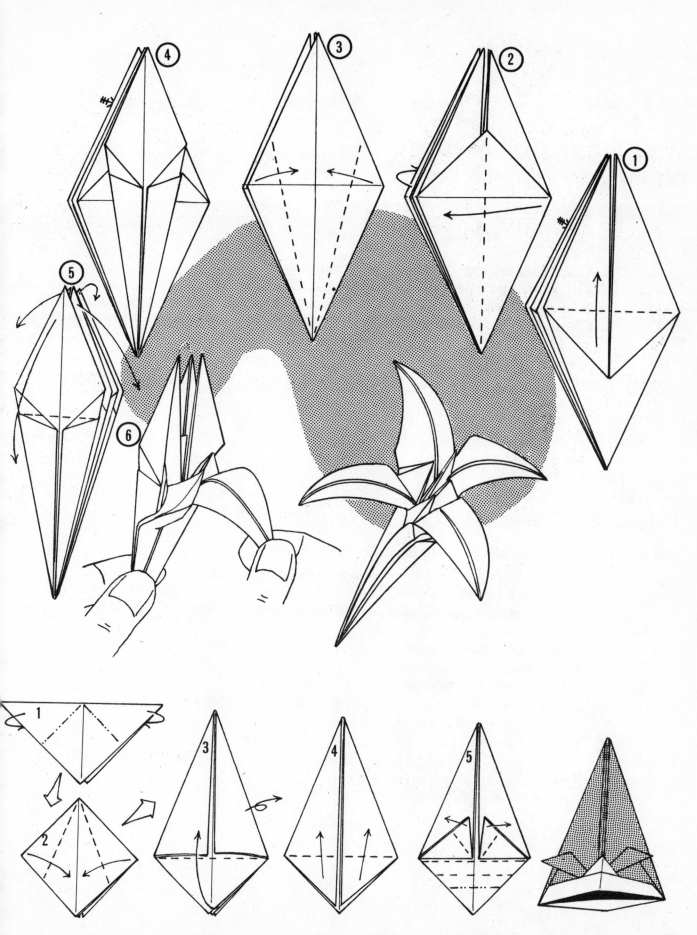

WATER BOMB

Origin: *Japan*. Traditional.

Use a square of paper.

1. Begin with the Water Bomb Base (*Page* 20). Valley-fold flaps in front, and repeat behind.
2. Valley-fold flaps again in front and behind.
3. Valley-fold small flaps upwards in front and behind.
4. Fold double flaps into the pockets indicated. Repeat with similar pockets behind.
5. Crease, by Valley-folding and Mountain-folding, the top and bottom triangles of the model. Hold the model as indicated, and then blow in at the point marked with a heavy arrow.

   This model will hold water, and if placed on a stove hot-plate the water will boil.

SNAIL

Origin: *Spain*. Elias Gutierrez Gil.

Use a rectangle of paper twice as long as it is wide.

1. Fold the rectangle in this manner and cut where indicated. Here, the Bird Base is applied to a diamond shape.
2. Valley-fold the resulting diamond shape downwards.
3. Squash-fold the point marked.
4. Petal-fold the flap marked.
5. Repeat folds with the other point.
6. The diamond Bird Base completed, Valley-fold the front flap downwards.
7. Mountain-fold the tip of the centre flap. Make a Rabbit's Ear out of the bottom flap. Take care; you are doing this backwards. Cut slit.
8. Rabbit's Ear completed, Mountain-fold the model in half.
9. Make a series of Crimps in the upright point, so forming the shell of the Snail. Reverse-fold neck and adjust the eyes.

   Finally, the completed Snail.

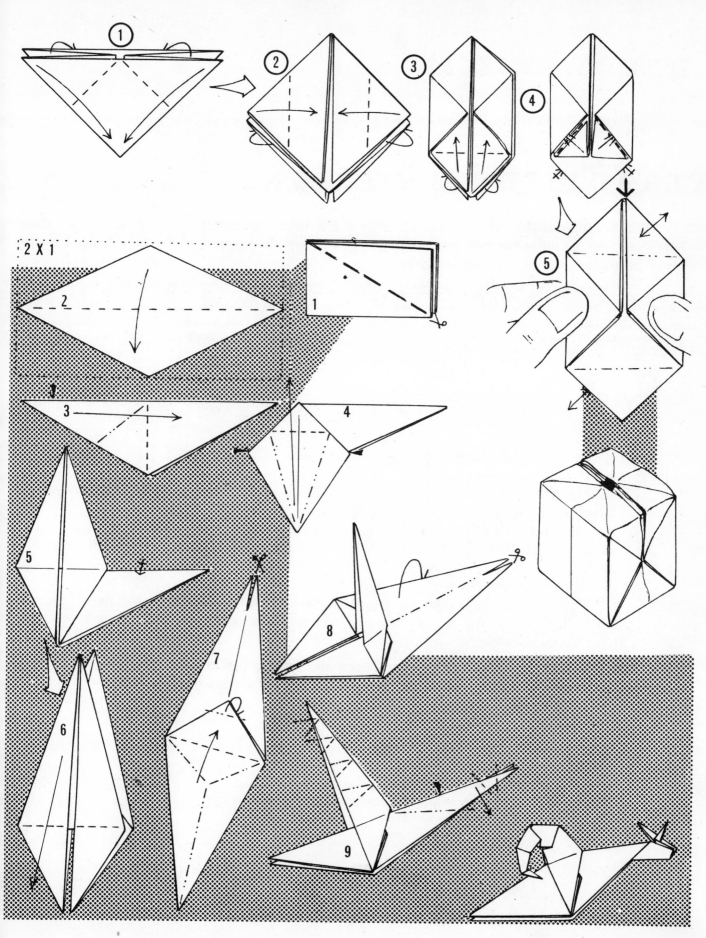

2 X 1

DECORATIONS (1)

TRADITIONAL DESIGNS

The decorations described below are only a few of the infinite number that can be made. Senorita Ligia Montoya has produced some really wonderful designs—so many, in fact, that they could be the subject of a complete book.

These decorations will give the student a lead in producing an endless number of designs.

Use a square of paper, coloured on one side only.

1. Begin with Fold 7 (*Page* 97). Valley-fold eight flaps to the centre line.
2. Squash-fold the eight little corners.
3. Valley-fold the four centre flaps.
4. Decoration complete.
5. Begin with Fold 7 (*Page* 97). Valley-fold along the Mountain Fold symbols—eight of them. Squash-fold the eight long flaps.
6. Decoration complete.
7. Begin with Fold 8 (*Page* 97). Valley-fold outwards the four flaps from the centre.
8. Valley-fold the four pointed flaps in to the centre.
9. Decoration complete.
10. Turn over Fold 7 (*on this page*), and Valley-fold inwards the four small flaps indicated.
11. Valley-fold the four sides inwards, and turn the model over.
12. Decoration complete.

When carefully made, out of attractive paper, these decorations can be pasted on to boxes, or used as coasters for example. Figs. 6 and 9 will fit on to the base of a wine-glass.

Many of these lovely and fascinating designs have been photographed together and are shown in Plate 2. Note that one design is used as a mat for a wine glass.

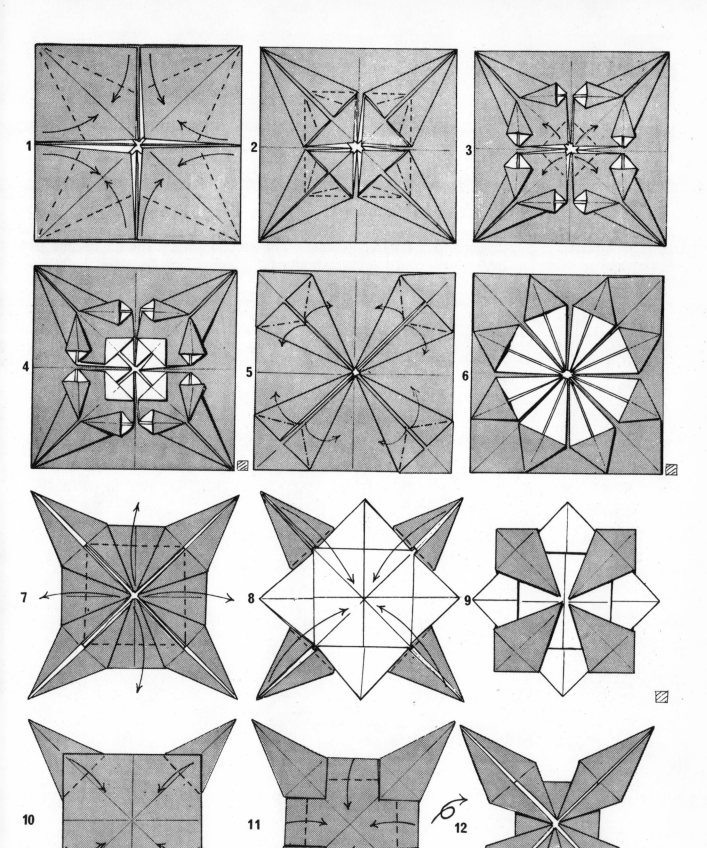

DECORATIONS (2)

MONTOYA STAR

Origin: *Argentina*. Ligia Montoya.

Use three squares of paper, each of a different colour. The second square should be one inch smaller than the first square, and the third square should be one inch smaller than the second. Fold each paper in the same way.

1. Begin with Fold 7 (*Page* 97). Squash-fold the four flaps indicated.
2. Valley-fold the Squash Fold in half.
3. Squash-fold the four flaps indicated.
4. Valley-fold the four Squash Folds.
5. Mountain-fold the four corner flaps.
6. You will notice that little gussets are formed. These must be flattened. Turn the model over, for it is now complete.

Make two more models with the other two squares, and paste together as shown in the illustration.

See also photograph reproduced in this book as Plate 2.

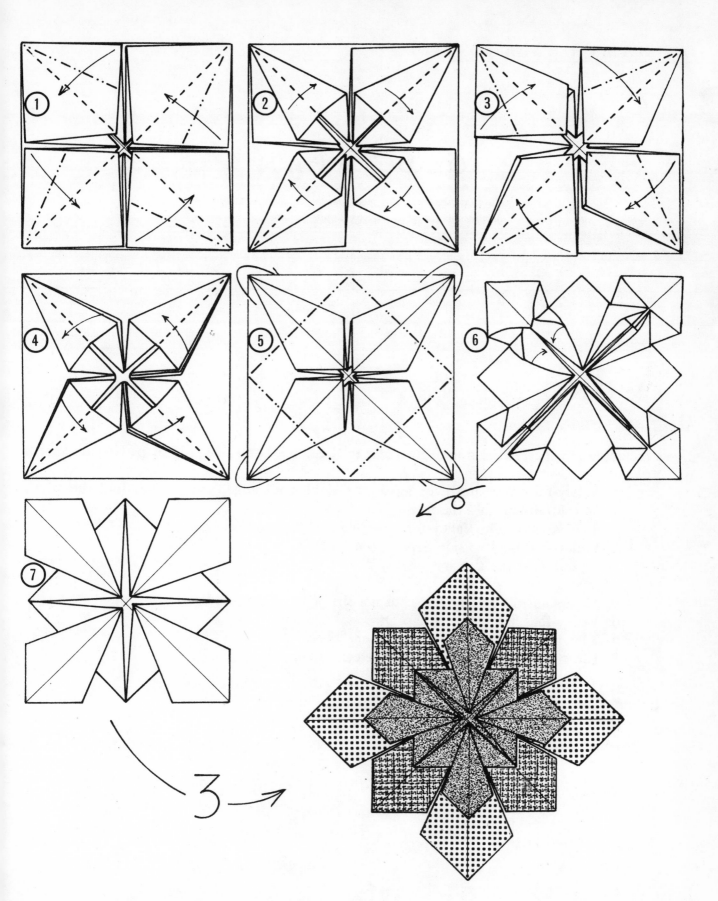

OLD JAPAN

The next five items are traditionally Japanese, and of them the Dragonfly on page 65 is quite the oldest.

KIMONO

Origin: *Japan.*

Use a rectangle of paper, in the proportions of 3 to 1, coloured one side only. A patterned paper is best.

1. Valley-fold over and over again the right-hand edge, then Valley-fold the whole flap. Mountain-fold the flap on left.
2. This is the result. Valley-fold the two corner flaps indicated.
3. Valley-fold the two side flaps to the centre.
4. Squash-fold the two long flaps, A and B, noting with care that they are squashed at an angle.
5. Mountain-fold the top flap, but not the point in the middle. Turn over.
6. Valley-fold flap C under flap D.
7. This is the result. Now turn it over.
8. Lift the lapels out from under the centre flaps.
   Finally, the completed Kimono.

Try to find a coloured flower design for this delightful model.

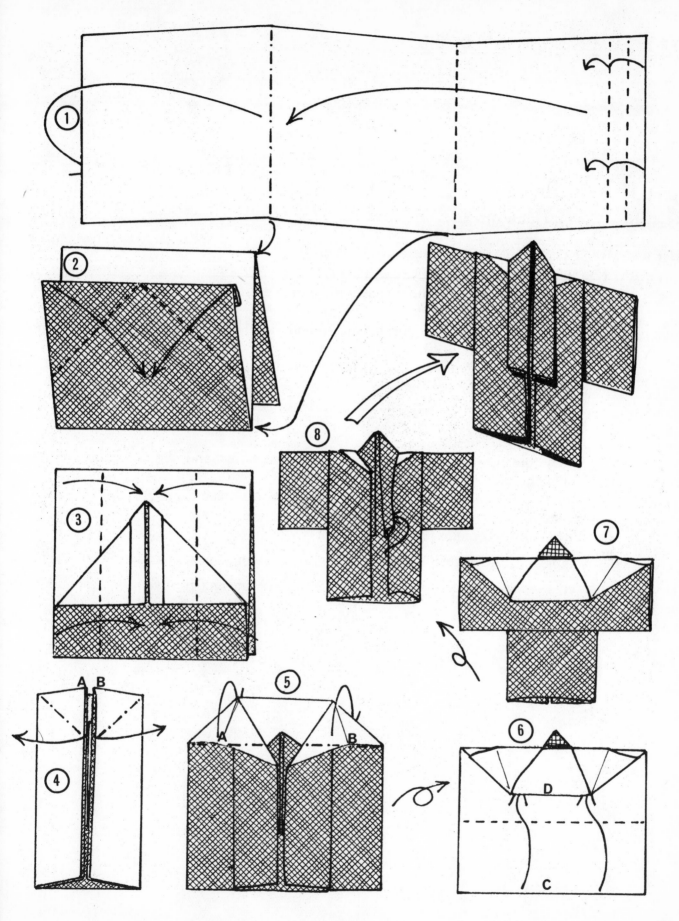

JAPANESE GENTLEMAN

Origin: *Japan.* Uchiyama.

Use a square of paper, coloured on one side.

1. The square is creased, ready to begin.
2. Cut each side in the manner indicated, and Mountain-fold the two flaps.
3. Valley-fold the pointed flap.
4. With a pencil, make the "neck" marks and cut the pieces away. Cut a hole for the neck directly underneath. Fold the flap back into place.
5. Valley-fold and Mountain-fold the two side flaps in and out, after the head has been passed through the neck-hole.
6. Valley-fold across the diagonal, letting the head flip round to the top.
7. Pull the arms upwards in the direction of the arrows. Valley-fold the bottom single flap under the chest.
8. Valley-fold upwards the little "belt". Mountain-fold and Valley-fold the point on top of the head.
9. Valley- and Mountain-fold the tips of the arms to make hands.
10. Valley-fold the arms into the lap.
11. The completed model.

This model is typical of the ancient Japanese art of doll-making, in which many cuts are made.

If your results are not satisfactory, it will probably be because the angles of your folds are not quite accurate. Try again.

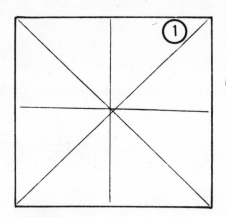

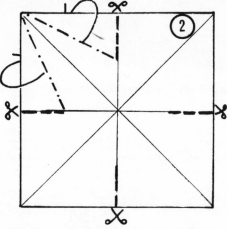

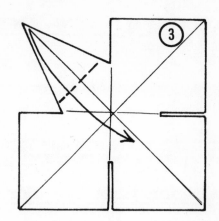

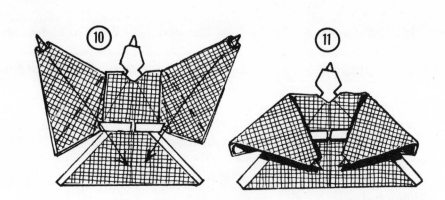

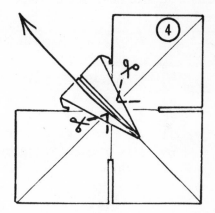

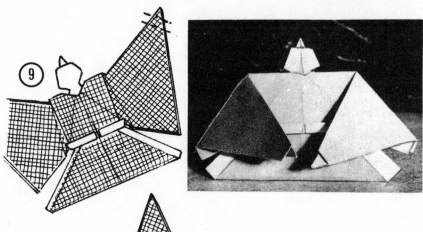

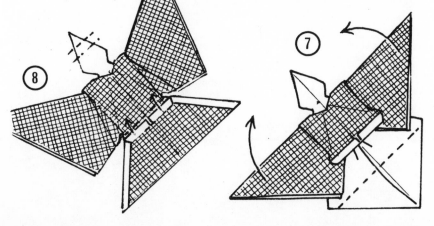

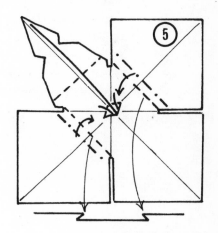

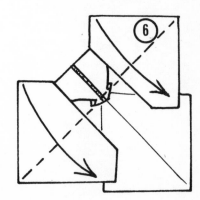

JAPANESE LADY

Origin: *Japan.* Uchiyama.

Use a square of paper coloured on one side. As this model is constructed to a typical doll-making technique, cuts are made, but these are used with great effect.

1. Crease the square along the diagonal. Valley-fold the two side flaps to the centre crease.
2. Mountain-fold two-fifths of the model to make a crease, and return to original position.
3. The crease made, Mountain-fold three-quarters of the top triangle.
4. This is the result. Turn the model over.
5. Cut away the portions indicated, and cut a neck-hole directly underneath. Fold the head back into position.
6. Valley-fold the head into the neck-hole. Cut away the edges, and cut nearly up to the neck-hole, single thickness only.
7. Operation completed. Valley-fold the top flap, letting the head flip over to the top.
8. Valley-fold the two side flaps, single layer only. The flaps will go under the chest at the top.
9. Valley-fold the next two flaps. Valley-fold the tip of the head and tuck in.
10. Mountain-fold the tips of the flaps just folded. Mountain-fold the bottom flap Finally, the completed figure.

This model must be very carefully folded, otherwise the result will be disappointing.

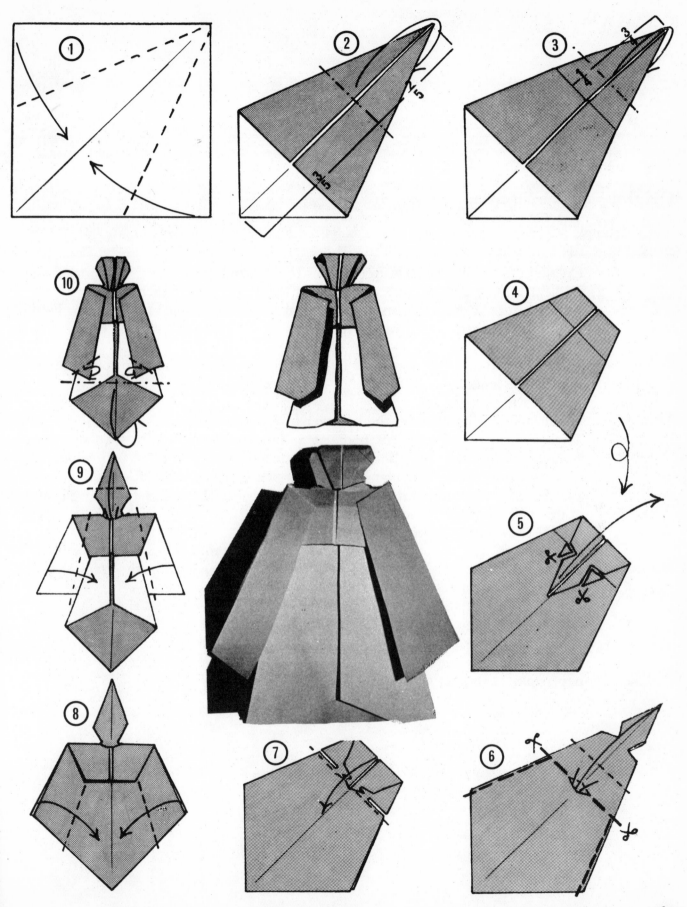

BOOK-CASE

Origin: *Japan.* Uchiyama.

Use a rectangle of paper, of proportions 2 to 1, coloured on one or both sides. Begin with the paper creased in thirds both ways.

1. Crease as indicated, by measurement, or by trial and error.
2. Add three more creases, each crease being the centre line of each third.
3. Add six more horizontal creases, each forming the centre line of each sixth. Fold the two vertical creases which are, in turn, formed by Valley-folding the edges in to the creases already there.
4. Make the two diagonal creases as indicated. Valley and Mountain-fold three times to pleat the model.
5. Push in the six corners.
6. Valley-fold the little flap on the left over to the right.
7. There are three shelves to the book-case. Valley-fold the bottom shelf downwards. Valley-fold the coloured flap to a vertical position. Valley-fold the flap A over to the right and into the model. Flap A will lock one side of the shelf.
8. Valley-fold the second shelf downwards. Valley-fold the flap B to the right and in to the model to lock the second shelf on one side.
9. Repeat the same folds with C and D.
10. Both shelves are now locked in place. Valley-fold the middle portion of the back flap downwards. The sides will Valley-fold across their diagonals in the creases in Fig.4 Valley-fold the base.
11. Enlarged view. Valley-fold the two upright flaps to the left and right.
12. Mountain-fold top flap and sides into the book-case.
13. Pleat a double strip of red paper to represent a row of books.
    Finally the Book-case completed. This, in my opinion, is one of the most remarkable paper-folding feats of all time.

See Plate 3, which demonstrates how convincing this model appears when finished.

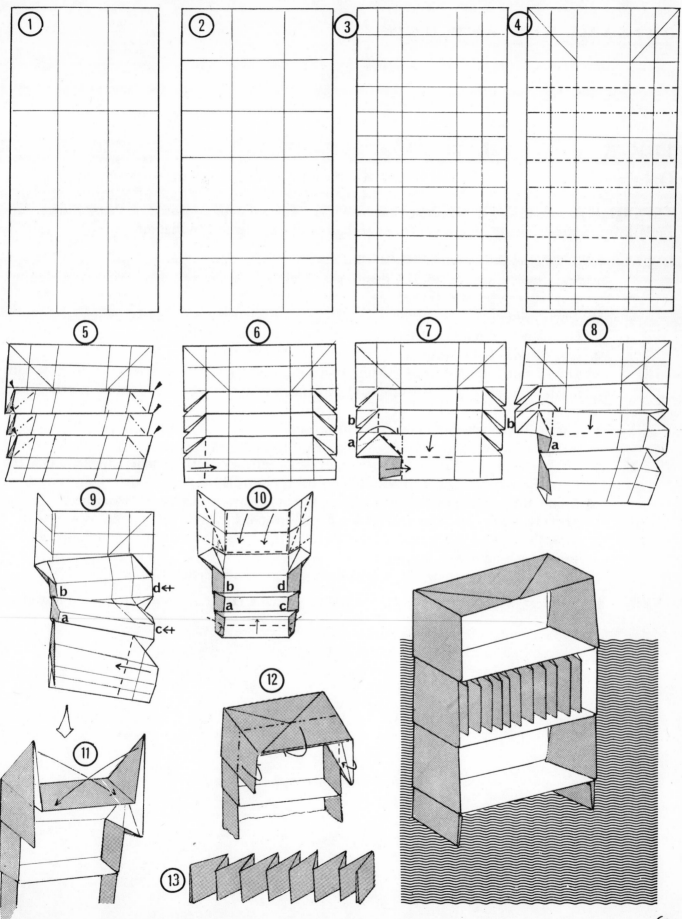

DRAGONFLY

Origin: *Japan*. From a section of the Kanomado, 1850 (Japanese Encyclopedia).

The original picture of this model, lent to me by Gershon Legman, appeared in *Paper Magic*. Ligia Montoya successfully discovered the method of folding from the diagrams.

Use a six-sided piece of paper, thin and strong.

1. Start with a square folded diagonally. Valley-fold the two flaps as indicated, thus dividing the triangle into three.
2. This is done.
3. Cut along the marked line, and open out into a six-sided sheet.
4. Cut the six slits indicated. Valley-fold the twelve flaps.
5. Crease along the Valley and Mountain-fold markings. Valley-fold the model in half.
6. With the creases now the opposite way, push into place as you would a Water Bomb Base.
7. This is the shape you should achieve. Squash-fold each flap.
8. The first flap is Squashed. Now Squash the other five.
9. Cut a slit in the top flap only, at the point indicated, using nail scissors. Push the head through the slit, and Mountain-fold the top flap A only. Turn the model over.
10. Mountain-fold the side flaps. Pull out the head, using fingers or tweezers.
11. Mountain-fold the small triangular flap. Reverse-fold the four wings, as arrowed.
12. Sink the tips of the wings. Mountain-fold the back under itself. Mountain-fold the two sides, and Sink the neck pieces.
    Finally, the completed Dragonfly, a really fine and realistic model.

As a matter of interest, Senorita Ligia Montoya has produced a Dragonfly without making any cuts.

For a photograph of this charming design, see Plate 4.

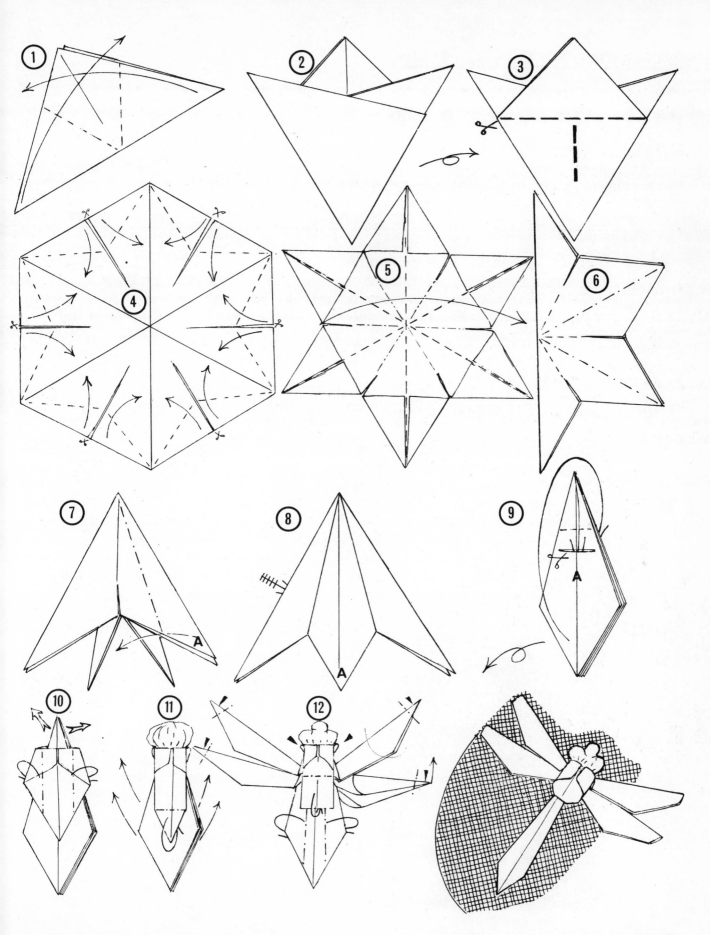

POP-UP RABBIT

Origin: *America.* E. D. Sullivan.

Use a square of paper, in any colour. Begin with a Water Bomb Base. (Page 20)

1. Study the notations or markings. Make this different Petal Fold.
2. Fold completed. Valley-fold the two triangular flaps downwards.
3. Valley-fold the two little tips outwards. Turn the model over sideways.
4. Make two Rabbit's Ears left and right.
5. Enlarged view. If folded with stiffish paper, this model will be a springy little fellow. When he is held down and then released, he will jump up.
   Finally, the completed Rabbit, with eye markings. This model gives great fun to the young.

SCISSORBILL

Origin: *America.* E. D. Sullivan.

Use a square of paper, any colour. Begin with a stretched Bird Base (*see Page 175*).

1. Reverse-fold points left and right.
2. Valley-fold flaps in front and behind.
3. Mountain-fold the model in half.
4. Mountain-fold and Valley-fold the lower portion into a Crimp. Crease heavily.
5. The Crimping completed. Flatten the model out. Mark in the eyes.
   Finally, the completed Scissorbill. Hold the model as shown, and move the legs to and fro, when the bill will open and close. Experiment carefully if the model seems to work a little stiffly. This model makes a fine toy for young children.

E. D. SULLIVAN

Supervisor at the Hydrofoil Laboratory of the Boeing Airplane Company. Married, with three teenage children. Forty years' experience with paper-folding. Has created some sixteen figures. Hobby: Woodcarving. Enjoys making paper-folds which amuse the young.

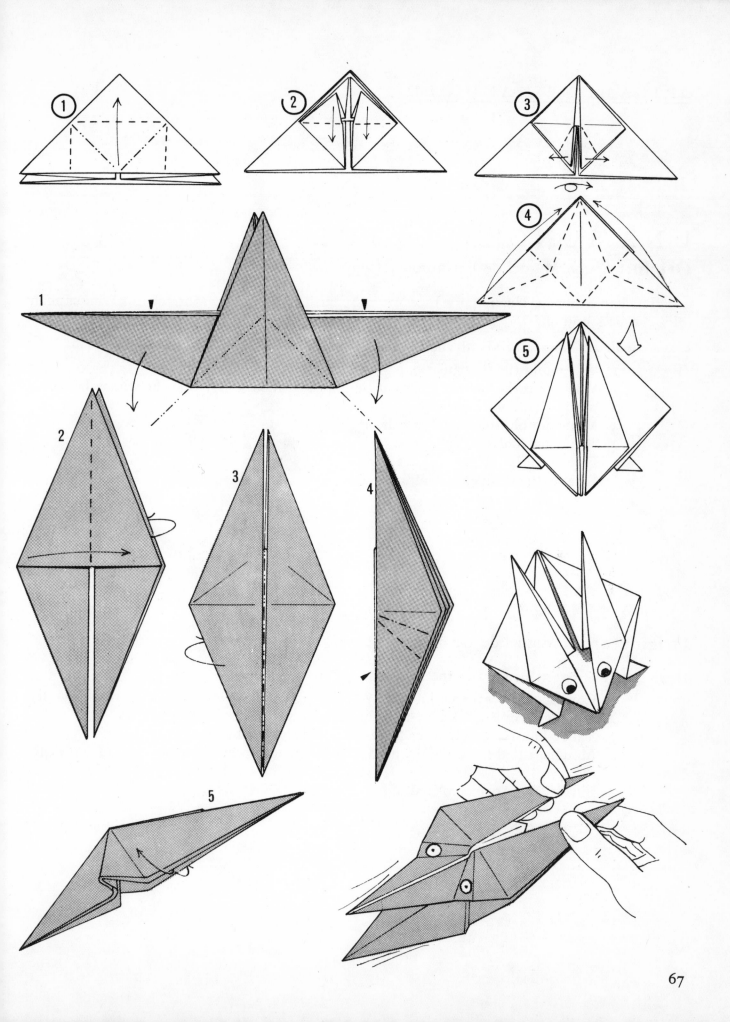

UNAMUNO'S VULTURE

Origin: *Spain*. Miguel de Unanumo y Jugo.

The late Senor de Unanumo y Jugo was a Spanish philosopher. More of this famous man's folds can be found in *Paper Magic* (*see Bibliography*).

Use a square of paper. Begin with the Bird Base, position 2 (Page 18).

1. Valley-fold the triangular flap at the top. Reverse-fold the feet.
2. Valley-fold the two little flaps at the top, and then Valley-fold the whole flap downwards. Bring the centre flap down as well.
3. Mountainfold the model in half.
4. Mountain-fold and Valley-fold to form the neck.
5. Fold the head. The two extra drawings show how.
   Finally, the completed Vulture.

UNAMUNO'S APE

Origin: *Spain*. Miguel de Unanumo y Jugo.

Use a square of paper. Begin with the Bird Base, position 2 (*Page* 18).

1. Consider the centre markings only. Valley-fold and Reverse-fold the two bottom legs.
2. Folding completed. Valley-fold the flap A right to the bottom behind.
3. Valley-fold the model in half. Reverse-fold the head and legs.
4. Mountain-fold the tip of the head into itself and repeat. Reverse-fold and Valley-fold the feet.
   Finally, the Ape completed.

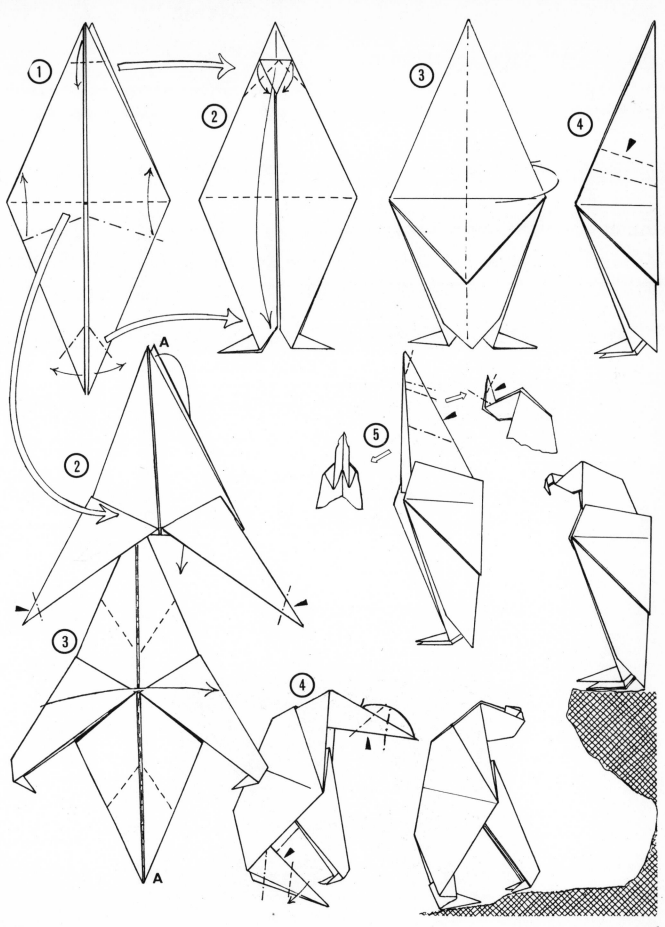

SOLORZANO'S ANGEL FISH

Origin: *Spain.* Dr. Vicente Solórzano Sagredo.

Dr. Solórzano Sagredo, possibly the finest living Spanish paper-folder, has just published his greatest book on the subject of Origami (*see Bibliography*).

Use a square of paper. Begin with the Fish Base, position 2 (*Page* 20).

1. Mountain-fold the top flap.
2. Mountain-fold the two flaps indicated, but do NOT fold the top layer.
3. Position when folded. Valley-fold the flap at the bottom—one layer.
4. Fold Rabbit's Ears top and bottom.
5. The top Rabbit's Ear folds to the left, the bottom one to the right. Valley-fold the top flap to the bottom.
6. Valley-fold both bottom flaps upwards.
7. Mountain-fold and Valley-fold the flaps left and right.
8. Shape the mouth of the fish. Turn the model over.
   Finally, the completed Angel Fish.
   This was one of the first models sent to me by Gershon Legman.

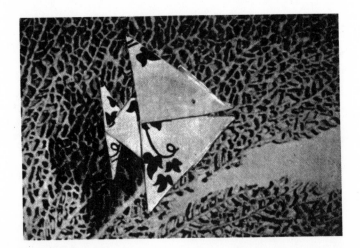

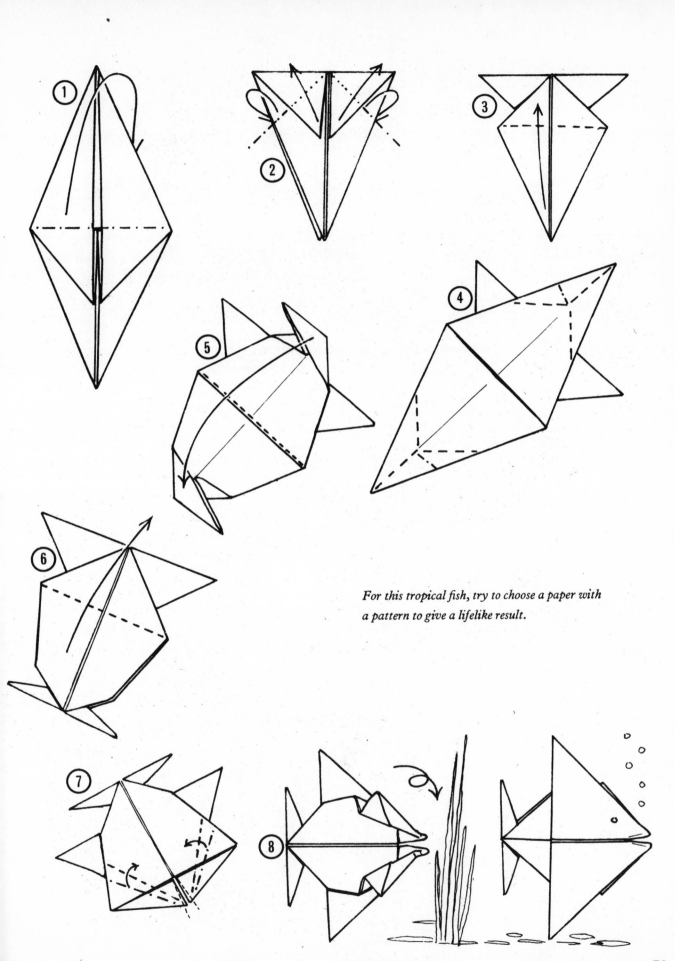

For this tropical fish, try to choose a paper with a pattern to give a lifelike result.

THREE-DIMENSIONAL WHALE

Origin: *Denmark.* Thoki Yenn. The method for folding was worked out by Ligi. Montoya. Thoki Yenn is reputed to be a wonder at paper-folding— but it is always difficult, and sometimes impossible, to locate hin precisely.

Use a square of paper creased into sixty-four small squares.

1. Mountain-fold over and over the thin flaps at the top (the quarters). Valley-fold th. two unequal flaps, starting with the one on the right.
2. Now Valley-fold the flap on the left and tuck the folded edge into the other folde. edge. Do this carefully.
3. Cut C and D as indicated. Valley-fold top layer of CD.
4. Valley-fold the four flaps to the centre.
5. Valley-fold the top triangular flap downwards.
6. Mountain-fold the model down the middle from both sides. In other words, Squas. the model from the sides.
7. Enlarged view of fold. Watch the letters for positions. Roll over and press flat.
8. Crease along the marked lines. Push in the top portion indicated, using Mountai. and Valley Folds back and front.
9. One tail pushed in. Now push in the bottom fin, using Mountain and Valley Folds
10. This is very difficult, so please study the symbols carefully. Valley-fold the middle back and front (watch X and Y). Flap O is Mountain-folded downwards. Flap 1 Mountain-folds under. The whole model takes a turn upwards in front and down. wards behind.
11. This is the result. O is now behind. P is in front. M and L, and X and Y hav. changed places. Push in after creasing X and Y as with the fins.
12. This is how it should look. Hold at X and Y and blow into the mouth.
Finally, the completed Whale.

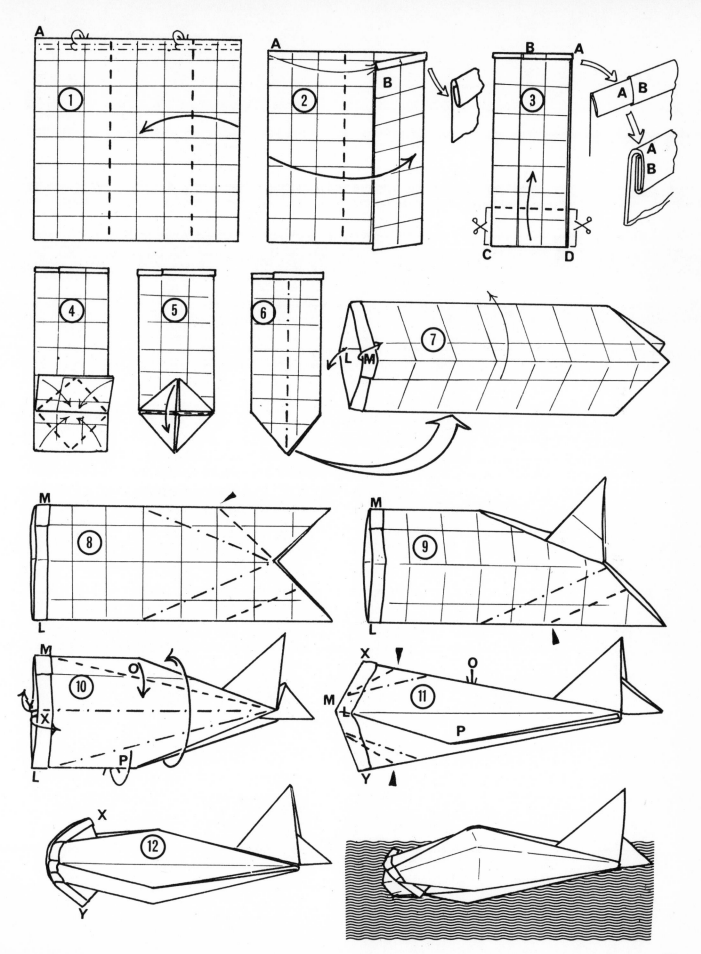

MOOR AT PRAYER

Origin: *Spain.* I understand from Senor Elias Guitierrez Gil that this model was folded by Miguel A. Salvatella, who is the author of a fine book on paper folding (*see Bibliography*).

This model is simpler, and more effective, than the Moor at Prayer explained in *Paper Magic*.

Use a square of white paper. Begin with a Bird Base (*Page* 18). Sink the top of the Bird Base (*Page* 21).

1. Valley-fold the flaps front and back to the right.
2. Fold Rabbit's Ears with the two flaps just folded, in front and behind. Reverse-fold the two long flaps on the left.
3. Squash-fold the Rabbit's Ear in front and repeat behind.
4. Reverse-fold the top pointed flap. Reverse-fold the bottom pointed flap. Valley-fold the arm downwards. Repeat with the flap behind.
5. Enlarged view. Reverse-fold the head point. Here you see the arm flap at the back being folded. Reverse-fold the leg portion.
6. Reverse-fold the head point. Turn the arm upwards under the sleeve. Watch X. and look ahead to position 7. Repeat behind. Reverse-fold the foot.
7. Form the hands with Reverse-folds. Reverse-fold the little point in front of the face,
8. Form a nose and beard with one Reverse Fold, as shown in the additional drawings. Finally, the Moor at Prayer completed.

A beautiful, clean-cut model.

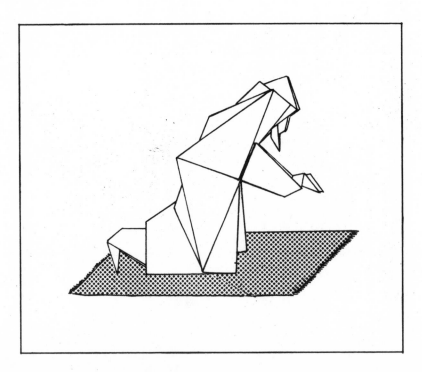

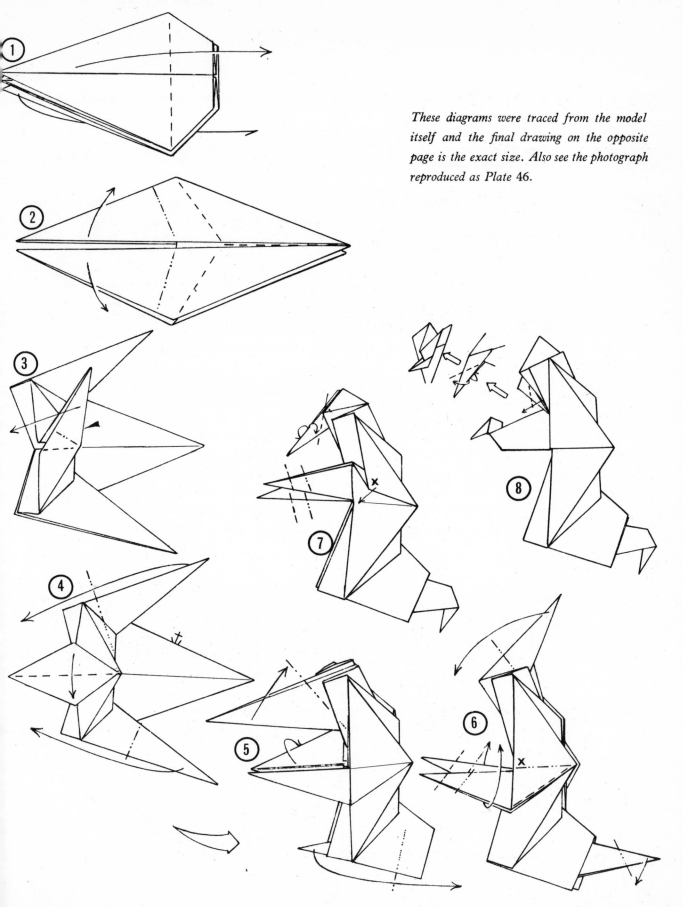

These diagrams were traced from the model itself and the final drawing on the opposite page is the exact size. Also see the photograph reproduced as Plate 46.

TUMBLING CHAN

Origin: *America*. Harry Weiss.

Use a square of paper, and begin with the Preliminary Fold (*Page* 18).

1. Valley-fold flap downwards in front, and repeat behind.
2. Fold a Rabbit's Ear on the flap in front, and repeat behind.
3. Squash-fold the upright flap, and follow-through the extra drawings to form a hand Repeat behind.
4. Valley-fold the white portion of the flap on the right, and push in the tinted part. Repeat behind. Mountain-fold the right flap into the model and repeat behind.
5. Reverse-fold the top left-hand flap, which is the head. Valley-fold the small flaps on the right and repeat behind, for the legs. Mountain-fold the little flap on lower left, and repeat behind.
6. Reverse-fold the head. Reverse-fold the leg portion three times. Sink the base. Finally, Tumbling Chan completed. Stand him on his head and give him a flip, and he will tumble.

RUBY-THROATED HUMMING BIRD

Origin: *America*. Harry Weiss.

Use two squares of paper placed together, the outside one green, the inside one red. The tint in the illustration represents the green paper. Begin with the Preliminary Fold as in Tumbling Chan (*Page* 18). Squash- and Petal-fold one side.

1. After creasing, push in the two sides indicated. Valley-fold the lower flap upwards
2. Pull down and Valley-fold the two flaps indicated. Valley-fold the small lower flap for the feet.
3. Valley-fold the curved flaps downwards. Petal-fold the top portion.
4. Valley-fold the head. Follow-through additional drawings, then Mountain-fold the model in half.
5. Mountain-fold the back flaps in front and behind into body. Valley-fold the neck flaps, and open out the head to disclose colour on throat. Sink the head. Finally, the Humming Bird completed.

①

②

③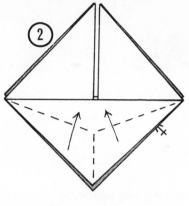

1

2

3

④

⑤

4

Mr. Harry Weiss, a newcomer to the Origami field, has produced some very fine models and these two, along with one other on page 82, arrived at the last moment.

4

5

⑥

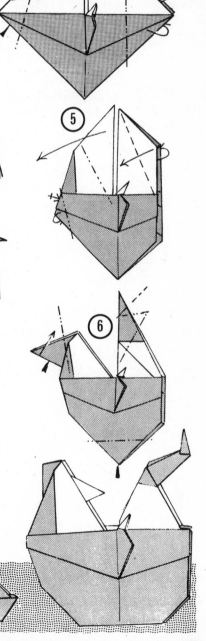

HUSKY DOG

Origin: *America.* Joint Work of Alan Cohen and Samuel Randlett.

This very fine dog is constructed out of the traditional fold popularly known as The Lover's Knot.

Use a square of white paper, and begin with position 5 (*Page* 29).

1. Squeeze all corners together so that the top four flaps Mountain-fold, and the interior Valley- and Mountain-folds.
2. Process taking place. Flattened, the model will look like position 3.
3. Pull X and X in the direction of the arrows so that they Mountain-fold in their natural creases. Repeat with similar flaps behind.
4. Valley-fold the two front flaps downwards to meet bottom centre. The X spots move to the sides. Repeat behind.
5. Lift up the model so that the base faces you. Insert thumbs either side of centre piece, and with fingers outside, begin to open the model out.
6. Centre opening out. Continue the opening movement until you flatten the centre completely. This is The Lovers' Knot.
7. Centre is now flattened. Note the path of the dotted line. First, Valley-fold top and lower flaps to centre. When this is done, Valley-fold the model in half.
8. At the hold points indicated, grasp the flaps marked, and lift them upwards. They will automatically move into shape. Refer to position 9.
9. At this point, examine the base, and see whether it is as shown in the additional drawing. Pull down the arrowed flaps in front and behind.
10. This is the result. Mountain-fold the flaps into the model and repeat with the similar two behind.
11. Left side of the model will become tail and hind legs, right side of the model head and front legs.
12. Fold Rabbit's Ears to form front and rear legs in front and behind. Be sure to fold these exactly. A detail of the folded hind leg is seen in the additional drawing. Push in the three little corner flaps. Under the tail you will find two flaps, A and B. Fold these up into the tail (*see second additional drawing*). Mountain-fold the tip of the nose into itself. The two additional drawings (*left*) show how the head is formed. Finally, the completed Husky Dog.

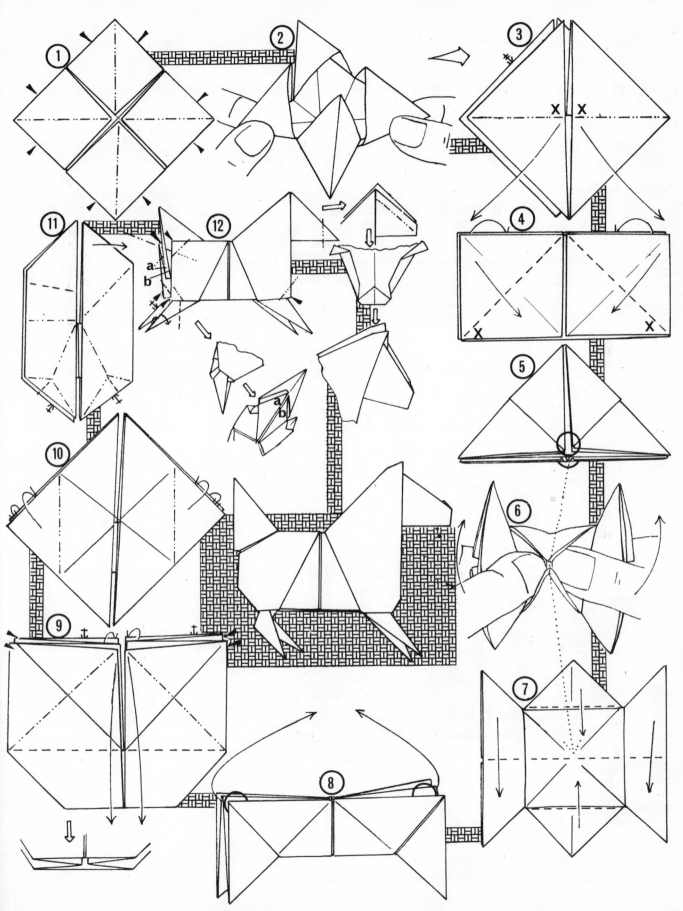

GARGOYLE

Origin: *America.* Samuel Randlett.

Use a square of paper, in brown or grey or any other colour to taste. Begin with the Bird Base, position 3 (*Page* 18).

1. Valley-fold the rear flap downwards.
2. Valley-fold carefully along the Valley Fold marks. The lower two folds are made with a single thickness only. (*see position* 3).
3. The creases made, Valley-fold the flap downwards.
4. Book-fold the flap on the left over to the right.
5. Crease heavily along the Valley Fold mark.
6. Crease along the Valley Fold heavily.
7. Book-fold the flap on the right over to the left.
8. Repeat the procedure with the flap on the right.
9. This is the result. Fold a Rabbit's Ear with the flap marked.
10. Reverse-fold the top points. Mountain-fold the lower flap.
11. Reverse-fold the beak, top and bottom.
    Finally, the finished Gargoyle.

Hold the Gargoyle at the back end, work like a pair of scissors, and the Gargoyle will open and close its mouth.

SAMUEL AND MRS RANDLETT

Samuel Randlett is a graduate of Northwestern University, like his wife, Jean, who illustrates his books. They have two children. University piano teacher, and is currently working for a Doctorate in Music.
Author of The Art of Origami, *and* The Best of Origami.
Began paper-folding in 1958, and within one year had figures of his own on display at the Cooper Union Museum for the Arts of Decoration, in New York City.

ALAN COHEN

A friend of the Randletts, who has been lucky enough to make personal contact with Akira Yoshizawa, in Tokyo.

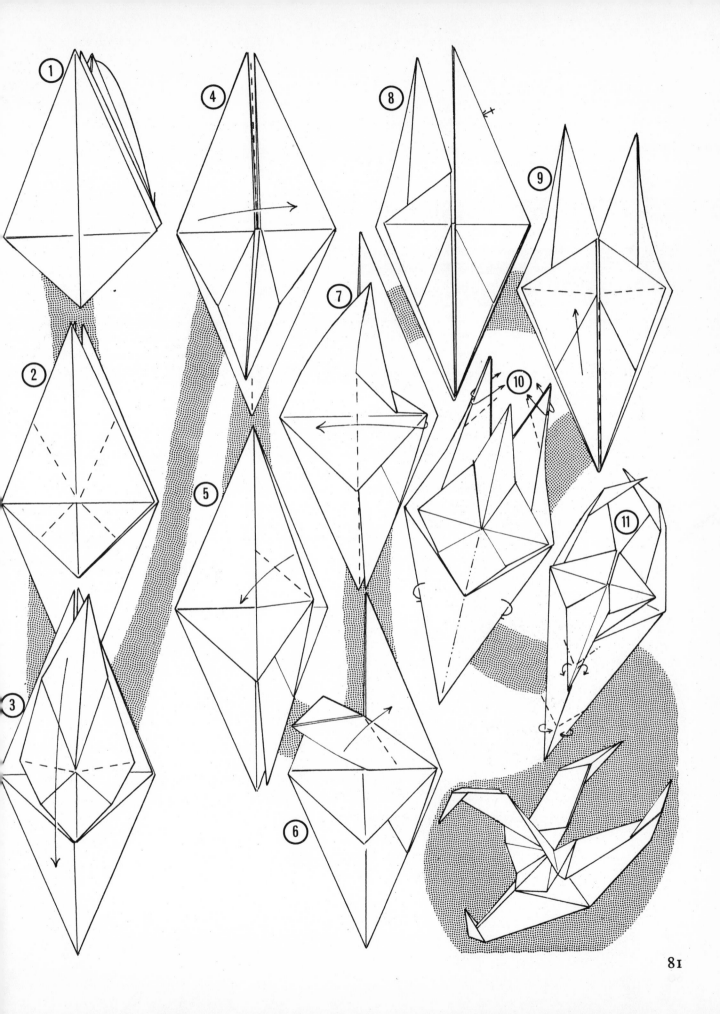

HARRY WEISS

Born 1915, in Newark, New Jersey, U.S.A. B.A. in Science from Antioch College in Ohio. Journalist, 7 years, with Cleveland, Ohio, paper. Now chief news officer for U.S. Department of Commerce in Washington, D.C. Married with three children. Hobbies include poetry writing and lifelong interest in parlor stunts capped by introduction to PAPER MAGIC.

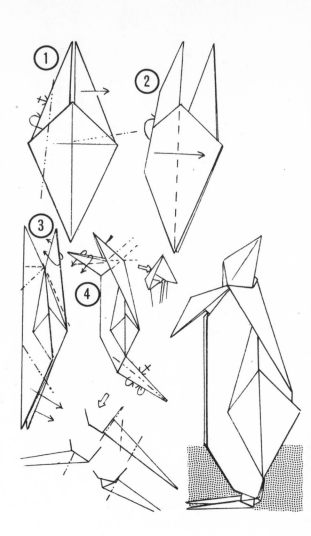

ORIGAMI NEW AND OLD

KIWI

Origin: *America*. Harry Weiss.

Use a square of paper. Begin with Bird Base, position 2 (*Page* 18), with flaps Book-folded.

1. Mountain-fold the flaps on the left in front and behind. Crimp the right point internally.
2. Valley-fold the flap to the right and repeat behind (Book Fold).
3. Reverse-fold twice the point on the left, to make the beak. Reverse-fold the point on the right for the head. Reverse-fold the legs.
4. Reverse-fold the beak. Form the head as shown in the extra drawing. Mountain-fold the legs. Extra drawings show formation of legs and feet.
   Finally, the completed Kiwi.

ORIGAMI

SECTIONS DEVOTED TO THE WORK OF

FLORENCE TEMKO
ROBERT HARBIN
LIGIA MONTOYA
JOHN M. NORDQUIST
JACK J. SKILLMAN
ADOLFO CERCEDA
NEAL ELIAS
FRED G. ROHM
REVEREND ROBERT EDWARD NEALE
GEORGE RHOADS

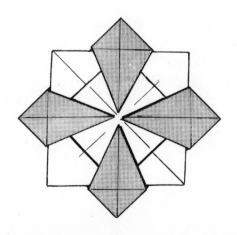

Florence Temko

British-born, and married to an American, she is famous for her lectures on Origami, in which she traces the development and application of paper-folding, at the same time teaching her audience and making a number of Origami figures.

Made a recent appearance on television in England.

STOCKING CASE

Origin: Popular fold adapted by Florence Temko.

Use a rectangle of decorated metallic paper, size 93×32 cm. (about $36\frac{1}{2} \times 12\frac{1}{2}$ in.). This model makes a very fine package for ladies' stockings.

1. Cut paper to size and divide up with pencil and ruler. The bottom flap is about 3 cm. Mountain- and Valley-fold where indicated.
2. This is how it should look. Sink six corners—three left and three right.
3. Valley-fold, and then Mountain-fold, the two front flaps.
4. Mountain-fold the two tips into the pocket behind. Now Valley-fold the first bottom flap.
5. Valley-fold the two side flaps to the centre.
6. This completed, Valley-fold the next bottom flap.
7. Valley-fold the two side flaps.
8. Valley-fold the arrowed flaps down again.
9. Valley-fold over and over the two side flaps. Note the portion which tucks under.
10. Sink the two corners indicated. Valley-fold flap at top.
    Finally, the finished model.

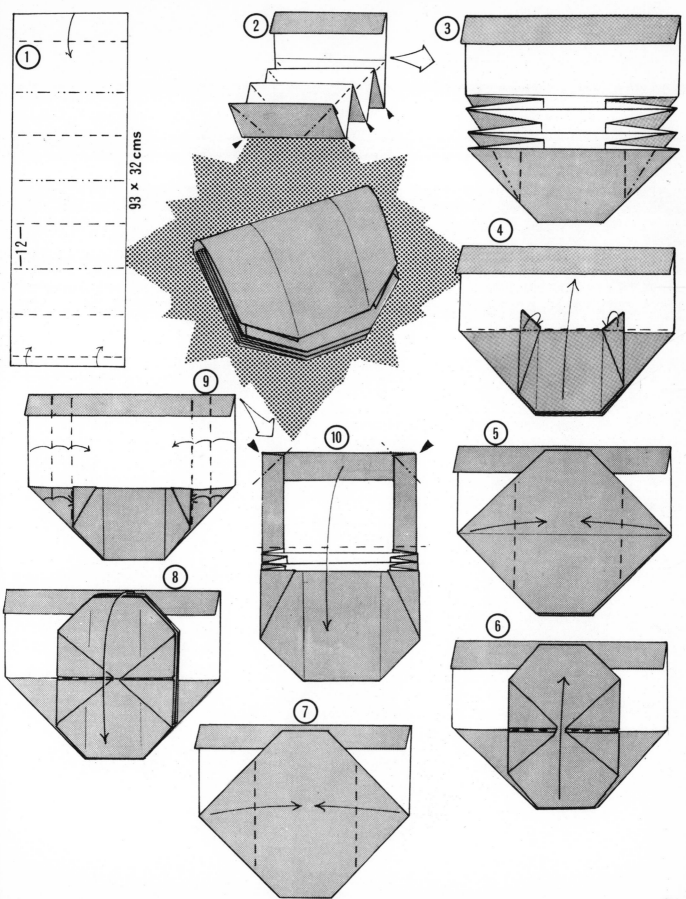

93 × 32 cms

85

For those who have difficulty in understanding the Reverse Fold, here is a lesson devised by Mrs. Temko. Assume that you are making a simple Swan. If you follow the first dark arrow, you see the information which is normally given to you. By following the second arrow, you will see how Mrs. Temko suggests making the Reverse Folds. This method cannot be applied in all cases, but it is helpful in understanding the fold.

THE SWAN

Use a square of paper.

1. Valley-fold side flaps to centre crease.
2. Mountain-fold side flaps.
3. Valley-fold the model in half.
4. Form the neck and head by making the two Reverse Folds.

Florence Temko Method

Start with Fold 3. Do not Valley-fold, but move over to . . .

4. Here, Valley-fold the pointed flap.
5. Valley-fold the pointed tip, which is to become the head.
6. Mountain-fold the model in half.
7. Grip the neck and head where indicated, and pull it into position. Now press the creases flat. Adjust the head and press it flat.
   Finally, the finished Swan.

THREE-PETALLED FLOWER

Origin: *America*. Florence Temko.

1. Begin with Bird Base, position 2 (*Page* 18). Valley-fold upwards one bottom flap.
2. Valley-fold two middle flaps to centre crease.
3. Fold completed. Turn the model over.
4. Valley-fold two side flaps to centre.
5. Valley-fold stem of the flower, and open out the flower. Roll the petals round a pencil for the best effect.

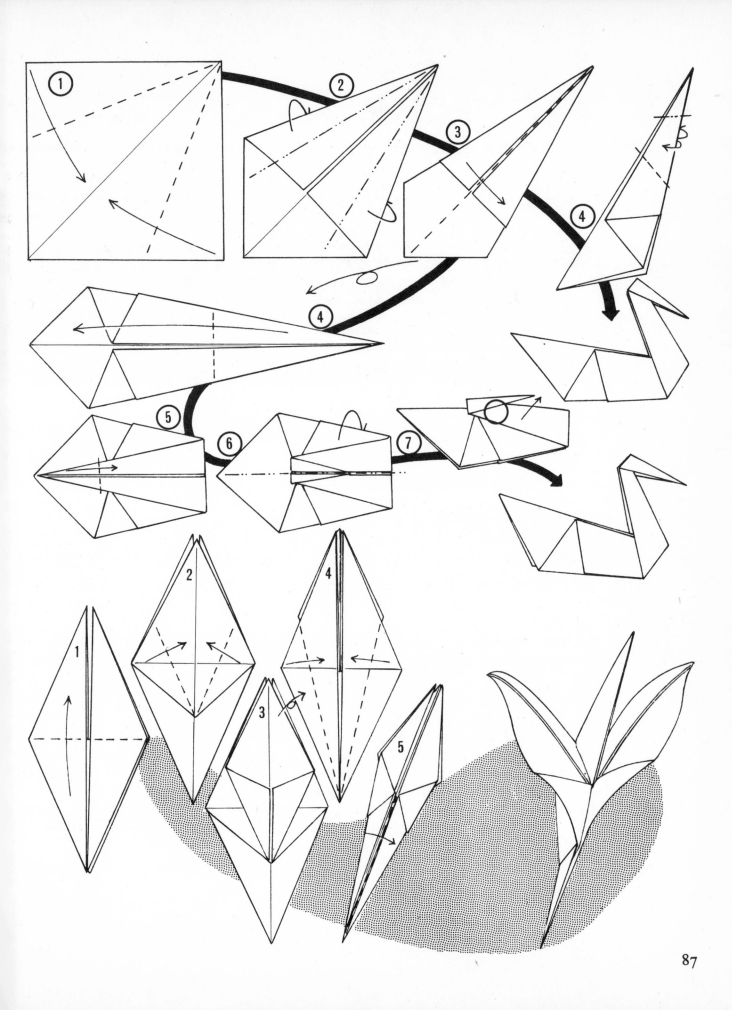

87

Robert Harbin

Born 1909—in South Africa, came to England at an early age and is today one of the World's leading magicians. Origami has become his all-absorbing interest and his one pleasure is to be able to illustrate and explain his own creations and those of the many friends he has made through this fascinating hobby.

BIRD IN FLIGHT

Origin: *England*. Robert Harbin.

Use a square of paper, coloured to choice. My series of folds are simple, and should be good training for the beginner.

1. The square has the standard markings of a Water Bomb Base.
2. The Base formed. Squash-fold the flap A.
3. Half done.
4. Petal-fold flap A. Repeat the same folds behind.
5. Here you see the creases being made before the Petal Fold.
6. Petal Fold half done. Repeat the same folds behind with B.
7. Point B is left up and point A down. Valley-fold the long flap indicated.
8. Valley-fold the model in half.
9. Carefully fold the wing. Valley-fold C in the direction of the arrow. Valley-fold the tail. Watch the new position of D.
10. Reverse-fold the neck.
11. Reverse-fold the head. Follow the group of folds to complete the head. Finally, the Bird in Flight.

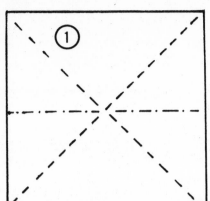
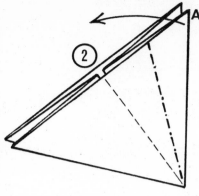
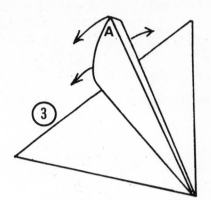
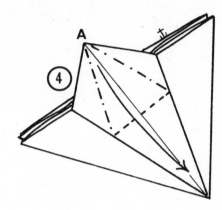
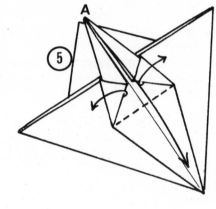
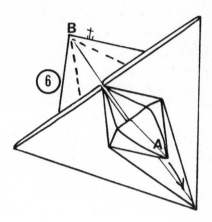
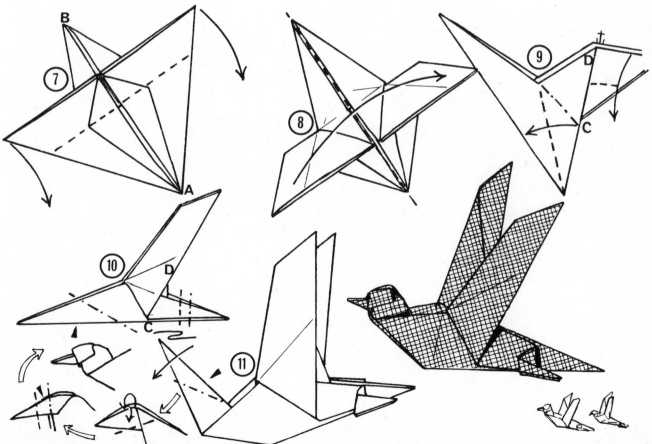

JAPANESE BLUE PHEASANT AND MATE

Origin: *England*. Robert Harbin.

Use a square of paper. Blue for male, brown for female. Begin with the Bird Base position 3 (*Page 18*).

1. Valley-fold the front flap upwards.
2. Squash-fold both leg flaps at right angles.
3. Valley-fold the four leg flaps inwards. Valley-fold the tail upwards (Hen only).
4. Valley-fold the leg flaps downwards. Valley-fold the model in half.
5. (Follow the right fork) Reverse-fold the neck. Reverse-fold the legs twice.
6. Reverse-fold the neck. Push in the tail portion. Reverse-fold the feet.
7. Reverse-fold the beak. Sink the top of the head (*see additional drawing*). Mountain-fold the stomach flaps inwards in front and behind. Push in the tail. Additional drawing shows how to sink the head.
Finally the completed Hen Pheasant.

JAPANESE BLUE PHEASANT

4. Reverse-fold the neck. Reverse-fold the tail. Cut away shows how to Reverse-fold the legs within the body. In front and behind. Additional drawing shows the leg formation.
5. Reverse-fold the neck. Mountain-fold the stomach flaps under, in front and behind. Valley-fold the tail flaps in front and behind. Reverse-fold both feet.
6. Reverse-fold the beak twice. Mountain-fold the whole neck behind. Reverse-fold the tail. Additional drawing shows how the head is crimped.
Finally the Blue Pheasant completed.

These two models show what can be done with the bird base. Using these procedures you can arrive at almost any bird imaginable, all you need is a little thought and a picture of the bird to work from.

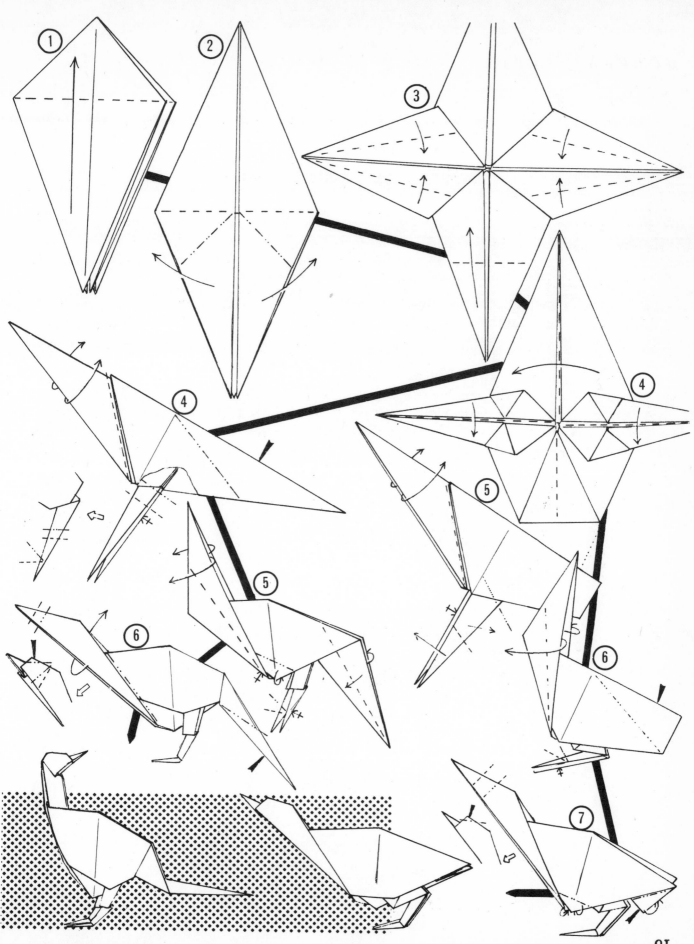

SEAL

Origin: *England*. Robert Harbin.

Use a square of grey or black paper.

1. Valley-fold the two sides to the centre crease.
2. Valley-fold the flaps to the centre.
3. Open out completely.
4. Valley-fold the paper across the diagonal.
5. Crease the two ends firmly.
6. Pinch the two corners together and bring them together.
7. This is the Fish Base, position 2 (*Page* 20), where another method is shown. Mountain-fold the model in half. Follow through the group of folds. Squash-fold the centre flaps in front and behind. Valley-fold the flaps on the Squash Fold inwards in front, and repeat behind. Reverse-fold the head. Reverse-fold the tail.
8. Crimp-fold the head (*Page* 16). Sink the chest front and back (*Page* 21). Valley-fold the front flipper over to the left. Repeat behind. Squash-fold the tail flipper.
9. Reverse-fold the tip of the head into itself. Mountain-fold the small flaps on the back in front, and repeat behind.
   Finally, the completed Seal.

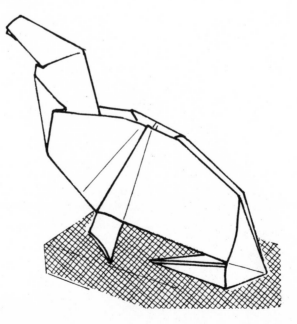

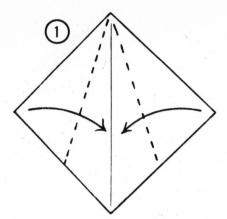

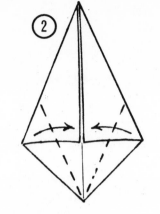

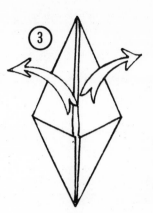

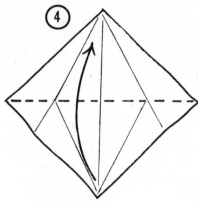

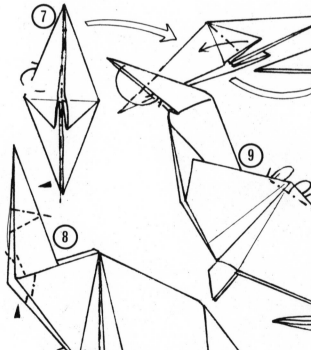

This seal was one of my earlier creations and you will find that there are many others very alike.

HARBIN'S MACAW

Origin: *England*. Robert Harbin.

Use a square of bright blue paper.

1. Begin with a stretched Bird Base (*Page* 175). Move fingers and thumbs inwards, and bring B up to A.
2. Fold a Rabbit's Ear with the triangular flap, and repeat with the similar flap behind.
3. Make Reverse Folds left and right.
4. Valley-fold the long tail flaps in front, and repeat behind. Watch the Sink symbol. Reverse-fold the head.
5. Reverse-fold the head. Valley-fold the tail in front and behind to meet again, as in Fig. 6.
6. Reverse-fold the head. Mountain-fold the two chest flaps in front and behind.
7. This group of folds shows clearly the formation of the head.
   Finally, the Macaw on its perch.

This particular bird seems to be a favourite with folders. I have seen many of them.

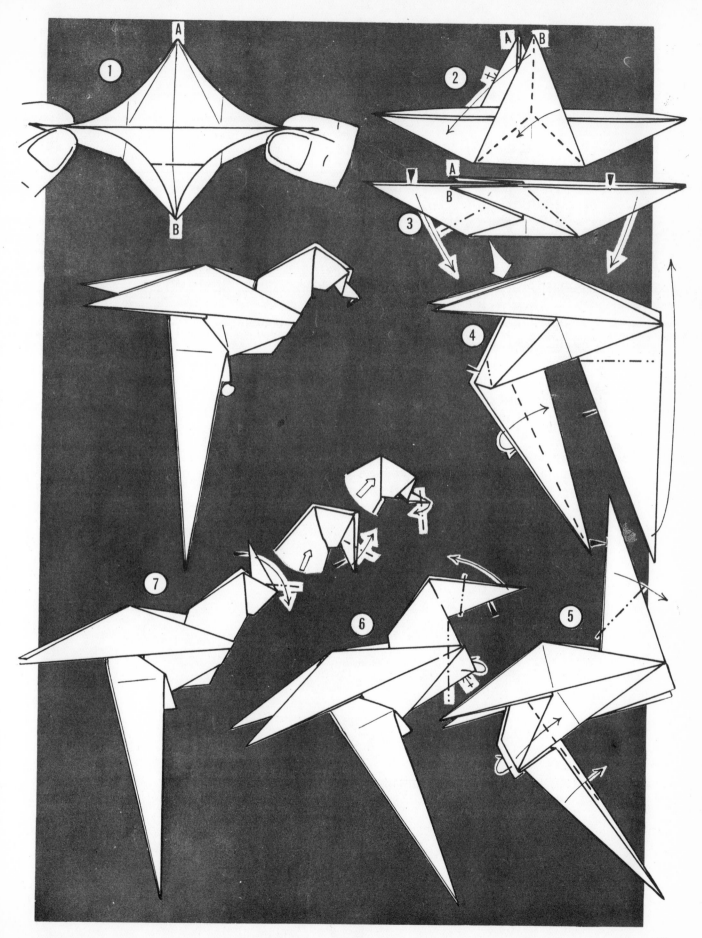

QUEEN ANNE TABLE

Origin: *England*. Robert Harbin.

Begin with a square of paper that is Blintzed (the corners folded to the centre).

1. The paper ready. Turn over.
2. Valley-fold the top and bottom flaps to the centre line.
3. Valley-fold the side flaps to the centre line.
4. Enlarged view. Crease heavily along the Valley Fold marks.
5. Pull out the four hidden corners in the direction of the arrow.
6. Squash-fold the four points.
7. Petal-fold the four flaps.
8. Hold at the points indicated and Sink (*Page* 21) the corner.
9. Sink begins.
10. Sink Fold almost complete. Repeat with the other three corners.
11. One corner completed. Fold the others. Turn over.
12. Valley-fold the little triangular flaps. These folds shape and stiffen the legs of the table. There are eight such folds.

Continued overleaf

When folding tables it is advisable to use somewhat stiffer, stronger paper.

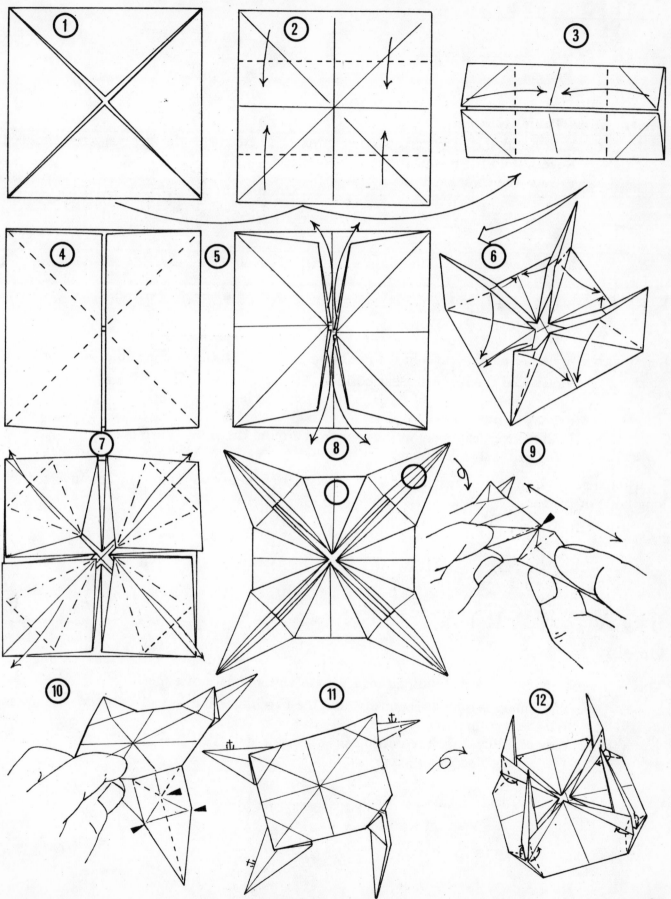

Queen Anne Table (*continued*)

13. Valley-fold the four narrow flaps inward. These make the legs very rigid indeed Reverse-fold the tips of the legs to form feet.
    Finally, the completed table.

CARD TABLE

Origin: *England.* Robert Harbin.

Begin with a square of paper, and fold it to position 12 of the Queen Anne Table. Now proceed:

12. Valley-fold the leg into a flat position.
13. Carry out this group of folds: Valley-fold the leg over right and repeat the folds. Repeat with the other three legs.
14. Fold to a vertical position the four flaps around the sides. Turn over.
    The Card Table complete.

By using a rectangle of paper, instead of a square, either of these two tables can be converted to a long table or bench.

BOAT VARIATION

Origin: *Japan.*

This is a variation of the boat described on Page 31. Use a square of paper.

1. The square is folded diagonally, and the flap illustrated is Valley-folded. Mountain-fold the bottom flap.
2. Very carefully, turn the portion shown inside-out.
3. The Sailing Boat completed.

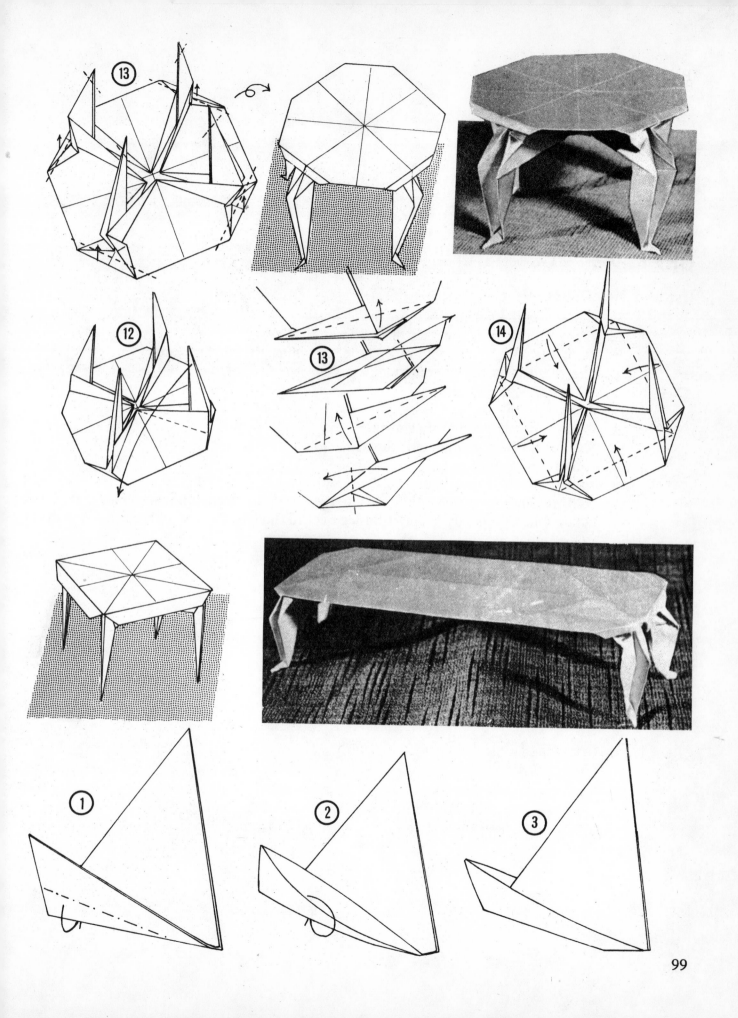

13

12

13

14

1

2

3

HARBIN'S BAT

Origin: *England*. Robert Harbin.

Use a square of black or brown paper.

1. Valley-fold the paper exactly in half.
2. Valley-fold both thicknesses of the flap indicated.
3. Using the edge of this fold as a guide, cut along the marked line.
4. The result is an equilateral triangle. You can use a compass and pencil to arrive at this triangle, if you prefer.
5. Valley-fold the top flap.
6. Make a special Rabbit's Ear of this.
7. The Rabbit's Ear completed. Squash-fold the centre upright.
8. Squash-fold complete.
9. Valley-fold left flap over to right.
10. Fold a Rabbit's Ear. Look right to the group of folds. Squash-fold. Petal-fold. Valley-fold, and finally Valley-fold leg over to the left. Repeat all these folds with the other similar flap.
11. The two legs completed, turn the model over.
12. Valley-fold the wing on the right over to the left.

Continued overleaf

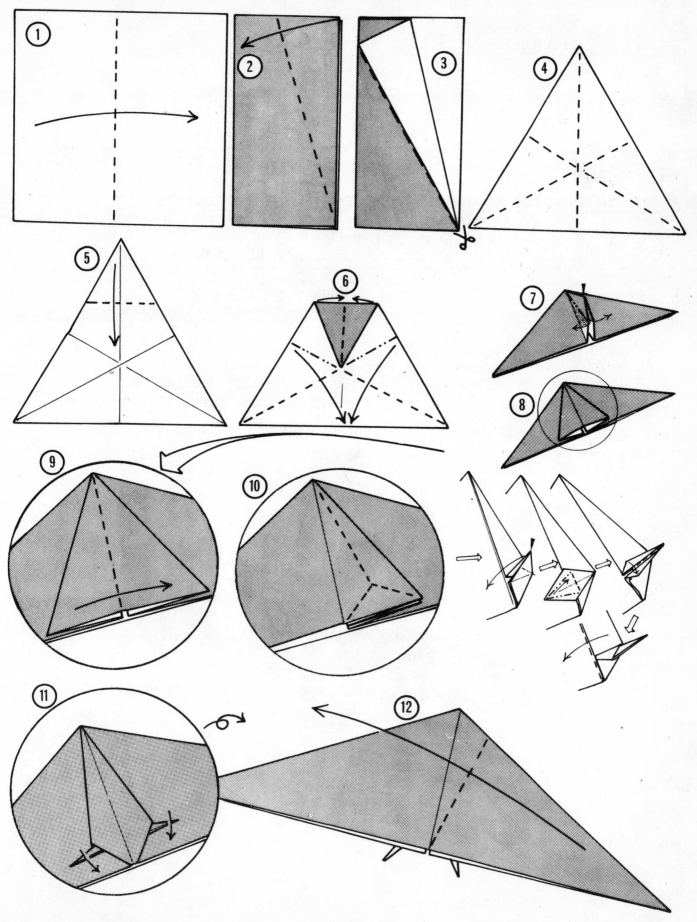

Harbin's Bat (*continued*)

13. Valley-fold the wing over to the right.
14. Valley-fold the left wing over to the right wing, so that tip meets tip
15. Valley-fold the top wing over to the left.
16. Mountain-fold the two back flaps, and the inside neck flaps.
17. Completed. Turn the model over.
18. Valley-fold the head downwards. Squash-fold both wing tips. Be careful! This is no ordinary Squash Fold. Watch the spots marked X. These spots stay where they are.
19. Valley-fold the two small flaps in the head. This fold will form the snout and the ears. Valley-fold the ends of the wings in an arc. Crease the body as marked.
    Finally, the finished Bat. If you place a small roll of cotton wool under the triangular flap (*see Fold* 6 *on previous page*) you will build the body up to the correct thickness.

I am very proud of this little model. So will you be, when you have made it up. It will be one of your show pieces.

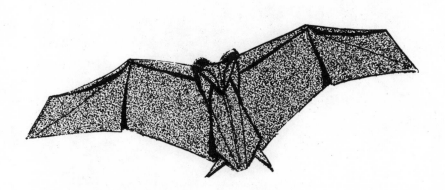

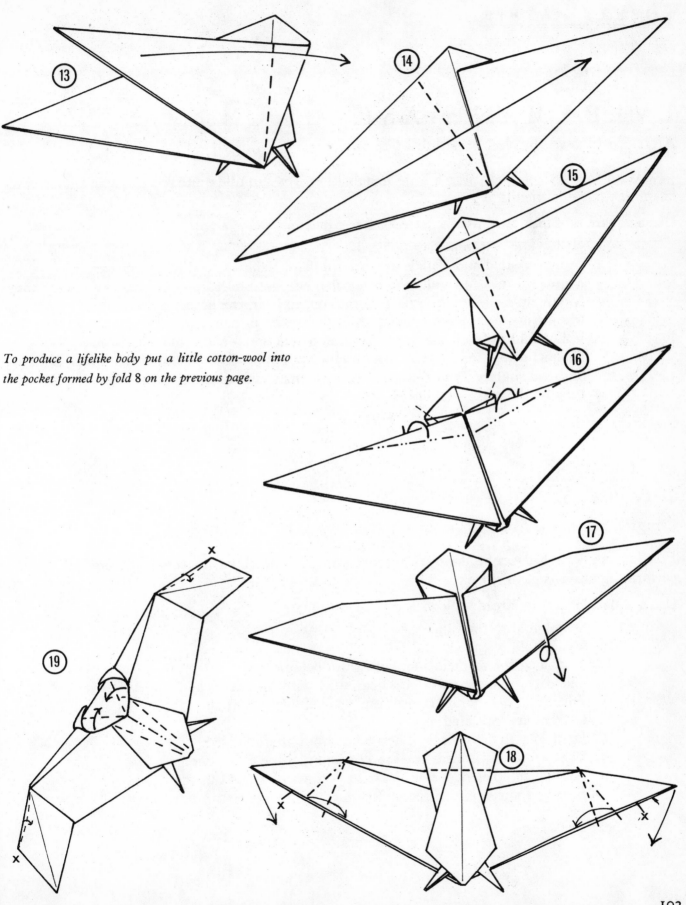

To produce a lifelike body put a little cotton-wool into
the pocket formed by fold 8 on the previous page.

EVERYMAN MASK

After Yoshizawa. Folded by Adolfo Cerceda.

With this system, and using a little imagination, you can fold quite recognisable and striking likenesses of your friends.

Use a square of paper. Begin with the Fish Base, position 3 (*Page* 20)

1. Valley-fold the front flap upwards.
2. Mountain-fold and Valley-fold the top flap. Valley-fold the bottom flap.
3. Mountain-fold and Valley-fold top flap and bottom flap.
4. Mountain-fold two little flaps at the top, to form the nose.
5. Mountain-fold the nose. Valley-fold the model in half.
6. Valley-fold the two top flaps. Mountain-fold and Valley-fold the arrowed flap.
7. Mountain-fold top of head. Mountain-fold both hair flaps and both cheeks. Squash-fold and slightly Petal-fold the two little flaps next to the nose.
   Finally, the mask completed.

FANCY BOWL

Origin: *England.* Robert Harbin.

This shows what can be done with a **octagon.** Upside-down, it makes a good base for the performing animals in this book.

Use a square of paper, already folded across its diagonal.

1. Valley-fold to the right.
2. Valley-fold to the left.
3. Cut along the marked line, both sides being equal.
4. Cut paper opened out. Crease carefully with Mountain and Valley Folds.
5. Form this base with creases just made. Squash-fold all eight corner flaps. The two in front are indicated.
6. Petal-fold all eight flaps. The two in front are indicated.
7. Valley-fold downwards the marked flap and the other one.
8. Folding completed, crease the base both ways. Open out the bowl.
   Finally, the completed Fancy Bowl.

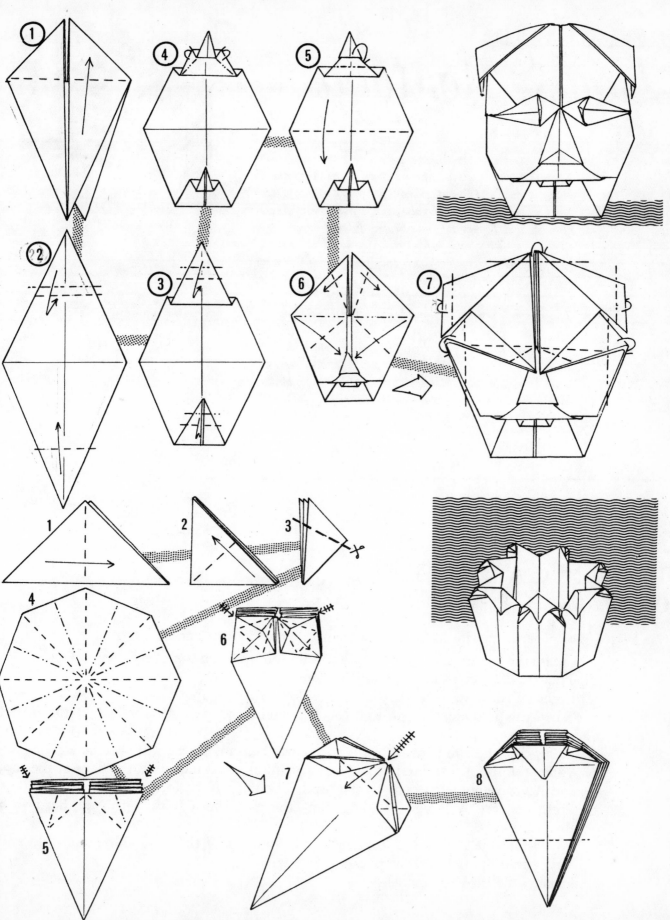

1

2

3

4

5

6

7

1

2

3

4

5

6

7

8

Ligia Montoya

Senorita Ligia Montoya, who was born in the Argentine, is regarded as the foremost woman paper-folder today. Her creations, which are innumerable, range from simple figures of birds and flowers to fantastically difficult insects. Her work is sensitive and ingenious, and her generosity in passing on her secrets to others is widely known. My great regret is that nobody will ever be able to set down on paper, or put into diagram form, the whole of her work.

This section is devoted to some of the work of Ligia Montoya. The models I have chosen are the ones I feel will be best suited to the student of Origami. The figures which form the Scene of the Nativity should delight everyone. We start the series devoted to Ligia Montoya, by one of her many birds— each different, each delightful, and each a pleasure to fold.

TROPICAL BIRD

Origin: *Argentina.* Ligia Montoya.

Use a square of paper (Senorita Montoya always uses white airmail paper).

1. Crease the square as indicated. Make a Rabbit's Ear on top of a Rabbit's Ear.
2. The two diagrams show how this is done.
3. Form a Fish Base with what is left (*see Second Stage, Page* 20).
4. When this is done, Squash-fold the flaps indicated, and Mountain-fold the model in half.
5. Valley-fold the two flaps in front, and repeat behind. These will become legs.
6. Valley-fold the leg to the left and repeat behind. Mountain-fold the flaps at the top, and Reverse-fold what is to be the head. The tail will be formed automatically.
7. Form the feet by Reverse-folding. Sink the chest both sides. Form the head with Reverse Folds.
8. Valley-fold the tips of the forehead. Sink the back of the head. Mountain-fold and Valley-fold the tail into the pocket of the tail.
   Finally, the Bird complete.

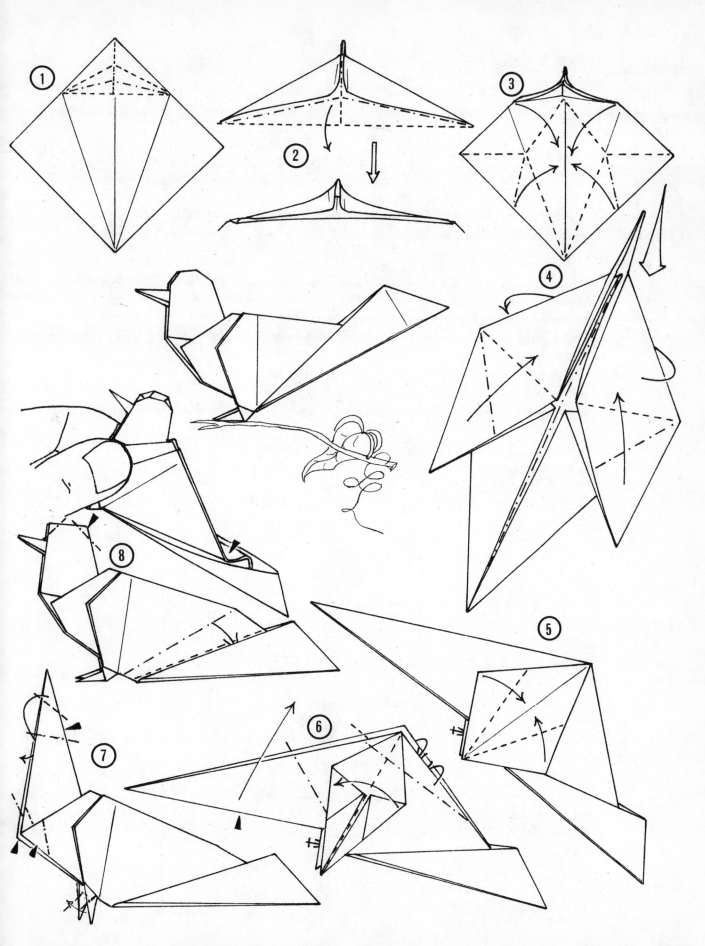

BIRD OF PARADISE

Origin: *Argentina*. Ligia Montoya.

Use a square of paper.

1. Start with the Fish Base, second position (*Page* 20). Valley-fold the bottom tip, and Mountain-fold the model in half.
2. Squash-fold the flap indicated, and repeat behind.
3. Valley-fold the tip of the tail in front and behind. Petal-fold the flap indicated, and repeat behind.
4. Valley-fold the flap to the left, and repeat behind.
5. Valley-fold the leg in front and behind. Reverse-fold the tail.
6. Reverse-fold the neck. Mountain-fold the tips on the back in front and behind. Mountain-fold and Valley-fold the legs.
7. Watch this group of diagrams! Sink the chest on both sides, and form the neck and head as illustrated.
   Finally, the completed Bird of Paradise.

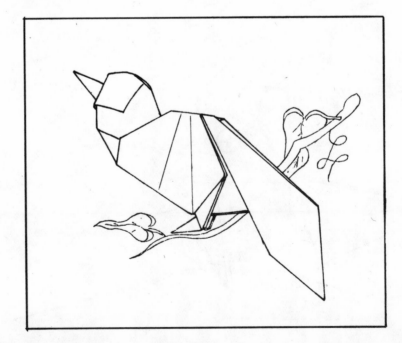

See Plate 16 for three delightful bird designs by Ligia Montoya.

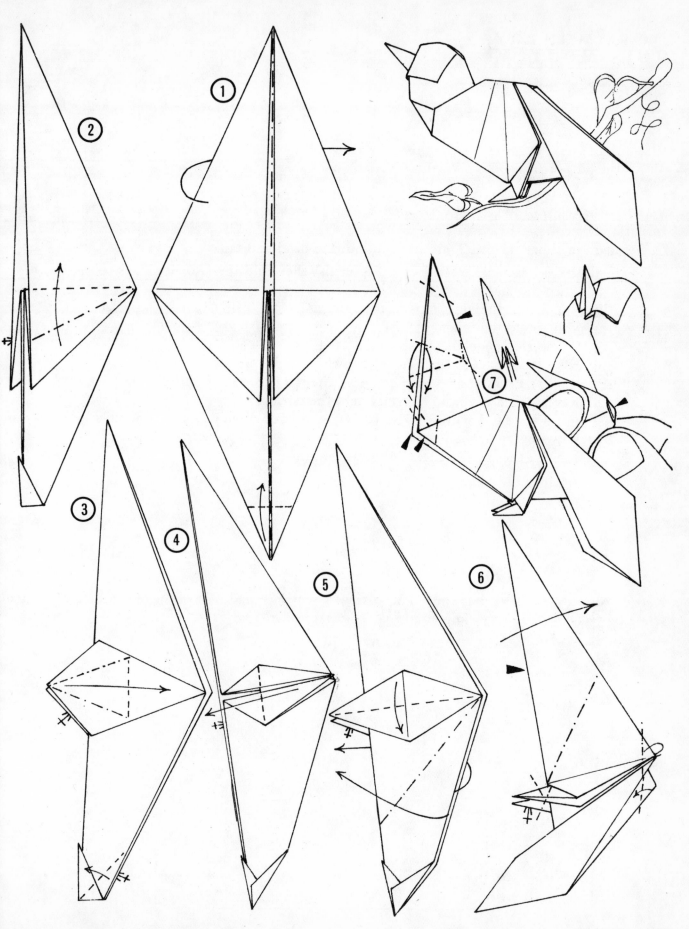

SWAN

Origin: *Argentina*. Ligia Montoya.

Use a square of paper. H and T are used to indicate head and tail.

1. Crease the square along the diagonal. Valley-fold the two side flaps to the centre.
2. Turn the model over.
3. Valley-fold the long flaps to the centre.
4. Valley-fold the model in half.
5. Crimp the model at the spot indicated.
6. Hold the model in the manner shown, and Reverse-fold the tail.
7. Reverse-fold the neck. Reverse-fold the tail (inside flap only).
8. Reverse-fold the head. Reverse-fold the tail.
9. Form the head with a series of Mountain and Valley Folds. The enlarged diagram shows every detail.
   Finally, the superb Ligia Montoya Swan.

Senorita Montoya is very proud indeed of this swan, which is made out of the old-fashioned original Schoolboy's Dart. It is very simple, and yet so very realistic.

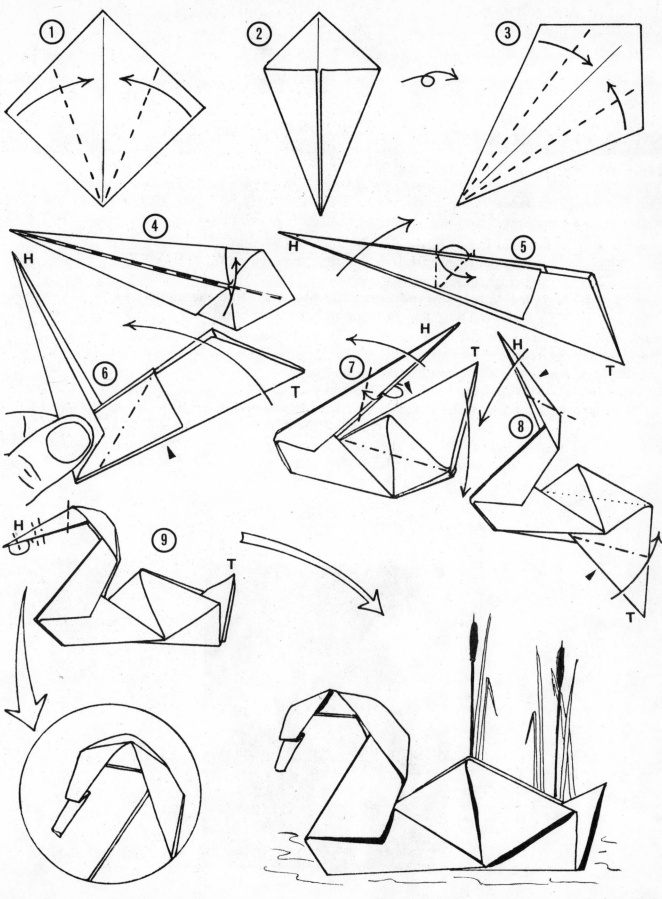

III

SEA HORSE

Origin: *Argentina.* Ligia Montoya.

Use a rectangle of paper.

1. Valley-fold the rectangle in half.
2. Valley-fold in half again.
3. Cut along the line indicated, and then open out completely.
4. Form a Fish Base, position 2 (*Page* 20).
5. Squash-fold the flaps indicated, and Mountain-fold the model in half.
6. Valley-fold the long flap in front and repeat behind.
7. Reverse-fold the head.
8. Reverse-fold the tail.
9. Reverse-fold the head. Reverse-fold the tail.
10. Reverse-fold the head. Reverse-fold the tail.
11. Sink the top of the head. Mountain-fold and Valley-fold the snout and tail. Pull out the flap behind the shoulder, and shape it as in 12.
12. Make a Rabbit's Ear of the snout on both sides. To do this, pinch it together with thumb and finger and push in.
    Finally, the finished Sea Horse.

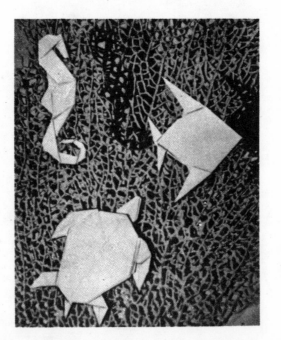

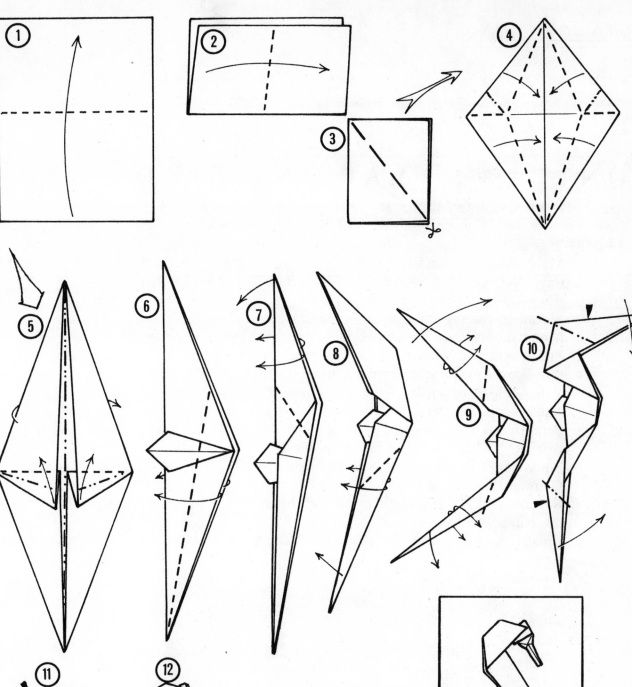

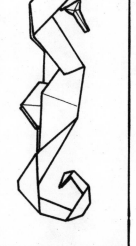

MONTOYA'S FLAPPING BIRD

Origin: *Argentina*. Ligia Montoya.

Use a square of paper.

1. Make the creases indicated—two diagonals and the square divided into three both ways. Valley-fold A and crease as indicated. B will rise.
2. With A down, lift B over to the arrowed position. Fold D over to the arrowed position, Mountain-folding the side in the process.
3. Mountain-fold and Valley-fold C down to the arrowed position.
4. Pull A out, and Valley-fold to the arrowed position.
5. Pull B over to the arrowed position.
6. Valley-fold A upwards.
7. Squash-fold A.
8. Petal-fold A.
9. Bring D under B to the arrowed position.
10. Squash-fold D. Make a square Petal Fold of D. Valley-fold flap D. Mountain-fold C around behind to B.
11. Reverse-fold A twice to form neck and head. Mountain-fold flaps on D to narrow the tail.
    Finally, hold the chest and gently move the tail in and out, causing the wings to flap.

This bird is improved if a more advanced head is added to it, as in other bird models. In fact, whenever you feel you can improve a model, by all means do so.

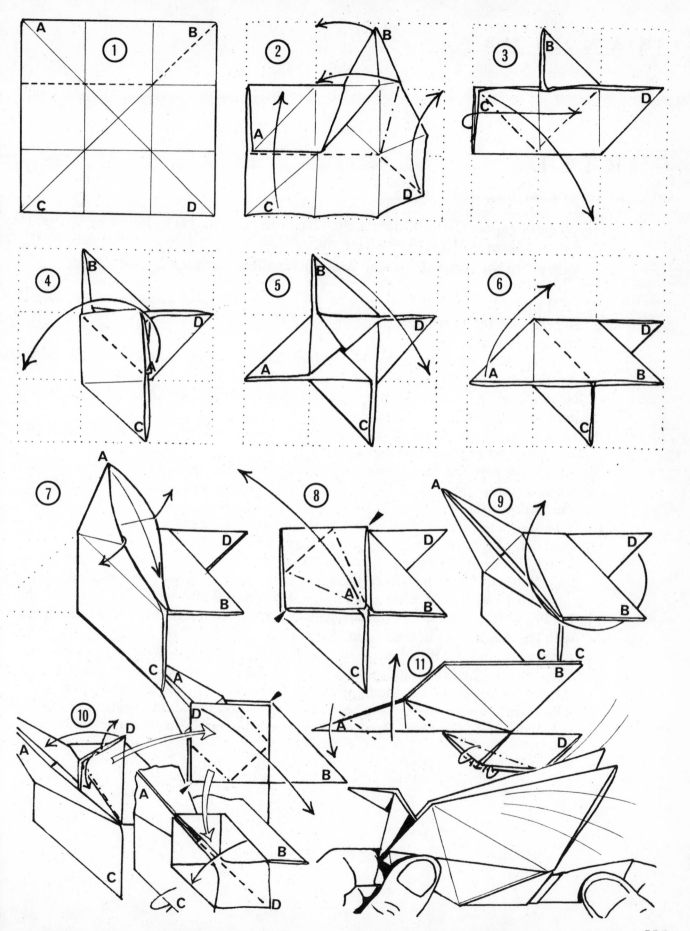

TURTLE

Origin: *Argentina*. Ligia Montoya.

Use a 2 : 1 rectangle of paper. The same double Bird Base can be arrived at by following instructions for The Moor on Horseback (*Page* 166).

1. Valley-fold the rectangle in half. Make a Bird Base with the doubled paper.
2. Squash-fold.
3. Petal-fold.
4. Repeat with the other side.
5. Open up completely.
6. The rectangle creased ready. Valley-fold flaps left and right downwards to meet centre base.
7. Now, using the creases, form a Bird Base left and right, and ease it out to look like position 8.
8. Hold the model at W and B. Pull, and make a stretched Bird Base (*Page* 175). Hold at W again, and at A, and stretch again.
9. This is the result. All important points are lettered, so that you can follow the movement. Bring points A and B together, pushing in as indicated. Note the Mountain and Valley Folds marked.
10. This shows the fold halfway done. Bring A and B together.
11. Fold completed, the other way up. Reverse-fold B and repeat with A.
12. Watch this carefully. Bring B down to W. Book-fold K over to the right, at the same time Valley-folding the centre triangle. This happens almost automatically. D will move up to V. Repeat with A behind. Lift up flap B and see if you have it right.
13. Fold completed. Book-fold the two flaps indicated from right to left, and do the same with the similar two behind from left to right.
14. Reverse-fold D, C, B and A.
15. Form the tail by bringing down the point at the top and pushing in the sides. Form the head at the bottom by doing the same thing. Squash-fold all the flippers.
16. The extra drawing shows how head and tail should look underneath. Petal-fold the tail. Valley-fold the head. Petal-fold the front flippers in the manner indicated.

Continued overleaf

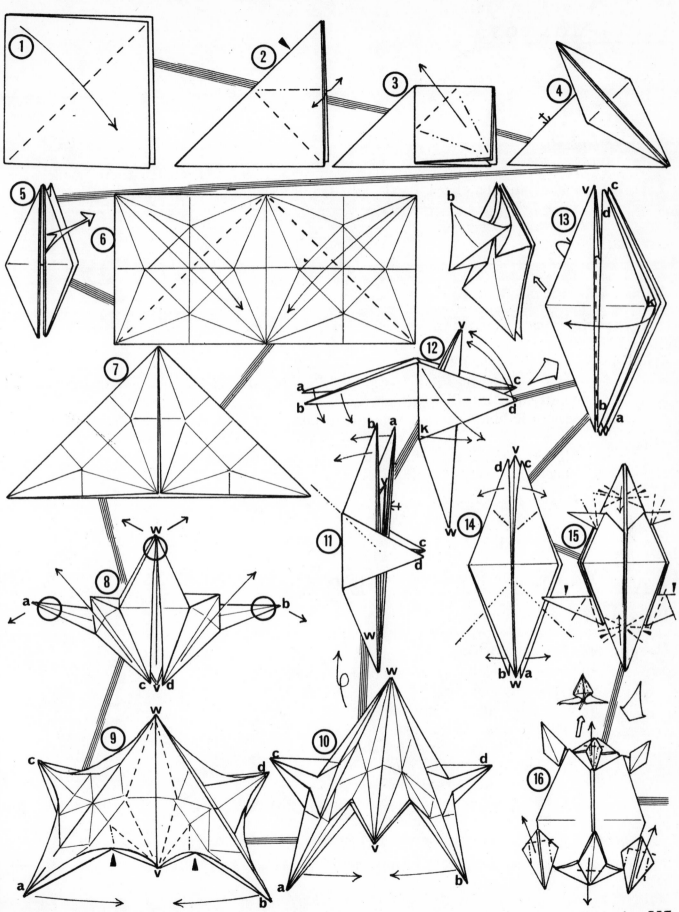

Turtle (*continued*)

    17. Here you see all underneath folds completed, in absolute detail. Turn the model over. Finally, the completed Turtle, as it should look on the right side.

ANGEL FISH

Origin: *Argentina*. Ligia Montoya.

Use a square of paper, of suitable colour.

    1. Begin with the Bird Base, position 2 (*Page* 18), this way up. Reverse-fold the bottom points, and fold back flap down.
    2. Make a Rabbit's Ear and Valley-fold right, at the top. Make a Rabbit's Ear and fold left at the bottom. Crimp the two fins left and right.
    3. All folds completed. Valley-fold the top tail fin down to the bottom fin.
       Finally, the completed Angel Fish.

JAPANESE LANTERN

Origin: *Japan*. Traditional.

Use a square of coloured paper.

    1. Valley-fold both sides to the centre crease.
    2. Valley-fold four corner flaps as indicated.
    3. With this done, turn the model over.
    4. Valley-fold top and bottom flaps, as arrowed.
    5. When this is done, turn the model over.
    6. Fold four corner flaps as indicated.
    7. Enlarged view. Turn the model over.
    8. Mountain-fold top and bottom four triangles by pulling outwards. Inside flaps will move into place automatically.
       Finally, the finished decorated Lantern.

These Japanese Lanterns make splendid items for decoration, and are usually coloured after folding.

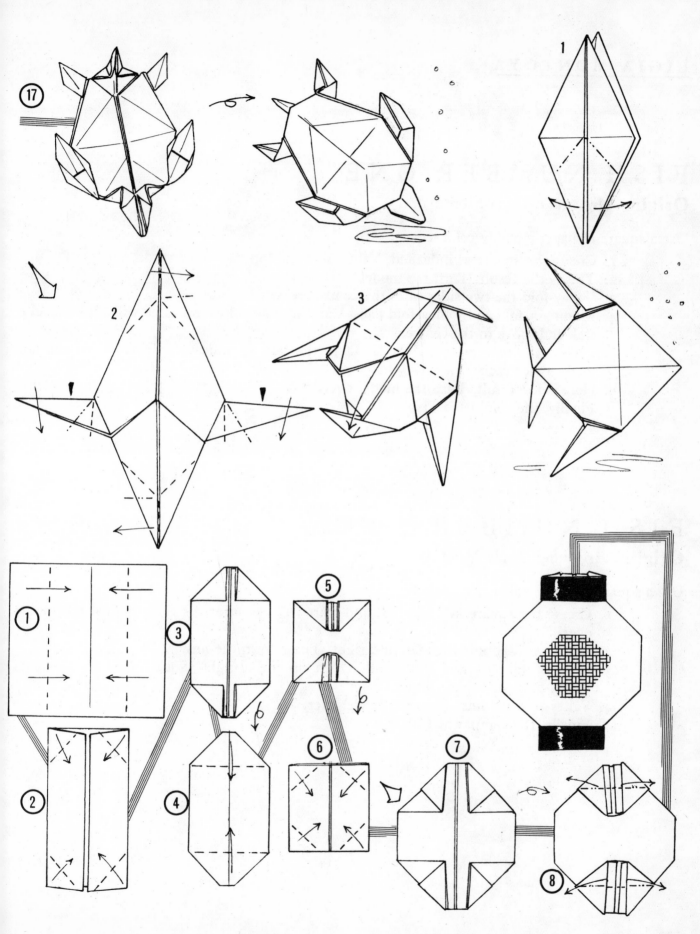

FISH NUMBER ONE

Origin: *Argentina*. Ligia Montoya.

Use a square of paper suitably coloured.

1. Crease the square as indicated. Valley-fold the top flap downwards.
2. This is the result. Turn the model over.
3. Valley-fold the two sides in to the centre crease.
4. Mountain-fold and Valley-fold flaps A and B. The points indicated will automatically sink and move to the centre.
5. This is the new position. Cut a slit in the tail, as indicated. Reverse-fold the tail pieces twice each.
6. Here is the result. Turn the model over.
   Finally, the completed Fish.

FISH NUMBER TWO

Origin: *Argentina*. Ligia Montoya.

Use a square of paper suitably coloured.

1. Crease the square as indicated, and start from position 2 (*above*). Turn the model over.
2. Make two Rabbit's Ears left and right. These form the fins.
3. Make a Rabbit's Ear of the tail. Open up the upright. Squash-fold the upright: Valley-fold the Squash Fold.
4. Valley-fold the fins. Turn the model over.
   Finally, the completed Fish.

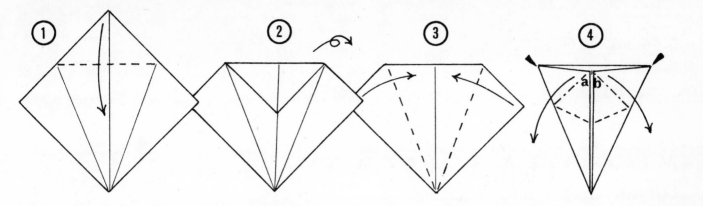

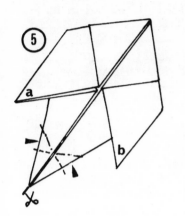

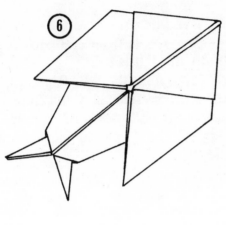

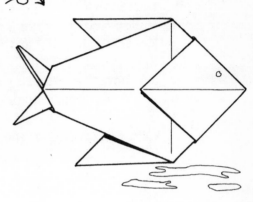

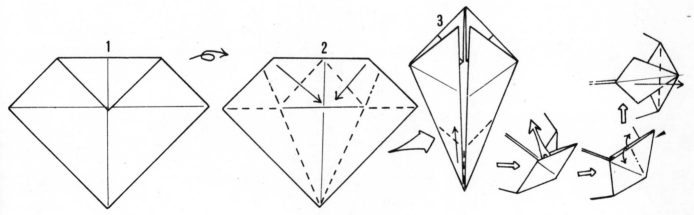

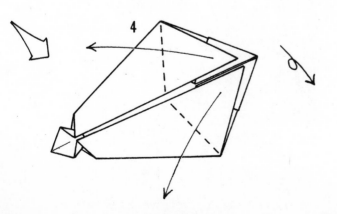

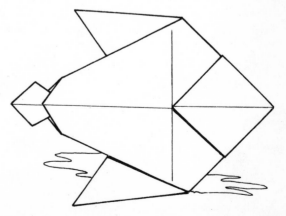

MONTOYA'S MACAW

Origin: *Argentina*. Ligia Montoya.

Use a square of blue paper.

1. Begin with the Fish Base, position 2 (*Page* 20). Mountain-fold the model in half.
2. Valley-fold the wing flaps downwards front and back.
3. Reverse-fold head at the top and tail below.
4. Sink the chest at the top. Valley-fold the long flaps of the tail front and back.
5. See how the chest is sunk. Reverse-fold the tail to position 6.
6. With this long triangle flattened, Valley-fold the tail downwards.
7. This series of drawings shows the details of the head formation. Two "Push-in" Crimps are used in the neck.
   Finally, the finished Macaw.

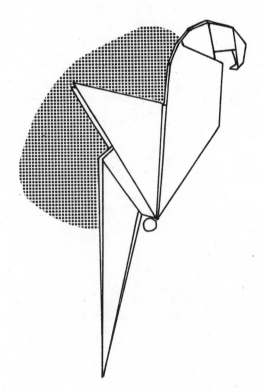

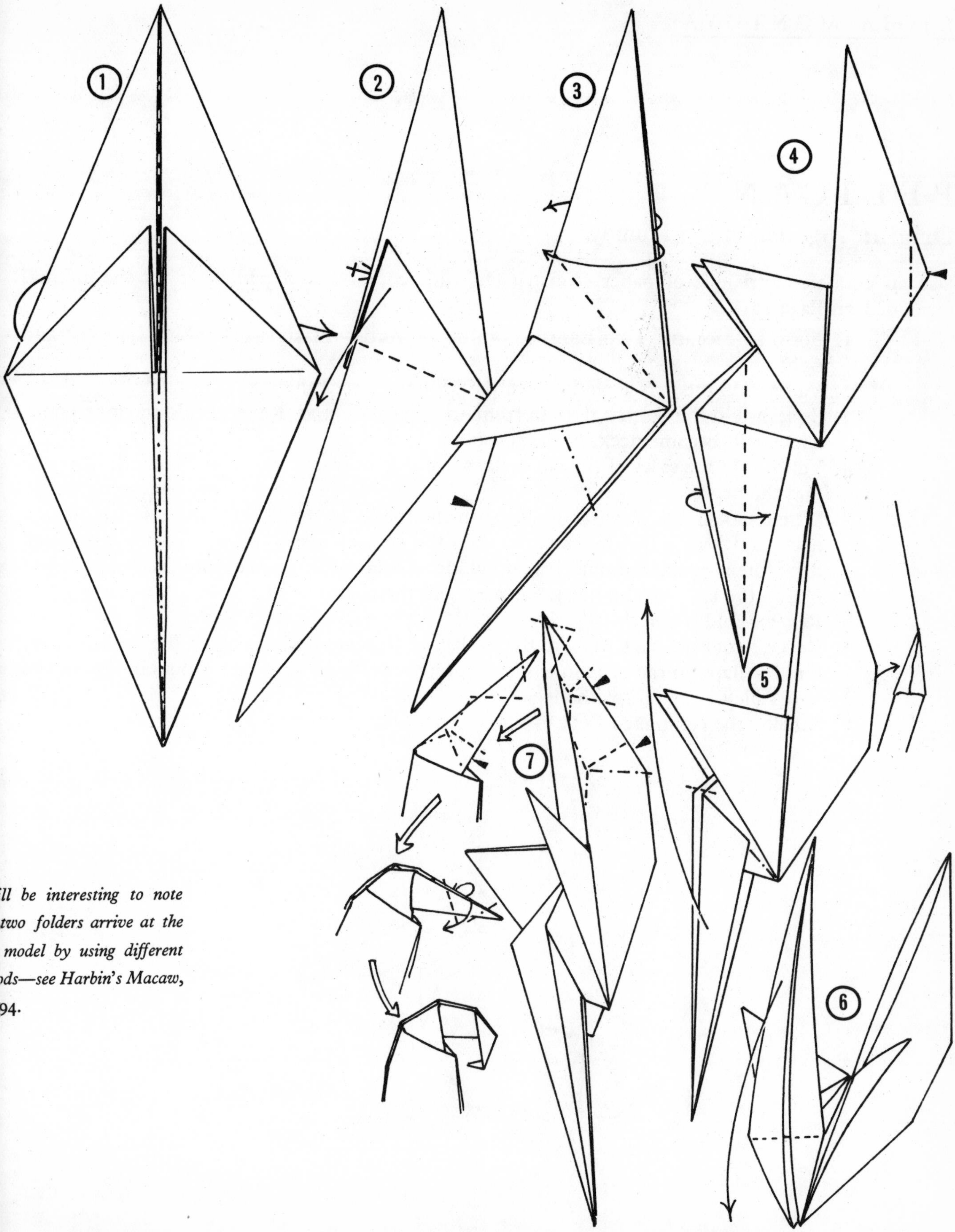

'll be interesting to note
two folders arrive at the
model by using different
ods—see Harbin's Macaw,
94.

PELICAN

Origin: *Argentina.* Ligia Montoya.

Use an equilateral triangle of paper, constructed with compass and pencil, or by the method explained on Page 101.

1. Form an eccentric Fish Base, or—in other words—make two Rabbit's Ears left and right.
2. Valley-fold the two flaps downwards. Mountain-fold the model in half.
3. Squash-fold the bottom flaps in front and repeat behind. Reverse-fold the long point, which will become neck, head, and beak.
4. Valley-fold the sides of the small flaps inwards in front, and repeat behind. Reverse-fold the neck.
5. When making the Reverse Folds, grip the model at the point shown. Open out the neck, and Valley-fold the long flaps in the centre crease. Valley-fold the two small flaps (the legs) in front and repeat behind. Reverse-fold the tail into the body.
6. Crimp the tail into the body. Reverse-fold the neck.
7. Reverse-fold the neck.
8. Reverse-fold the neck to form the beak, and Reverse-fold the tip of the beak. Valley-fold the flaps on the back in front, and repeat behind. With two Mountain Folds and two Valley Folds, form the legs.
Finally, the completed Pelican—a very fine model indeed.

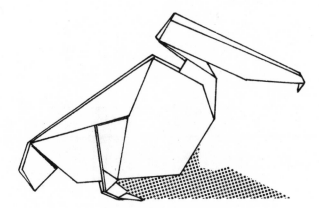

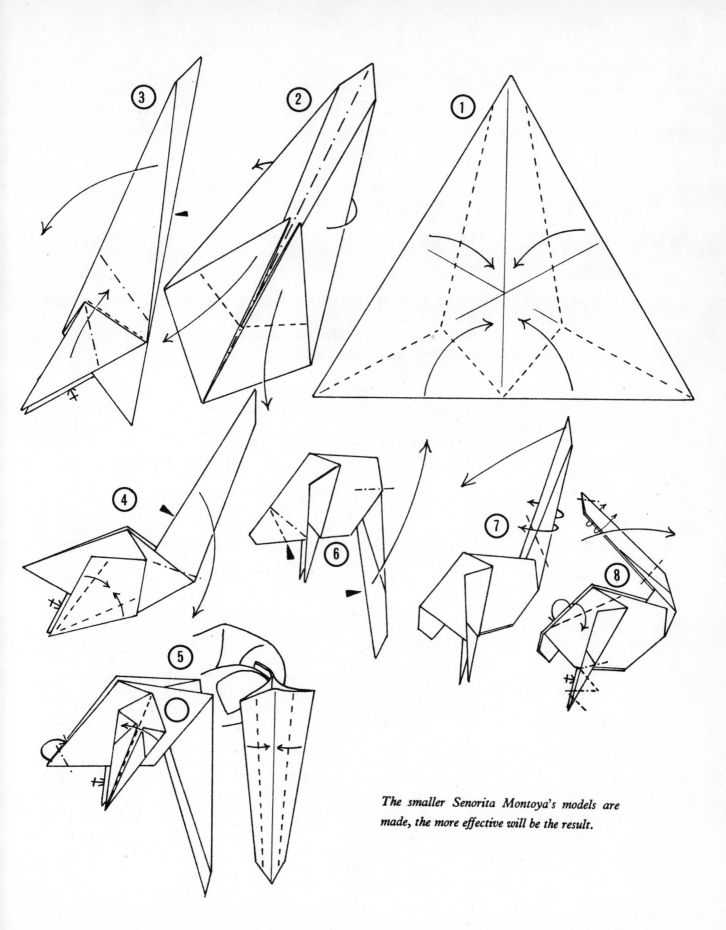

The smaller Senorita Montoya's models are made, the more effective will be the result.

HUMMING BIRD

Origin: *Argentina*. Ligia Montoya.

Use a square of paper.

1. Begin with a Fish Base, position 2 (*Page* 20). Squash-fold the two flaps indicated.
2. Make this special Rabbit's Ear out of the bottom flap.
3. Here the Rabbit's Ear is completed. Mountain-fold the model in half. While you do this, push in the chest, making a Valley Fold.
4. This is how the model is held.
5. Reverse-fold the neck. Mountain-fold the two stomach flaps. Reverse-fold the tail.
6. Mountain-fold and Valley-fold the beak. Mountain-fold the tail into itself and Reverse-fold the tail.
   Finally, the Humming Bird, feeding on honey.

Take great care with fold 3. The drawing may not indicate clearly enough that the next section is upright when the fold is made, resulting in 4.

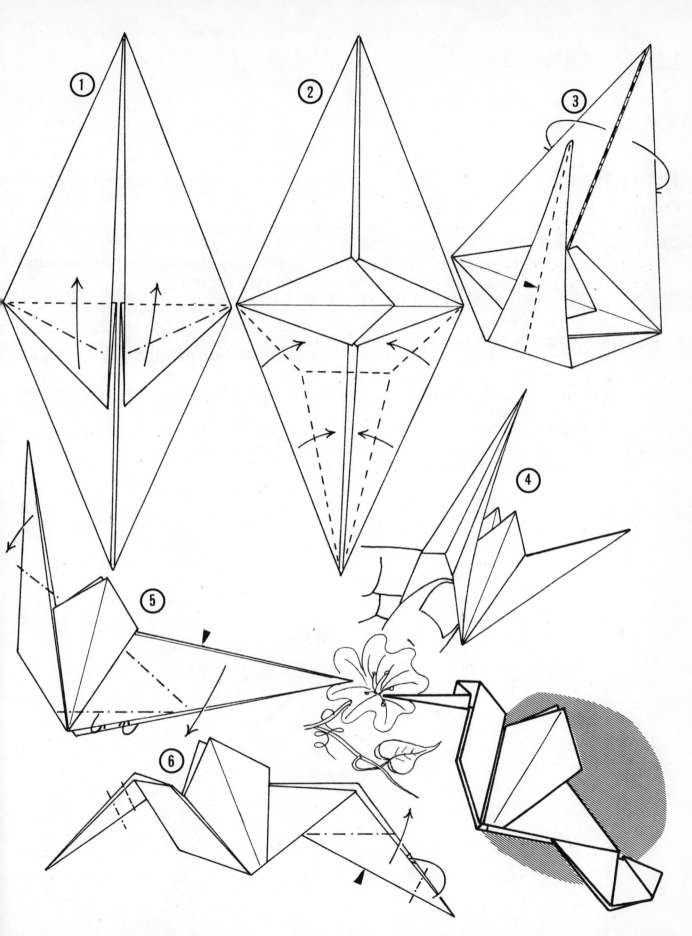

PIGEON

Origin: *Argentina*. Ligia Montoya.

Use a square of paper.

1. Begin with a stretched Bird Base (*Page* 175, position 4, the other way up and turned over). Valley-fold the tip of the bottom flap. Turn the model over.
2. Squash-fold both pointed flaps, which will be the wings.
3. Mountain-fold the model in half.
4. Crimp-fold the tail, which goes under the wings in front and behind.
5. Valley-fold the wing at the root, and Mountain-fold the right edge. This is really half a Petal Fold. Repeat with wing behind.
6. Crease the neck as marked, then Crimp the neck into itself, forming the two little inward gussets in the crop.
7. Reverse-fold the head.
8. Form the beak with a Mountain Fold and a Valley Fold.
   Finally, the finished model, a perfect bird.

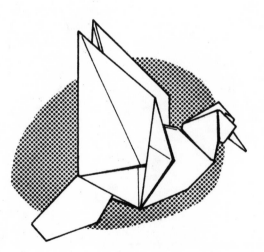

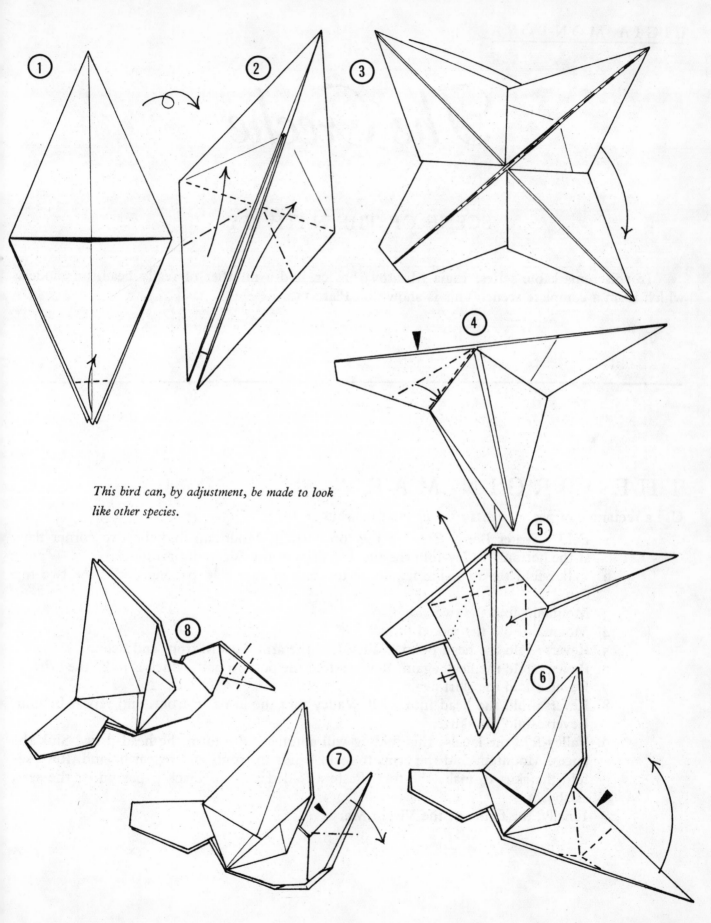

This bird can, by adjustment, be made to look like other species.

The Creche

SCENE OF THE NATIVITY

In this remarkable series, Ligia Montoya has created a number of really beautiful models, which form a complete scene. This is shown on Plate 15.

THE VIRGIN MARY

Use a rectangle of paper, size 19.5 × 11 cm., in white.

1. Fold a Water Bomb Base on the top portion. Mountain-fold the two corner flaps at the bottom. Valley-fold the two top flaps of the Water Bomb Base.
2. Valley-fold the two side flaps, the top half of each flap passing under the two top flaps.
3. Mountain-fold the two side flaps.
4. Mountain-fold the model in half.
5. Reverse-fold the head point. Valley-fold the arm flaps in front and behind.
6. Reverse-fold the head again. Reverse-fold the bottom half, which is to be the skirt.
7. Reverse-fold the skirt again.
8. Reverse-fold the head into itself. Valley-fold the arms in front, and repeat behind. Reverse-fold the skirt.
9. Valley-fold the lapels; this folding will automatically form the head-dress. Sink the knees. Mountain-fold the arms to form hands in front, and repeat behind. Reverse-fold the skirt to make the foot. Paste a folded strip of black paper under the seat, as shown.

Finally, the figure of the Virgin Mary.

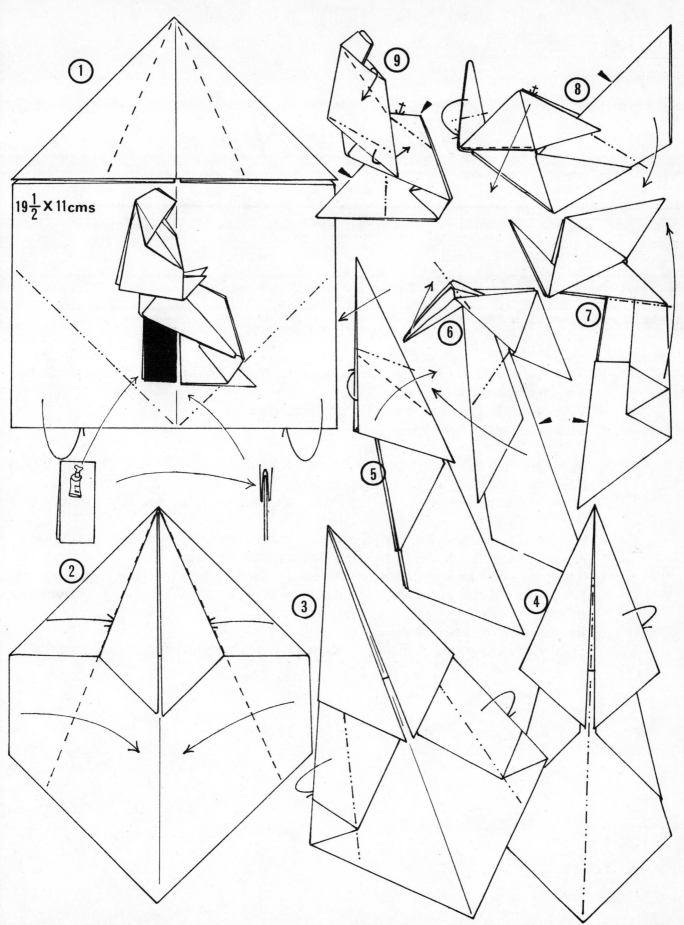

1

$19\frac{1}{2} \times 11$cms

2

3

4

5

6

7

8

9

131

The Creche

STANDING ANGEL

Origin: *Argentina*. Ligia Montoya.

Use a rectangle, size 15 × 11·5 cm., in white.

1. Fold a Water Bomb Base on the top portion. Valley-fold to the centre line the two bottom corners.
2. Valley-fold the flaps under the Water Bomb Base.
3. This is the result.
4. Valley-fold the two long side flaps.
5. Mountain-fold and Valley-fold the bottom. Snip the tip to form feet. Turn the model over.
6. Study the notations or markings on the wing flaps. Crease and fold carefully two Rabbit's Ears.
7. Form a small Rabbit's Ear with the hidden centre point, to represent hands in prayer. Mountain-fold the model in half and Reverse-fold the head.
8. This group of drawings shows how the head is formed, by a top view of the Reverse-folded head. Petal-fold the head. Mountain-fold the tip of the wing in front and behind.
9. Reverse-fold the head into itself.
   Finally, the completed Angel. This drawing is a tracing from the actual model.

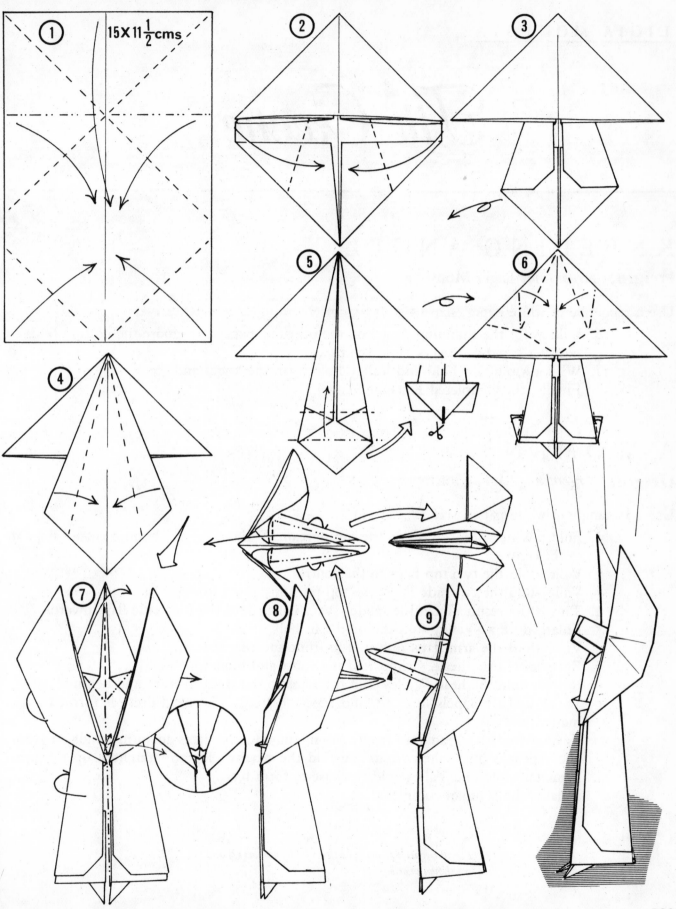

The Creche

KNEELING ANGEL

Origin: *Argentina*. Ligia Montoya.

Use a rectangle of white paper, size 15·5 × 11·5 cm.

10. Fold as for the Standing Angel on the previous page, but ignore the bottom folds in position 5 and 6. Reverse-fold the base.
11. With a Mountain Fold and Valley Fold form the knees and feet.
    Finally, the completed Kneeling Angel.

A WOMAN

Origin: *Argentina*. Ligia Montoya.

Use a rectangle of white paper, size 18 × 11 cm.

1. Fold a Water Bomb Base on the top portion. Valley-fold the bottom corner flaps in to the centre.
2. Valley-fold the two top flaps to the centre.
3. Valley-fold the two side flaps, the top portions going under.
4. This is the result. Turn the model over. Valley-fold the long side flap inwards.
5. Enlarged view. Valley-fold the model in half.
6. Valley-fold the arm flaps upwards in front and repeat behind.
7. Reverse-fold the head. Crimp-fold the waist and push in.
8. Reverse-fold the head. Valley-fold the arms to the right in front and behind.
9. Valley-fold the lapels in front, and repeat behind. The head-dress is formed automatically.
10. Reverse-fold the head into itself. Mountain-fold the arms to form hands in front, and repeat behind, then Mountain-fold the narrow flap to straighten up the arm. Mountain-fold and Valley-fold the base to form feet.
    Finally, the Woman completed.

The illustrations for the last two folds, numbers 9 and 10, are shown overleaf.

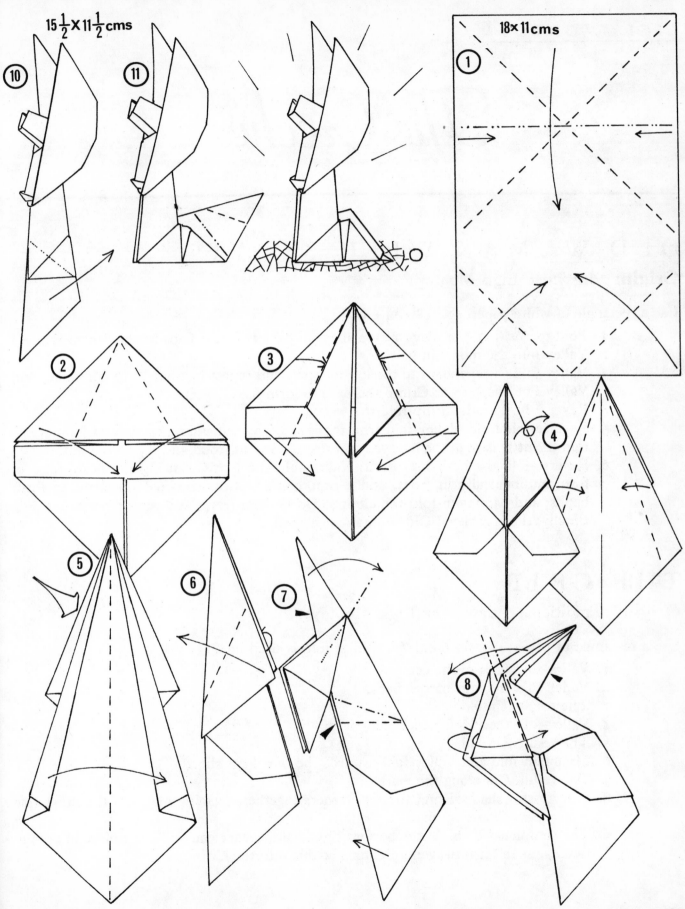

15½ X 11½ cms

18 x 11 cms

The Creche

OLD WOMAN WITH STAFF

Origin: *Argentina*. Ligia Montoya.

Use a rectangle of white paper, size 18 × 11 cm.

1. Fold to position 4 on Page 139. Valley-fold the two side flaps to the centre crease.
2. Valley-fold the model in half.
3. Valley-fold the arm flaps to the left in front, and repeat behind. With Mountain and Valley Fold push in or Crimp the base to form feet.
4. Reverse-fold head. Crimp-fold the waist.
5. Reverse-fold head. Valley-fold arms to the right in front and repeat behind. Mountain-fold the little flaps at the base to complete the feet in front, and repeat behind.
6. Reverse-fold the head into itself. Valley-fold the lapels, causing the head-dress to form automatically in front, and repeat behind. Mountain-fold the arms to form hands, and Mountain-fold the elbows. Do both in front, and repeat behind. Finally, the completed Old Woman with Staff.

THE CRIB

Origin: Traditional. Adaptation: Ligia Montoya.

Use a rectangle of paper, size 8 × 6 cm. (A similar fold is used on Page 209.)

1. Valley-fold flaps to the centre.
2. Valley-fold the four corner flaps.
3. The result. Unfold.
4. Valley-fold the two flaps left and right.
5. The result. Unfold.
6. Mountain-fold and Valley-fold inwards the four flaps shown.
7. The result. Cut along the marks.
8. Fold to this shape. Bring the top corners together, pushing one into the other (*see enlargement*). Paste in place.
9. The completed Crib. At the bottom right-hand corner you will see a piece of orange tissue, cut to form heavenly lights. Fix this into the Crib.

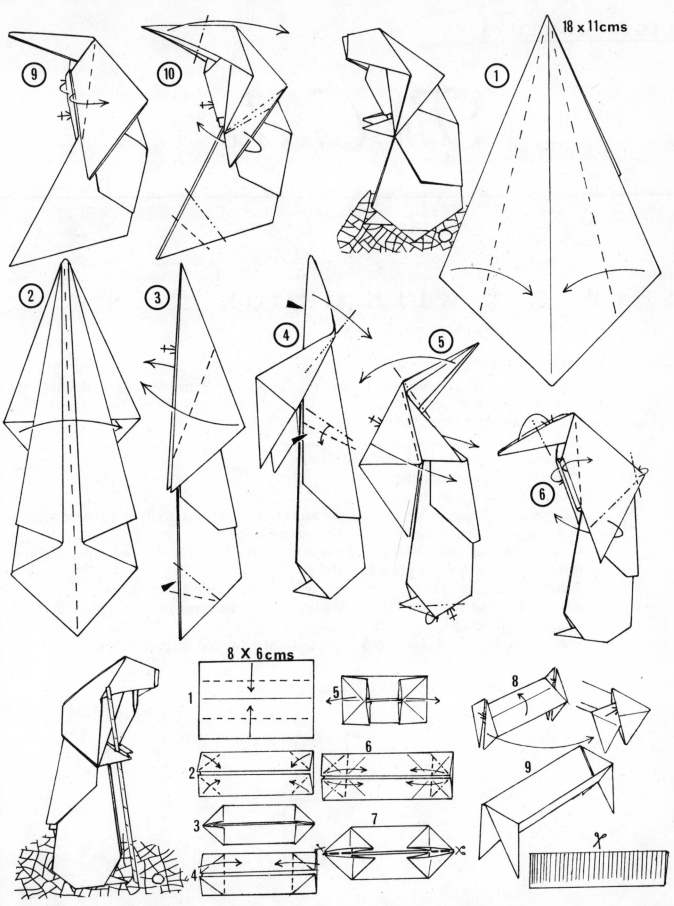

18 x 11cms

① ② ③ ④ ⑤ ⑥ ⑨ ⑩

8 X 6cms

1
2
3
4
5
6
7
8
9

The Creche

SHEPHERD WITH CROOK

Origin: *Argentina.* Ligia Montoya.

Use a rectangle of paper, size 18 × 11 cm.

1. Fold a Water Bomb Base on the top portion of the rectangle, and Valley-fold the bottom corner flaps to the centre. Valley-fold the two flaps of the Water Bomb Base, and the two inside flaps below.
2. Valley-fold over and over, and under the two side flaps.
3. The fold completed. Turn the model over.
4. Valley-fold the two side flaps.
5. Mountain-fold the model in half.
6. Reverse-fold the head. Valley-fold the arms to the right in front, and repeat behind. Mountain-fold and Valley-fold the base to form the feet.
7. Reverse-fold the head. Valley-fold the arms to the left in front, and repeat behind. Reverse-fold the bottom point into itself.
8. Valley-fold the lapels in front to form the head-dress, and repeat behind.
9. Reverse-fold the head into itself. Mountain-fold the arms to form hands in front, and repeat behind.

    Finally, the Shepherd. His crook is made from a twisted strip of paper.

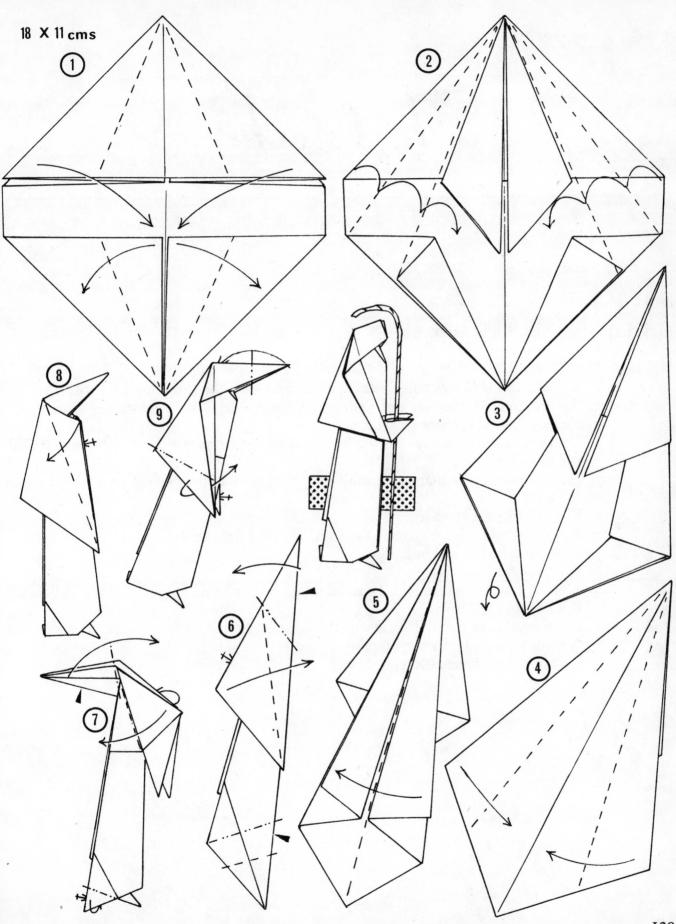

18 X 11 cms

139

The Creche

SHEEP

Origin: *Argentina*. Ligia Montoya.

Use a square of white paper, size 9 × 9 cm. Begin with the Frog Base, position 2, shown on Page 19

1. Valley-fold the centre flap downwards. Repeat with the three similar flaps.
2. Reverse-fold, or open up and Valley-fold, the two legs at the front.
3. Reverse-fold both these legs again.
4. Valley-fold the long flaps on the legs in front, and repeat behind. Mountain-fold the two bottom legs.
5. Enlarged view. Mountain-fold and Valley Reverse-fold the two top legs. Reverse-fold the bottom legs.
6. Reverse-fold the hind legs.
7. Mountain-fold the two small flaps on the hind legs in front, and repeat behind, Valley-fold the model in half.
8. Reverse-fold the neck.
9. Sink the tail. Mountain-fold the small flaps into the belly in front, and repeat behind. Reverse-fold the head.
   Cut from the nose to the middle of the head. Make sure that the same portion is cut behind. Valley-fold these points to form ears.
   Finally, the completed Sheep.

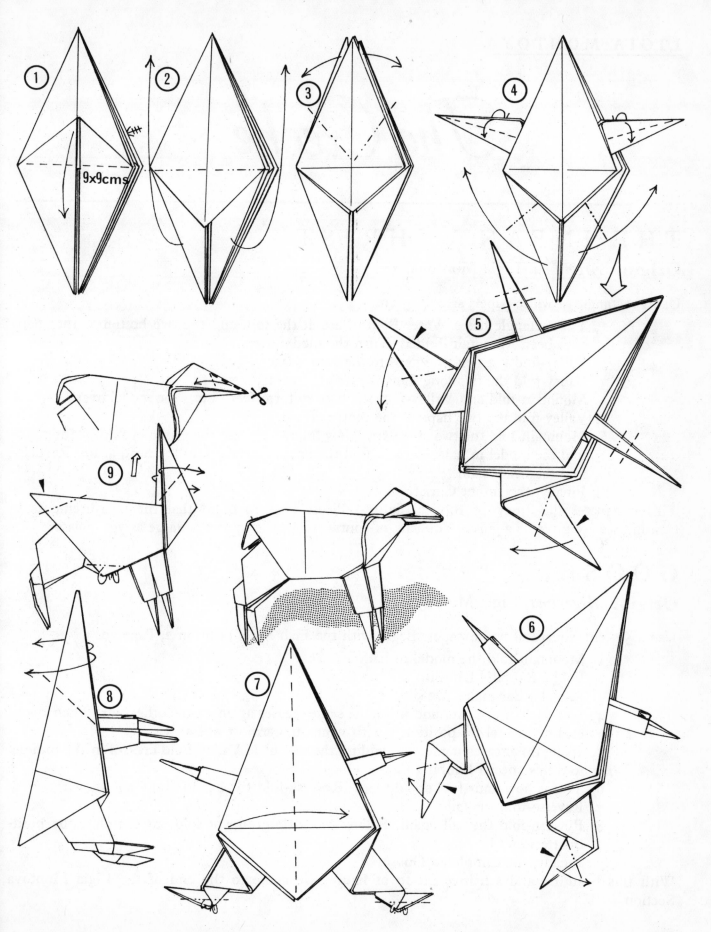

9x9cms.

The Creche

THE INFANT CHRIST

Origin: *Argentina*. Ligia Montoya.

Use a rectangle of white paper, size 8 × 5 cm.

1. The rectangle has a Water Bomb Base at the top, and the two bottom corner flaps have been Mountain-folded. Turn the model over.
2. Valley-fold the two side flaps to the centre line.
3. Valley-fold the two long flaps towards the centre.
4. Mountain-fold and Valley-fold the base to form feet. Turn the model over.
5. Valley-fold the two flaps to the centre crease.
6. Mountain-fold the two side flaps. Now follow through the group of folds. Mountain-fold the model in half. Reverse-fold the head. Reverse-fold the head again. Reverse-fold the head again.
   Finally, the Infant Christ.

This completes the group of Biblical figures. Please bear in mind that the measurements in centimetres are given as a guide. You can, of course, make the figures as large as you please.

GOOSE

Origin: *Argentina*. Ligia Montoya.

Use a 5·5 cm. square of white paper. Begin with the Fish Base, position 2, Page 20.

1. Mountain-fold the model in half.
2. Fold a Rabbit's Ear with the top flap.
3. Rabbit's Ear made. Unfold.
4. Unfolded. Turn over and make the same creases again on the other side. Then Book-fold the model for position 5 with wings uppermost not as 5.
5. Using the creases made, and adding the two little Valley Fold creases in the middle, fold this special Rabbit's Ear.
6. This is how your fold should look. Reverse-fold the head (wings not shown).
7. Reverse-fold the tail.
8. Reverse-fold the tail again. Follow the little group of folds to complete the hindquarters and leg.
   Finally, the completed Goose.

With this beautiful and sensitive group of figures we come to the end of the Ligia Montoya Section.

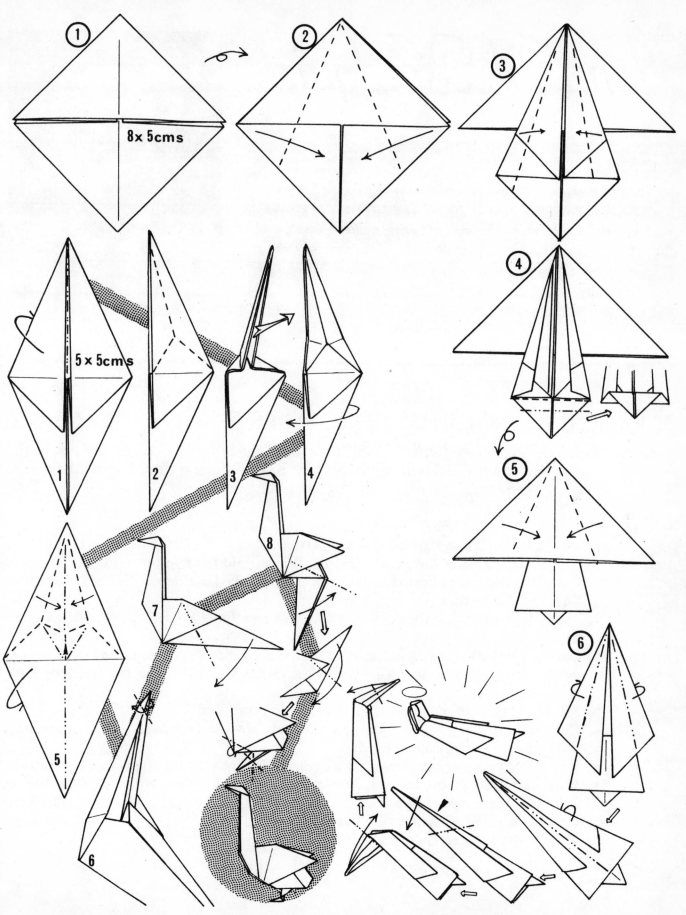

8x 5cms

5 x 5cms

John M. Nordquist

Born 1904, Portland, Oregon, U.S.A. Degree (M.Sc.) from the University of Oklahoma, and studied further at the California Institute of Technology, Pasadena. Now Assistant at the Seismological Laboratory in Pasadena, Cal. His real interest in Origami started in 1957, after a meeting with Yasuo Sate, a Japanese seismologist, Nordquist participated in an Origami exhibition in Pasadena, and at the Cooper Union Museum in New York City.

HELMET, WITH TORTOISE AND CRANE

Origin: *Japan.* Collected by John M. Nordquist, and made by Yoshinaga Ogawa, of the Ogasawara School, probably in Kyoto during the Early Meija Era (1868–1912). The helmet signifies long life.

Use a rectangle of paper, in the proportions of 3 to 2.

1. Fold a Water Bomb Base on the top portion.
2. Cut one thickness at the point indicated. Valley-fold the flap upwards.
3. Cut along the line indicated. Fold over and over the base flaps.
4. Squash-fold the triangular cut flap.
5. Valley-fold inwards to the centre the four corners (Blintz Fold). Squash-fold the other flap.
6. Cut the two little flaps as indicated. Cut the Squashed flap as indicated (*see enlarged view*). Mountain-fold and Valley-fold the base. Mountain-fold the two side flaps (*see finished model*).
7. Proceed with enlarged view of the flap above Petal Fold.
8. Cut carefully along the marked lines. Valley-fold the two flaps to the centre line.
9. Valley-fold the long flap upwards.
10. Valley-fold the long flap across its length. Valley-fold the top right flap downwards.
11. With the crane almost formed, Reverse-fold the head. Now go back to position 6, and make the tortoise. The folds are the same as for the Table (*Page* 97). Just keep the head and tail of the tortoise out of the way.

Finally, the finished Helmet.

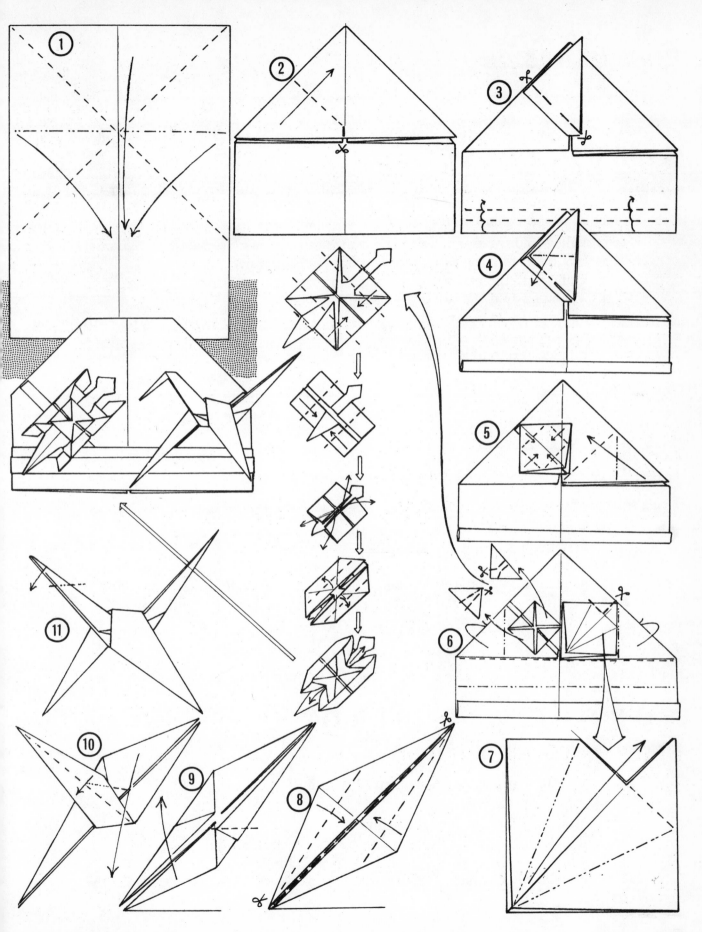

RABBIT VASE

Origin: *Japan*. Obtained by John M. Nordquist from the Frederick Starr Collection.

Use a square of paper, coloured on one side.

1. Valley-fold the two sides to the centre line.
2. Mountain-fold the bottom flap. Turn the model over.
3. Valley-fold the two triangular flaps to meet at the bottom.
4. Mountain-fold the two corner flaps.
5. Mountain-fold the two arrowed flaps and bring the top corner down. Turn the model over and decorate.
   Finally, the completed Rabbit Vase.

JAPANESE VASE

Origin: *Japan*. Collected by John M. Nordquist.

Use a square of paper, coloured on one side. Begin with the Preliminary Fold (*Page* 18).

1. Valley-fold the two side flaps to the centre crease.
2. Mountain-fold the two side flaps.
3. Squash-fold the two corners marked, and repeat with the same two behind.
4. Mountain-fold the two squashed flaps, then Valley-fold the two behind.
5. Carefully open out the vase and roll the four pointed tips with a pencil.
   Finally, the completed Japanese Vase.

NORDQUIST'S BIRD

Origin: *America*. John M. Nordquist.

Use a square of yellow paper. Begin with the Preliminary Fold (*Page* 18).

1. Petal-fold the front flap.
2. Mountain-fold the model in half.
3. Valley-fold the right flap over to the left. Repeat behind.
4. Valley-fold the front flap in half. Repeat behind.
   Finally, the completed Bird, with the head Reverse-folded. Open out the wings.

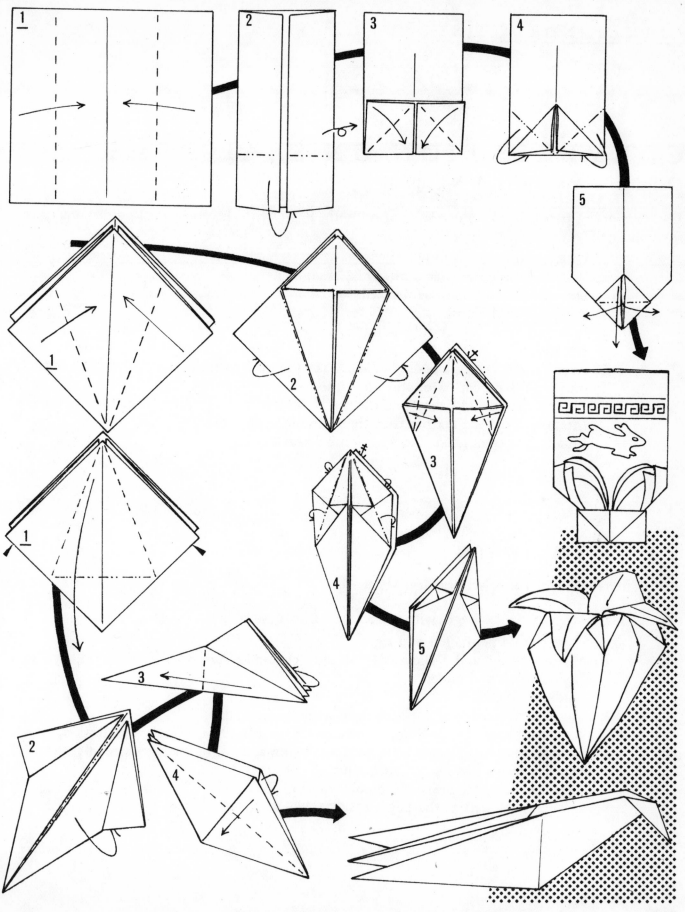

CONVERSATION ON SEAL ROCK

Origin: *America*. John M. Nordquist.

Use a square of paper, black on one side, or on both. Begin with the paper creased diagonally and folded in half.

1. Valley-fold the flaps to meet.
2. Valley-fold the same flaps upwards, at an angle.
3. Squash-fold both flaps as marked.
4. Petal-fold both flaps.
5. Enlarged view. Valley-fold both flaps upwards. Mountain-fold and Valley-fold the top base flap.
6. Reverse-fold the two seals' heads. Make the cuts to form the tail fins. Valley-fold the folded base flap. Mountain-fold the two front flippers.
7. Mountain-fold and Valley-fold the heads. Mountain-fold the two back flippers behind. Mountain-fold the bottom flap, then Mountain-fold the two sides.
   Finally, the completed Conversation on Seal Rock.

PICKLE-PUSS

Origin: *America*. John M. Nordquist.

Use a square of green paper. Begin with a stretched Bird Base this way up (*see Page* 175).

1. Reverse-fold points left and right.
2. Mountain-fold and Valley-fold the sides left and right. Valley-fold the two side flaps inwards and under.
3. Folds completed.
4. Fold an eccentric Water Bomb Base with the front flap.
5. The completed Pickle-Puss, which looks, in Mr. Nordquist's description, like a man who has just eaten a sour pickle. When made out of a large piece of paper, this model makes a fine Davy Crocket hat.
   To form the face, press the model flat and look at it. The face will soon become apparent. Now turn the page upside down and then look at 5.

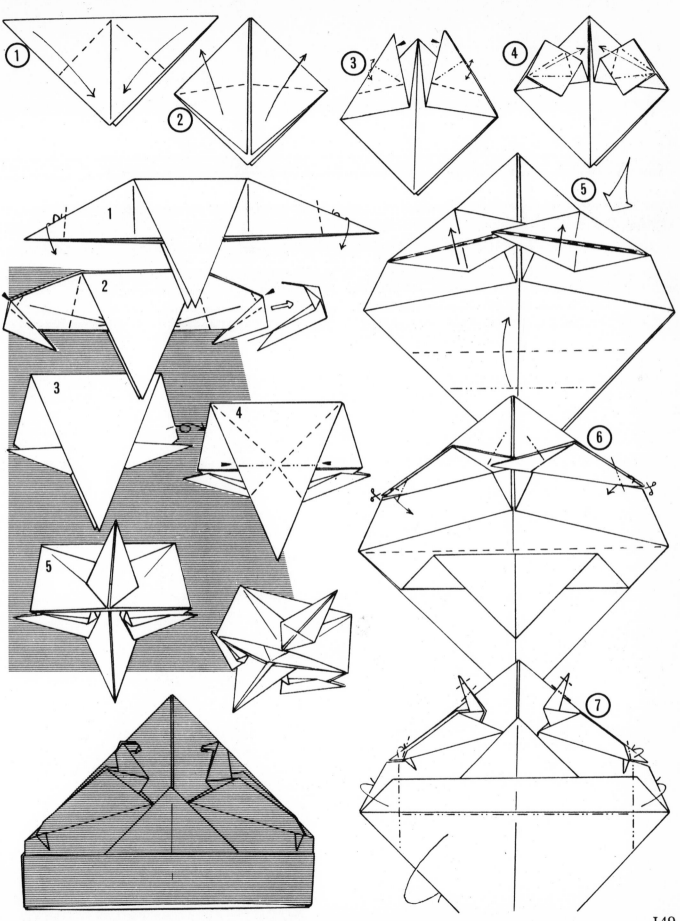

GIFT PACKAGE

Origin: *Japan.* Yoshinaga Ogawa. Collected by John M. Nordquist.

Use a rectangle of paper, in the proportions of 3 to 2. Begin with the paper folded in half and creased down the middle.

1. Valley-fold the flap in front upwards, and repeat with the similar flap behind.
2. The folds made. Valley-fold the small long flap at the bottom.
3. Mountain-fold the two corner flaps to the back.
4. Cut off the two end pieces. Turn the model over.
5. Enlarged view. Fold over and over the bottom flap.
6. Folds completed. Turn the model over.
7. Valley-fold the corner flaps and tuck into pocket.
   Finally, the finished Gift Package, front and back.

With space to spare, here is a simple Whale.

WHALE

Origin: *Japan.*

Use a square of paper. Begin with a Fish Base, position 2 (*Page* 20).

1. Valley-fold the model in half.
2. Valley-fold the middle fin. Repeat behind.
3. Reverse-fold the head into itself. Reverse-fold the tail. Finally, the completed Whale.

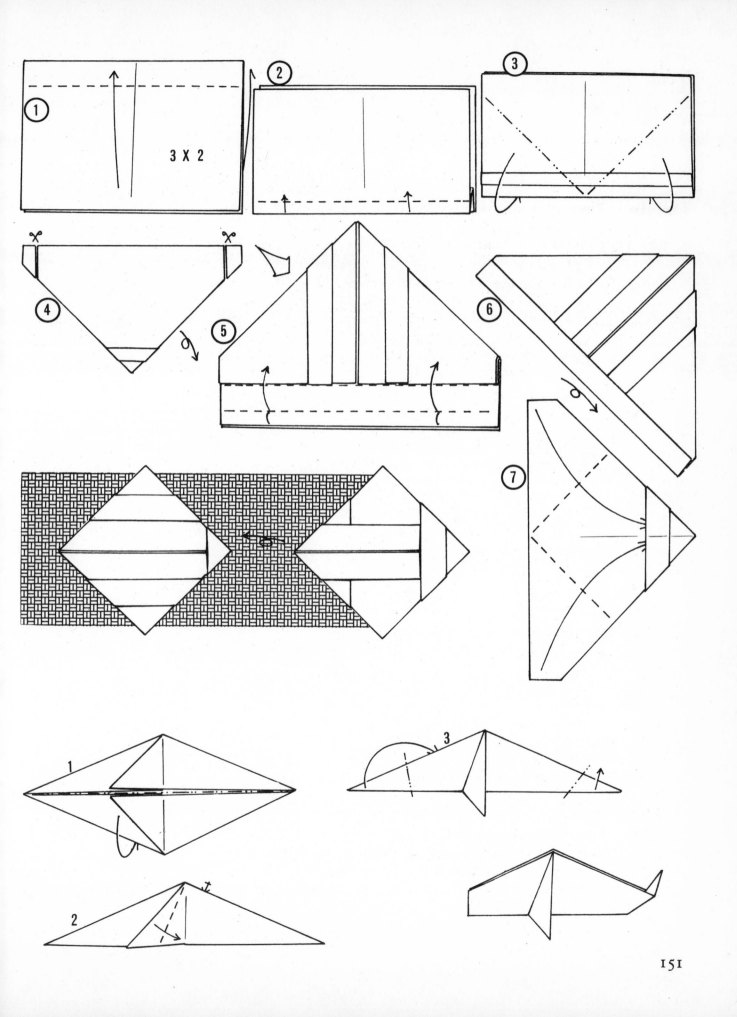

3 X 2

MAPLE SEED

Origin: *America.* John M. Nordquist.

Use a square of paper, creased along the diagonal.

1. Valley-fold the top flap to the centre crease. Crease firmly and open up.
2. Valley-fold the top flap to the crease just made.
3. Valley-fold in half the fold just made.
4. Valley-fold the folded flap downwards. Cut as indicated. Valley-fold the flap just cut.
5. Mountain-fold the flap just folded.
6. Valley-fold the same flap.
7. Valley-fold the whole triangular top flap—all thicknesses.
8. Valley-fold the flap into the pocket opposite.
   Finally, the completed Maple Seed. In England, the Sycamore seed is more common. When thrown into the air, either of these seeds descends with a gentle spinning motion. If you have folded this model correctly, it will perform just like the Maple or Sycamore Seed.

This model ends the John M. Nordquist Section.

Room for one more by the Reverend Robert Neale.

WATCHFUL DOG

Origin: *America.* Rev. Robert Neale (*see Page* 224)

Use a square of paper, creased diagonally, and the two sides Valley-folded to the centre crease.

1. Valley-fold the model in half.
2. Reverse-fold the head part. Squash-fold the tail part.
3. Reverse-fold the head. Petal-fold the tail.
4. Valley-fold the tail to the left. Mountain-fold the muzzle into itself. Crimp the head.
   Finally, the Watchful Dog completed.

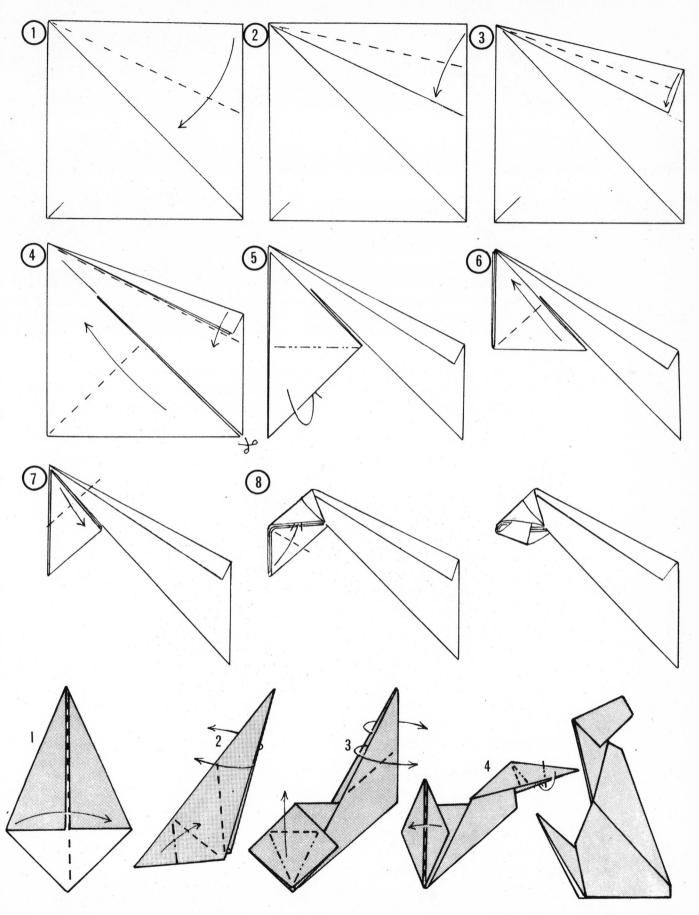

Jack J. Skillman

Jack Skillman was born in 1915 in Terre Haute, Indiana. Educated Terre Haute. Served in the U.S. Army for six years, and later signed on in the Regular Army. Now a clerk in the Department of Health Education, Board of Health, City of Chicago. Mr. Skillman explains his work as follows: "I do an explorative type of mechanical folding, observing what paper will do as to line, symmetry, plastic properties, and I measure the response to sequential changes, reversals, or other procedural innovations, in an effort to discover and fix the most economic spatial definitions."

PHOTO : FABIAN BACHRACH

COUCH

Origin: *America*. Jack J. Skillman.

Use a rectangle of paper, in the proportions of 2 to 1. Begin with the rectangle creased into thirty-two squares.

1. Crease along the marked lines.
2. Crease again along the new marked lines.
3. Valley-fold the two corner flaps.
4. Valley-fold along Line 1 first, and unfold. Valley-fold along Line 2.
5. Valley-fold the flap, unfold, and Valley-fold as in Fig. 6.
6. Valley-fold flap to the right.
7. Mountain-fold the flap, top and bottom, and Sink the two corners.
8. Valley-fold the square flap over to the left.
9. With the flap held in an upright position, Valley-fold the flap at the bottom, and Mountain-fold the flap at the top, i.e., as you see it in the illustration. Press down.
10. Valley-fold the flap inside, and open out the sides.
11. When in this upright position, Squash-fold the flap.
12. Lift up and Squash-fold the flaps top and bottom.
13. Petal-fold the two Squashed flaps. The result is eccentric.
14. Valley-fold inwards the narrow flaps around the Petal Folds. Then lift the legs upright, at the same time flattening the folds round them to stiffen the leg, which is also Valley-folded. Now repeat all folds from 1 on the arrowed side.
15. Here, both sides have been folded and four legs formed. Valley-fold the two narrow side flaps.
16. Mountain-fold the two end flaps. Turn the model over.
17. With a pencil, curl the ends to form arm-rests.
    Finally, the completed Couch.

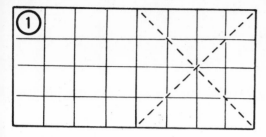

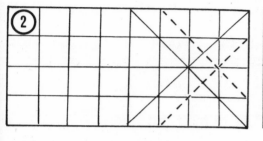

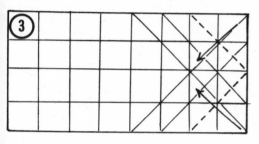

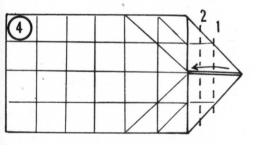

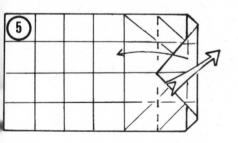

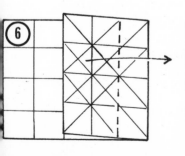

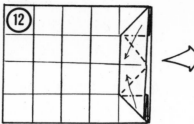

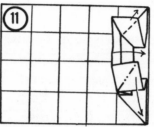

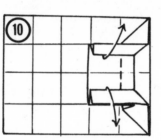

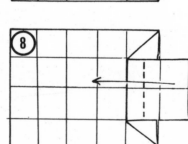

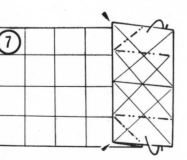

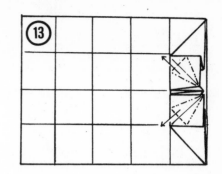

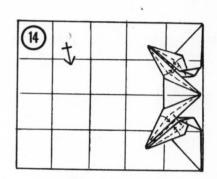

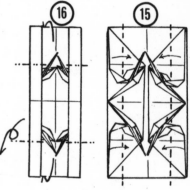

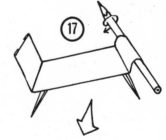

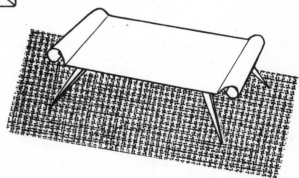

155

DOUBLE BOAT

Origin: *America*. Jack Skillman.

Use a rectangle of paper in the proportions of 5 to 4. Begin with the rectangle creased into twenty squares. Crease the two bottom diagonals.

1. Valley-fold the side flaps to the centre crease.
2. Pull outwards the two arrowed corners. Valley-fold inside.
3. This is the result. Pull down the two arrowed flaps to meet the points.
4. Enlarged view of the result. Turn over.
5. Valley-fold the top front flap downwards.
6. Pull the arrowed corner flaps and the centre flap downwards to meet at the bottom.
7. This is the result. Mountain-fold the bottom flap and Valley-fold this flap into the boat.
8. Flap almost in. Valley-fold the top flap into the boat.
9. Push in the bottom.
10. Like this.
    Finally, the Boat completed. With ballast, it will float.

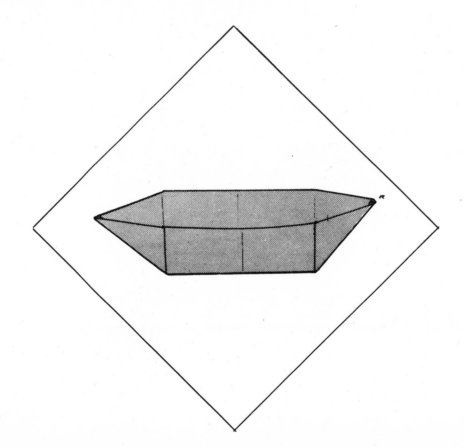

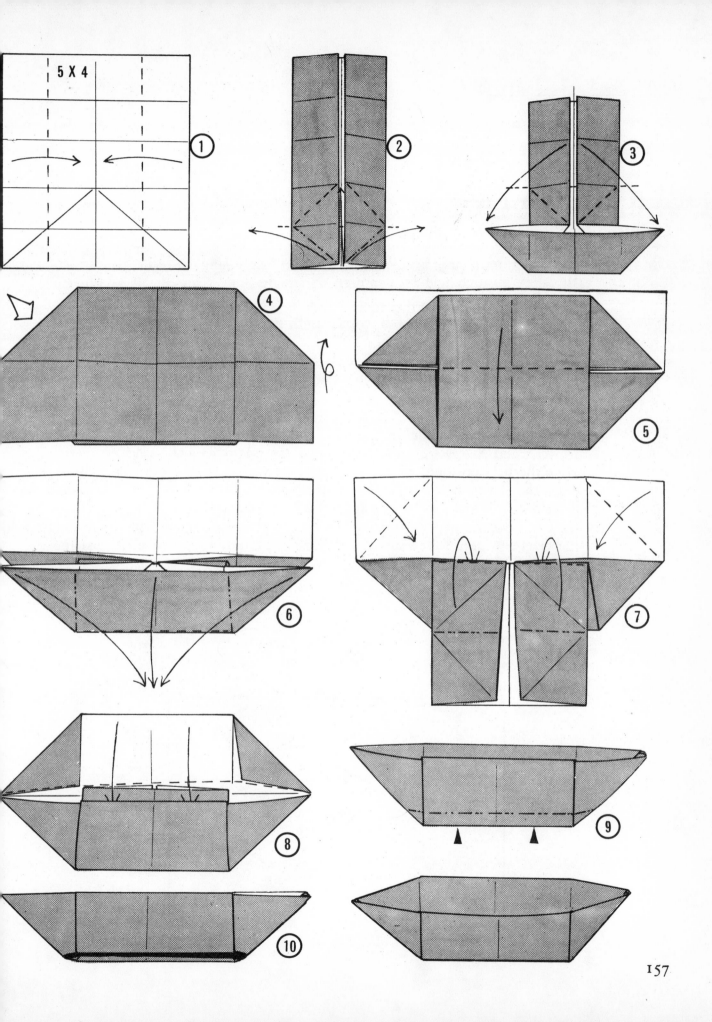

5 X 4

① ② ③ ④ ⑤ ⑥ ⑦ ⑧ ⑨ ⑩

ARMCHAIR

Origin: *America.* Jack J. Skillman.

Use a rectangle of paper in the proportions of 5 to 4. Begin by creasing the rectangle into 80 squares. To do this easily, crease a rectangle 2×1 into 16×8 squares, and then cut off 48 squares.

1. Valley-fold the top flap downwards. Valley-fold the bottom flap upwards.
2. Valley-fold the bottom flap upwards. Both flaps meet.
3. Valley-fold side flaps inwards.
4. Crease the model along the Valley-fold lines. Turn over.
5. Crease the model along the Valley-fold lines. Valley-fold triangles X to the arrowed point. Push in the corners.
6. Note the new position of Xs. Valley-fold the X flaps to meet in the centre.
7. Mountain-fold the model in half.
8. Move X and X upwards, and Valley-fold the side flaps.
9. Note the new positions of Xs. Lift up the square flap to form chair shape 10.
10. Turn the chair shape over.
11. This is how it looks. Open out from the bottom completely.
12. This is what the paper will look like. Study the markings carefully. Mountain-fold the diagonals and, following all the symbols accurately, fold the chair shape.

Continued overleaf

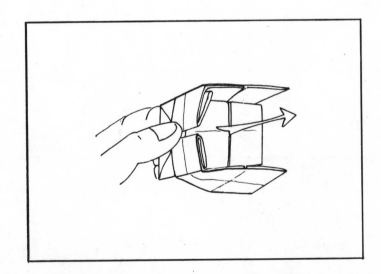

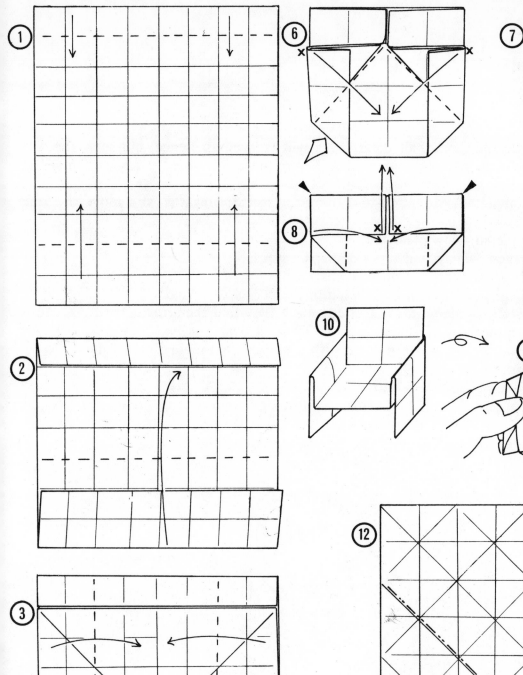

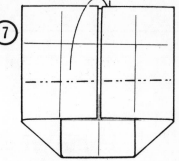

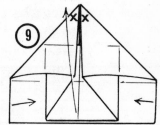

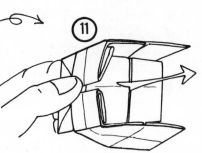

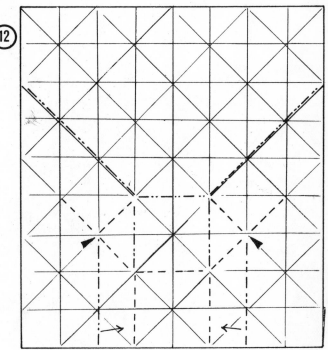

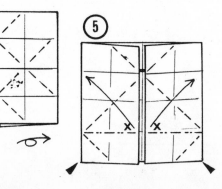

159

Armchair (*continued*)

13. Here you see the shape half done. This will tax your patience, but look ahead to Fig. 14, and then back to your model. Try to get the arrowed triangles behind the chair back.
14. The fold completed. Mountain-fold the chair seat downwards, and move the arms to the back.
15. Nearly completed. Now press flat.
16. Fold completed. Valley-fold two side flaps inwards.
17. Valley-fold the two corner flaps inwards.
18. Valley-fold the bottom flap, and tuck into the pocket indicated.
19. Hold the model at the points indicated, and Valley-fold the arms inwards. X and X will move upwards. The seat will move forward from the back (*see follow-through drawing*). Roll the back of the chair with a curved Mountain Fold. Valley-fold the arms outwards.

Finally, the completed Armchair.

This is a really wonderful model, and the business of folding it is most satisfying.

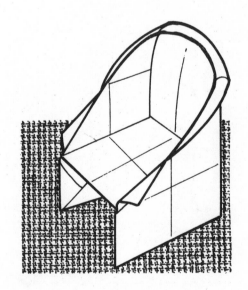

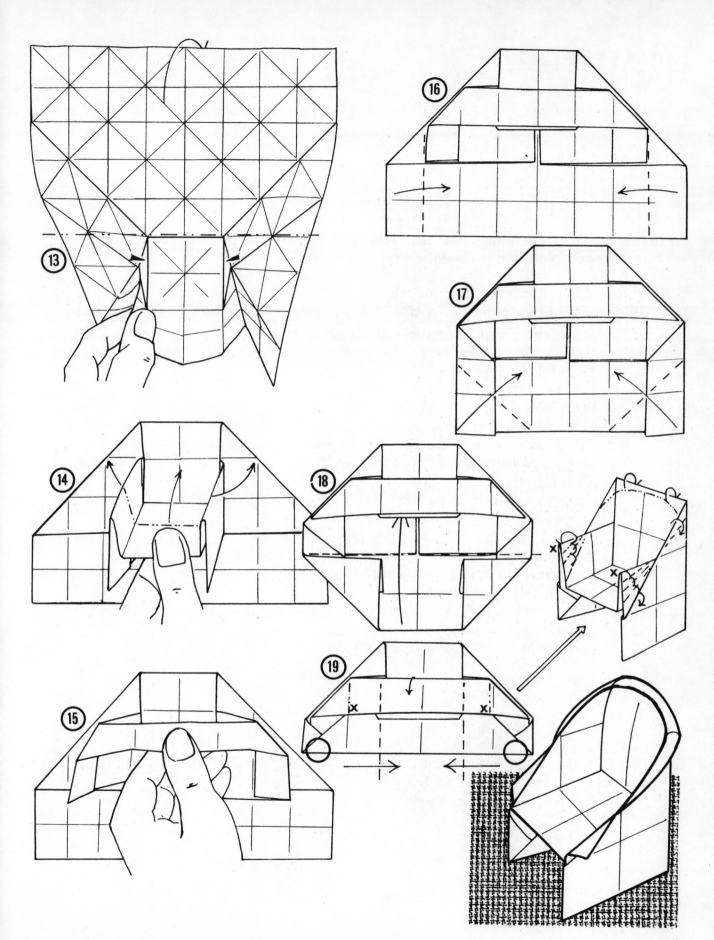

SALT CELLAR TABLE

Origin: *Japan*. Uchiyama. *America*. Jack J. Skillman. Both folders created this quite remarkable table independently.

Use a square of brown paper. Uchiyama achieves his result by pre-creasing the paper as in Fig. 10. Jack Skillman makes a series of "Salt Cellar" folds to prepare the creases for the final assault.

1. Crease the square along the Valley Fold lines. Turn the paper over.
2. Fold the four corner flaps to the centre.
3. Flaps folded, turn the model over.
4. Fold the four corner flaps to the centre.
5. Flaps folded. Open out to 6.
6. Make a Preliminary Fold.
7. There are four faces like this. Crease each face along the Valley Fold lines.
8. Valley-fold flaps X and X to the sides. Bottom point moves up. Make this fold on the three other similar faces.
9. Here you see the new positions of the Xs. With all sides folded, open out the model completely.
10. Using all the creases made, study the symbols and form the table. First, Valley-fold the inside square and the corner diagonally, and form Fig. 11.
11. Mountain-fold the eight flaps of the legs into themselves. Start with one leg at a time (*see follow-through drawing*).
12. All legs folded. Pull each leg out to the dotted position and press together the creases at the base of each leg.
    Finally, the completed Salt Cellar Table.

In my opinion, this model is the finest table in the whole art of Origami. It is a fitting model on which to close this Jack J. Skillman Section.

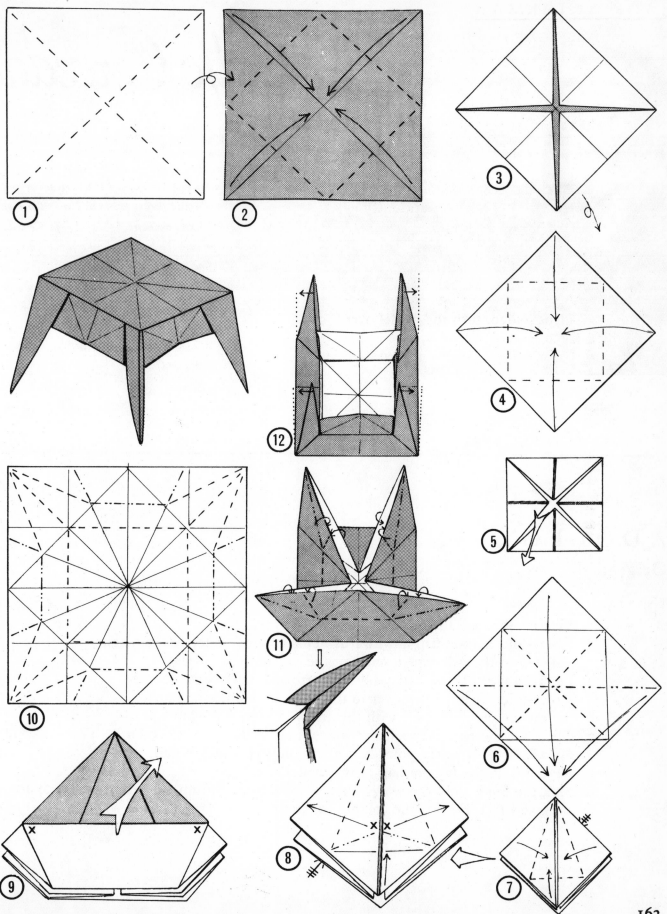

Born in Buenos Aires. Known primarily through his Night Club, Television and Theatre performances as Knife Thrower "Extraordinaire." But Adolfo Cerceda is also the creator of a large collection of fine paper folds.

Has made a serious study of hypnotism. Devotes much time to his great love, painting. A charming man who, with his delightful partner, Martha, is now living in Chicago.

ADOLFO'S ANGEL

Origin: *Argentina.* Adolfo Cerceda.

Use a square of paper.

1. Valley-fold along the diagonal.
2. Valley-fold the top flap downwards. This is one quarter of the height.
3. Valley-fold the two flaps to meet at the centre. Sink corners.
4. Enlarged view. First, Valley-fold the arrowed flap over to the left.
5. Valley-fold the same flap over to the right at an angle.
6. Repeat the previous folds with the arrowed flap on the left.
7. Open out the part between the wings, and Valley-fold downwards. This is a wide Squash Fold. Note the point X. Valley-fold the model in half.
8. Reverse-fold the bottom half of the model.
9. Sink the head. Fold the wings forward and back. Crimp the rear portion to form back and feet. Finally, the completed Angel.

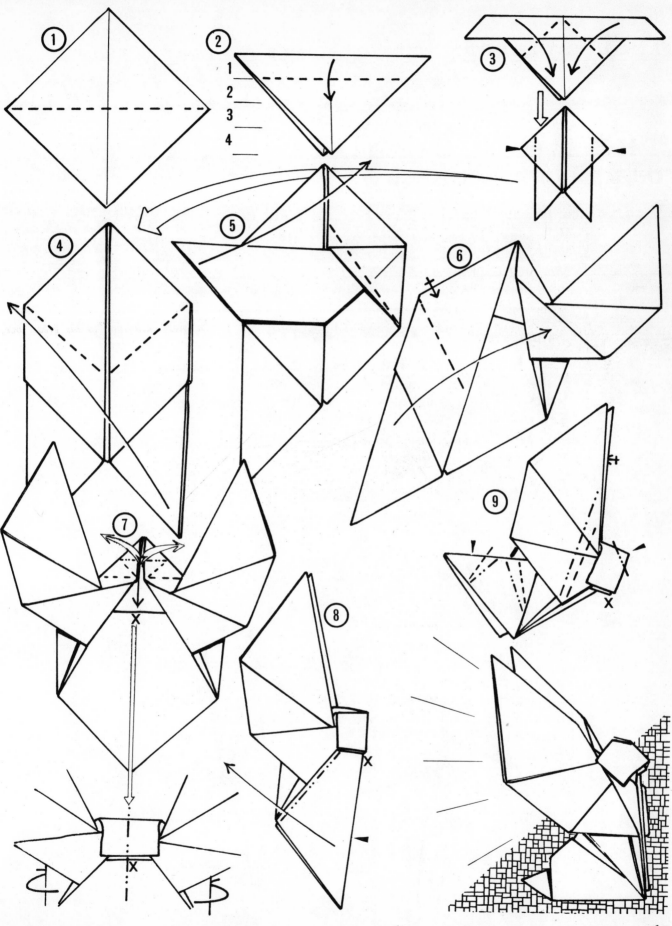

THE MOOR ON HORSEBACK

Origin: *Argentina.* Adolfo Cerceda.

Use a rectangle of thin, strong white paper 2 × 1. Begin with the rectangle creased down the middle.

1. Valley-fold the two side flaps to the centre line.
2. Valley-fold the four triangular flaps in the direction arrowed.
3. Mountain-fold the model in half.
4. Push in the arrowed corners. (This is a Water Bomb Base.)
5. Squash-fold the two front flaps.
6. This shows the fold happening. Repeat with the other three similar flaps.
7. Petal-fold the front flap.
8. Valley-fold the Petal Fold downwards. Repeat with the similar flap behind.
9. Push, with Mountain Folds, the corners indicated.
10. Valley-fold the top flap upwards with the two points underneath.
11. Reverse-fold the two points at the angle shown.
12. Mountain-fold and Valley-fold the top triangle. (This will be a tail.)

Continued overleaf

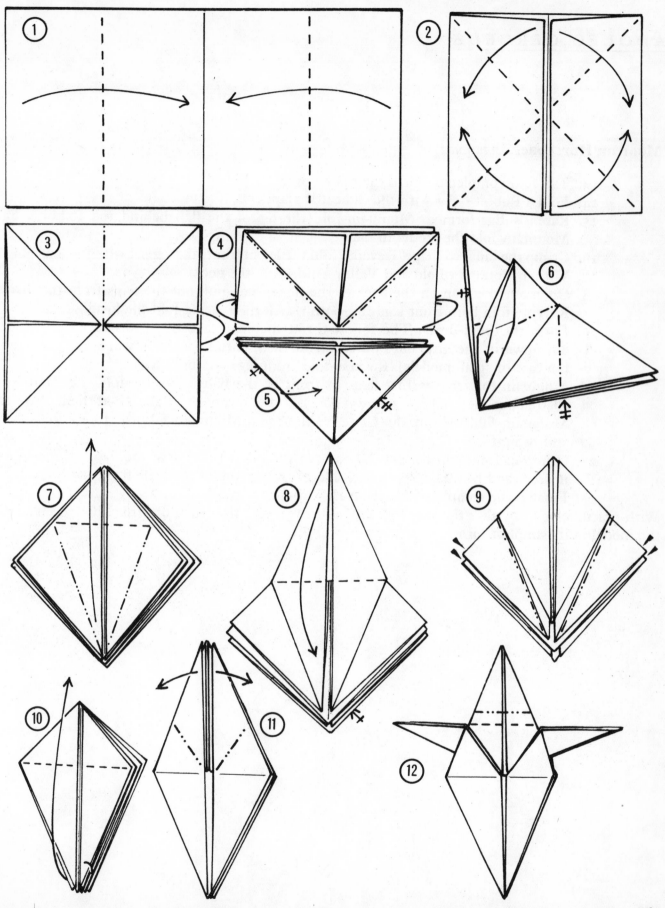

Moor on Horseback (*continued*)

13. Tail fold completed. Turn the model over.
14. Fold a Rabbit's Ear with the indicated flap.
15. Rabbit's Ear formed. Mountain-fold the tip of the flap behind the Rabbit's Ear. Mountain-fold the model in half.
16. Crimp the tail into shape. Reverse-fold the leg in front, and repeat with the leg behind.
17. With a Mountain Fold and Valley Fold, Sink the neck.
18. Open out the man on the back of the horse, i.e., pull out the flaps from the inside. Reverse-fold both front legs and both rear legs. Reverse-fold the head.
19. Form the head-dress. The follow-through folds make this procedure clear. **Open out upwards the little flaps on each side of the head** (tweezers will assist this job in the case of small models). Reverse-fold front legs and back legs.
20. Mountain-fold the narrow flaps in front of the body. Reverse-fold the front legs. Flatten out the head (*see enlarged view*). Cut two ears and Valley-fold them upwards. Mountain-fold the muzzle. Close up the head. Mountain-fold the forehead in front and behind.
21. Crimp in front and behind the body of the man. Valley-fold the flaps on the legs—in front and behind on both legs. Note how the top of the little flap tucks in.
    Finally, the completed Moor on Horseback.

With practice, you can alter the shape of the head-dress and the arms, but this illustration shows the model in its simplest form.

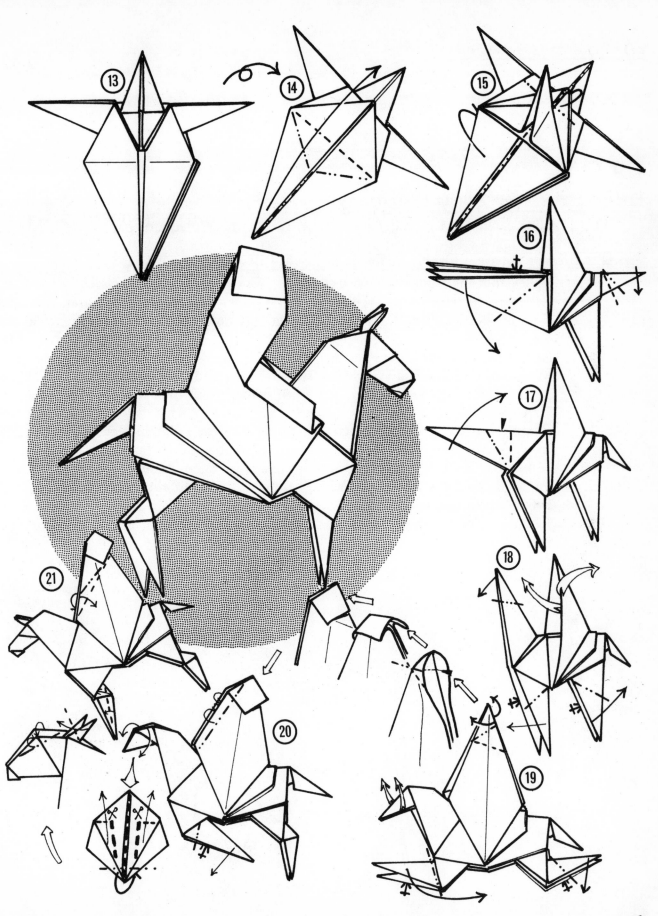

LION

Origin: *Argentina*. Adolfo Cerceda.

This is a fine example of a model made from two separate pieces of paper.

First Part: Use a square of paper. Begin with the Bird Base, position 3 (*Page* 18).

1. Valley-fold the front flap upwards.
2. Reverse-fold the two arrowed legs.
3. Fold in the tips of each leg (*see also Page* 43, Fold 12). Valley-fold model in half.
4. Reverse-fold the head.
5. Reverse-fold the head.
6. Mountain-fold and Valley-fold the tip of the head to form muzzle and tongue. Now open out the flap on the right, and turn it inside-out over the head.
7. Half-way folded.
8. Completely folded and flattened. Mountain-fold the point into the main part. Sink the neck. Mountain-fold the leg flaps in front and behind.
9. When this fold is completed, the muzzle is revealed. Mountain-fold and Sink the forehead. Fold the legs in front and behind with **Mountain and Valley Folds**.
10. Front half of lion completed.

Continued overleaf

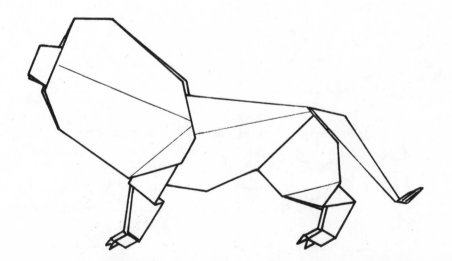

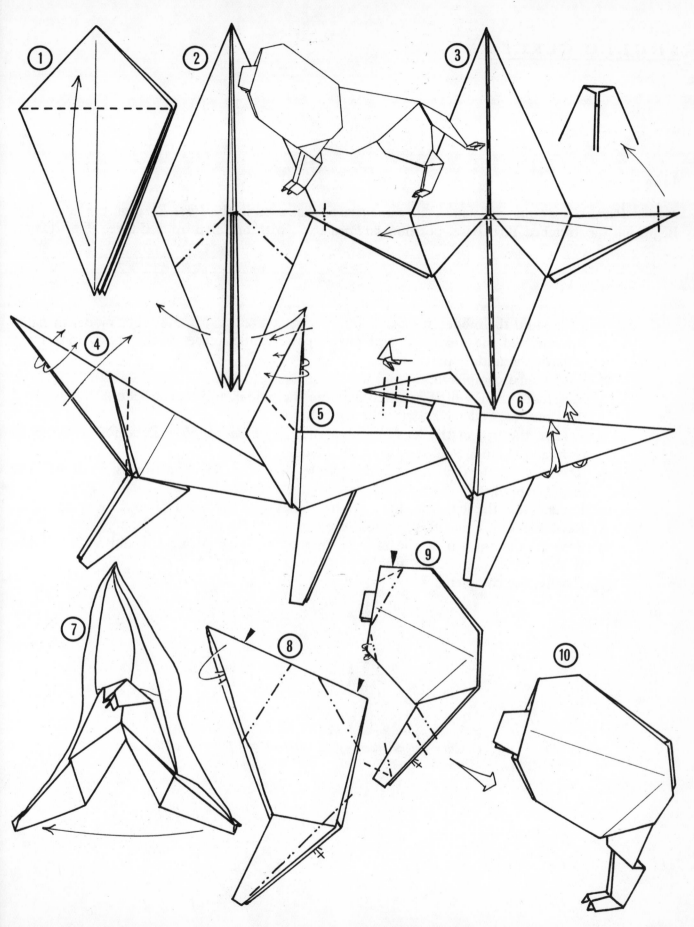

Lion (*continued*)

Second Part: Use a square of paper, the same size as that used in the *First Part*, on previous page. Begin with a stretched Bird Base, position 5 (*Page* 175), with one flap up and three flaps down.

1. Valley-fold the model in half.
2. Reverse-fold the top point and push in the centre piece. Crease first, and crimp inwards the middle portion.
3. Fold almost completed.
4. Mountain-fold the little arrowed flap into the model, and repeat behind. Squash-fold the front leg, and repeat with the leg behind.
5. Fold in the tips of the legs (*see previous page, Fold* 3). Now Petal-fold the legs in front and behind. Sink the tip of the model.
6. Reverse-fold the half-hidden tail. Valley-fold the leg downwards in front, and repeat behind.
7. Reverse-fold the legs from left to right. Valley-fold the tail flaps in front and behind.
8. Reverse-fold the tail. Reverse-fold the legs.
9. Reverse-fold the tip of the tail. Form the feet with Mountain and Valley Folds. With a small spot of glue, fix the two halves together.
   Finally, the completed Lion.

When you have completed this Lion, try making some of the other animals described in this book and form a Menagerie

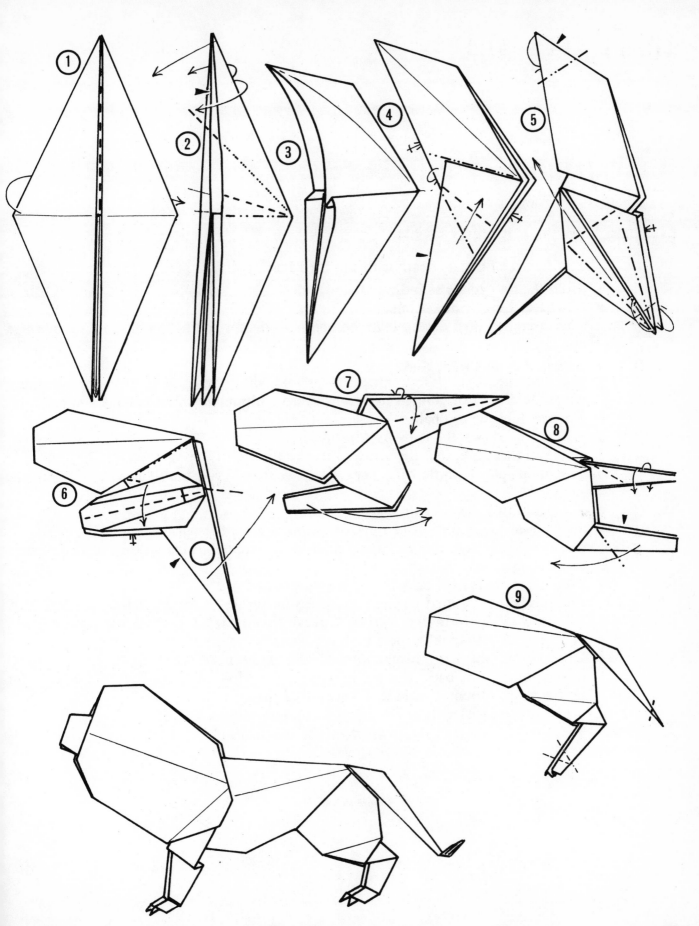

ADOLFO'S PIG

Another fine example of a two-piece model.

Origin: *Argentina*. Adolfo Cerceda.

First Part: Use a square of paper. Begin with the Bird Base, position 3 (*Page* 18).

1. Hold the two points as indicated, and pull.
2. The stretching commencing.
3. The stretched Bird Base. Move the points to the top, and Mountain-fold the centre triangle.
4. The fold almost completed.
5. The stretched Bird Base complete. This fold will be referred to on many occasions Valley-fold the two pointed flaps downwards. Mountain-fold the model in half.
6. Reverse-fold the top half.
7. Pull out and open the flaps from inside.
8. When in this state, fold the arrowed flap to the right. Repeat the folds behind.
9. Mountain-fold the little belly flaps. Use tweezers if you find it hard to do with the fingers.
10. Book-fold two leaves of the flaps.
11. Valley-fold this centre-piece upwards. This is to be the tail.
12. Valley-fold inwards the two arrowed flaps on the tail. This will cause two gussets to be formed.
13. Fold completed. Fold back the flaps into position 9.
14. Pull the tail into dotted position and press into place. Crease carefully the legs back and front, then form the legs by Squash-folding front both sides, pulling back, and Mountain-folding. Repeat with leg behind.
15. Reverse-fold the legs. Mountain-fold the point near the belly front and back. Mountain-fold the back near tail in front and behind. Sink the back. Sink the point on the right. Mountain-fold and Valley-fold the tail.
16. Tail completed. Details of Reverse-folding feet. Repeat behind.

Continued overleaf

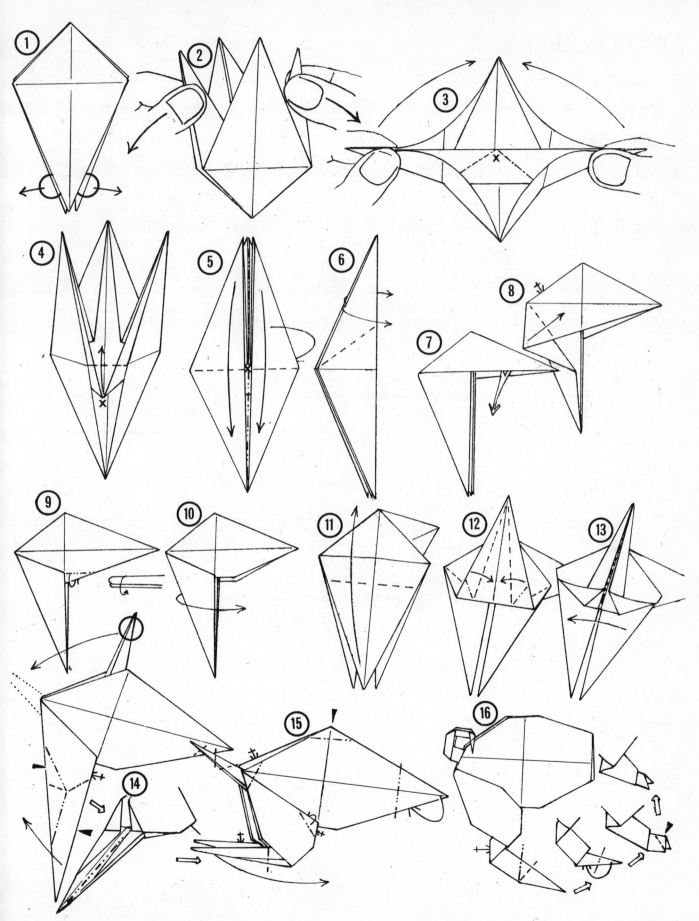

Adolfo's Pig (*continued*)

Second Part: Use a square of paper the same size as that used in *First Part* on previous page. Begin with a Bird Base, position 3 (*Page* 18).

17. Sink the top.
18. Valley-fold the front flap upwards.
19. Valley-fold and Mountain-fold the top flap into itself.
20. Valley-fold the top flap downwards.
21. Reverse-fold the legs upwards.
22. Reverse-fold the legs.
23. Crease along the Valley Fold lines. Fold the inside folds to the left and right.
24. Lift up the arrowed flap and Valley-fold. Now move on to the enlarged view.
25. This ingenious fold makes the ears. Hold down where indicated. Pull down the arrowed flaps, watching carefully the new positions of the Xs. Mountain-fold the little flap into the model.
26. The fold completed. Mountain-fold the model in half.
27. Reverse-fold the legs. Form the snout with Mountain and Valley Folds.
28. Reverse-fold the legs. Mountain-fold the little flap in the chin, and repeat behind.
29. Push in the front of the cheek, and repeat behind. Mountain-fold the thin flap along the leg, and repeat behind with both legs. Form the legs with the same folds shown at Fig. 16 on the previous page. With a little glue, fix the two parts together. Finally, the completed Pig—with those wonderful ears!

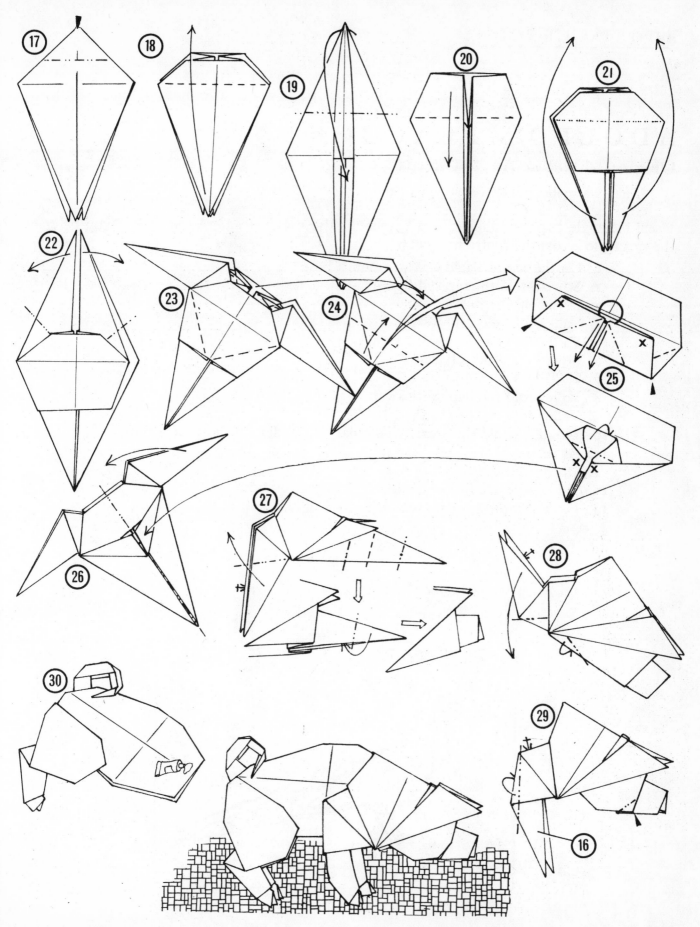

ADOLFO'S PEACOCK

Origin: *Argentina*. Adolfo Cerceda.

This is a really wonderful action model.

Use a rectangle of paper, about 2 × 1. You could also use, instead, a bank-note. Begin by creasing the rectangle across the centre both ways.

1. On the top half fold a Water Bomb Base.
2. Squash-fold the marked flap.
3. Petal-fold the flap.
4. Valley-fold the flap downwards.
5. Valley-fold the flap to the right.
6. Squash-fold the left flap.
7. Petal-fold the flap.
8. Valley-fold the flap downwards.
9. Valley-fold the flap to the left.
10. Mountain-fold the centre triangular flap under and into the model.
11. Reverse-fold the legs.
12. Open up the legs.
13. Valley-fold the little flaps top and bottom on both legs.
14. Folds completed. Valley-fold the legs in half.

Continued overleaf

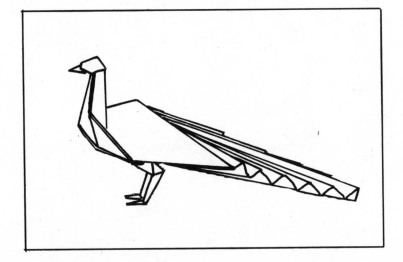

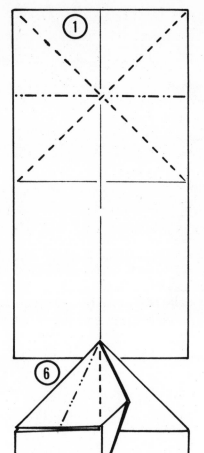

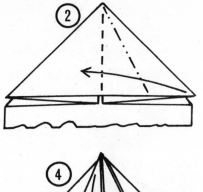

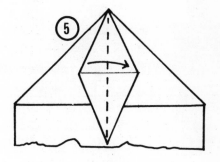

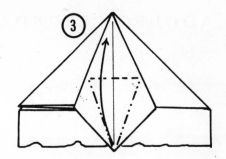

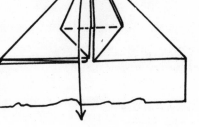

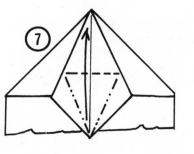

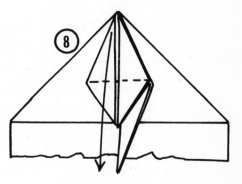

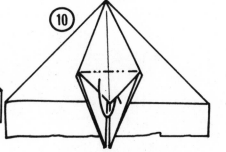

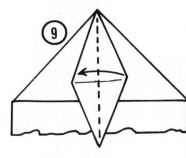

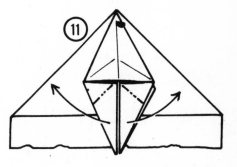

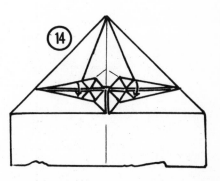

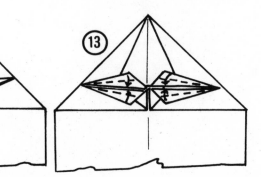

Adolfo's Peacock (*continued*)

15. Valley-fold the side flaps inwards and under the legs.
16. Valley-fold the model in half.
17. Reverse-fold the bottom half.
18. Crease this fold heavily; it will be used later. Open out to position 19.
19. Valley-fold bottom flap up to the arrowed points.
20. Valley-fold top flap, with legs downwards.
21. Open up to position 22.
22. Pleat the tail sixteen times. This is done by folding in half, then in half again, and so on until you have made sixteen creases. Making the creases, be sure to begin with a Mountain Fold first.
23. Enlarged view of the tail creased. Turn the model over.
24. Valley-fold the pleated tail upwards.

This charming design is shown, with its tail in another position, in the photograph, Plate 21.

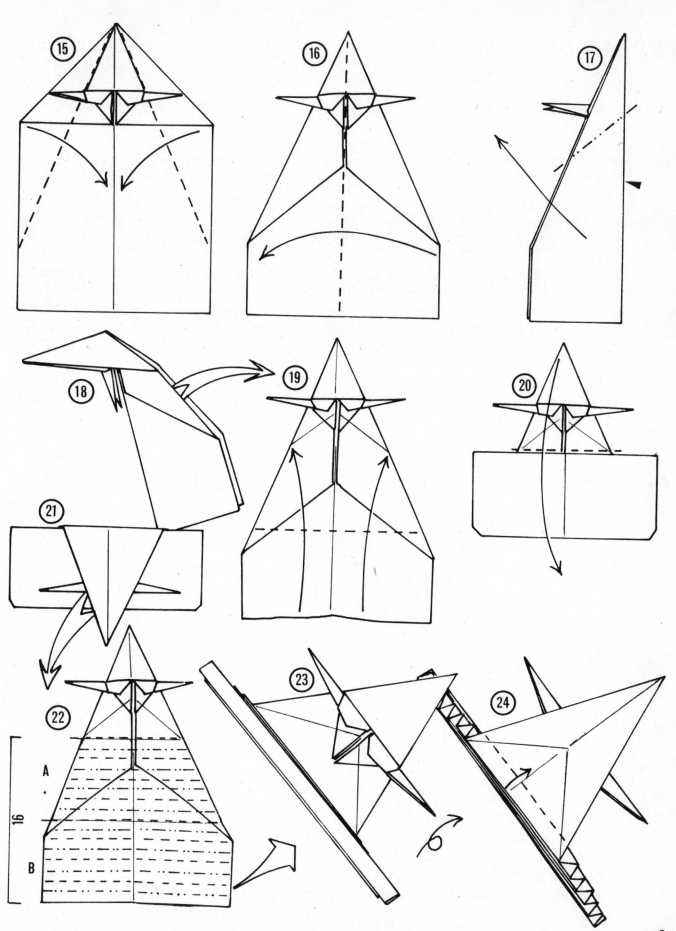

Adolfo's Peacock (*continued*)

25. Valley-fold the tail and Mountain-fold the model almost at the same time.
26. Fold completed. Glue the tail together as indicated.
27. This group of drawings shows how to form the neck. Valley-fold the top flap. Valley-fold the sides, forming two gussets left and right. Mountain-fold the model in half.
28. Grip the neck and pull it forward. Sink the chest. Reverse-fold the head, and complete it as shown. Form the legs with Reverse Folds, and repeat behind. The follow-through drawings show how to do this.
29. Here, the Peacock is completed. To fan the tail, hold the chest, and push the tail up.

This delightful model—which brings many "Ooh's!" and "Ah's!"—makes a fitting end to the Adolfo Cerceda Section.

W A T E R   F O W L
Origin: *Japan.*

Use a square of paper creased across its diagonal.

1. Valley-fold the top and bottom flaps to the centre crease.
2. Valley-fold the two narrow flaps inwards.
3. Mountain-fold the model in half.
4. With Reverse Folds form the head and tail.
   Finally, an enlarged view of the completed Water Fowl.

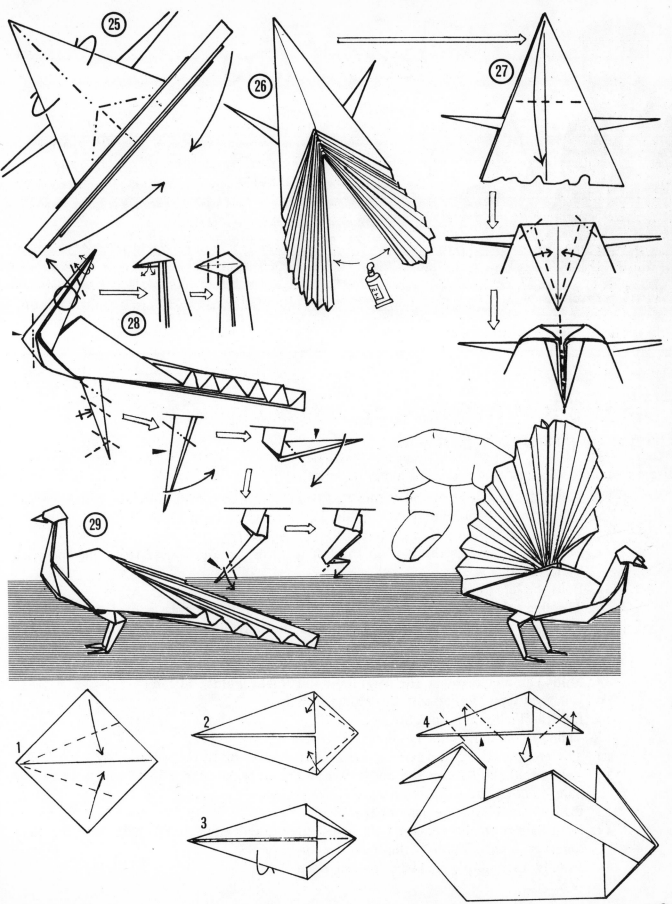

Neal Elias

Married, has two daughters, and lives in Brunswick, Ohio, where he is employed by the Nickel Plate Railroad. Mr. Elias is a fine magician and is the author of a book on Card Magic. In 1960 Mr. Elias began folding and has created some three hundred models, all of which are highly ingenious, and display a sense of humour.

The first fold in this section—my Fisherman in a Boat—is included under this heading because I sent it with great pride to Neal Elias and a few weeks later it came back to me, wonderfully improved by a genius. His version is shown on page 186.

FISHERMAN IN A BOAT

Origin: *England*. Robert Harbin.

Use a rectangle of paper, 4 × 1, creased along its length.

1. Valley-fold top right-hand corner and the top and bottom flaps to the centre crease.
2. Crease the left end with Valley Folds. Lift up the top layer on the left.
3. Valley-fold flap on left. Valley-fold flap on right.
4. Fold over and over the flap on the left to form a mast. Crease the right end with Valley Folds.
5. Fold the left top flap back into place. Pull out the corners on the right.
6. The flap folded back, and the corners pulled out into the creases made.
7. Enlarged view of right end. Squash-fold the flap indicated. Make a Rabbit's Ear on the flap underneath. Mountain-fold the flap on the top portion. Then pull this part out to the right to form the hat.
8. Folds completed. Make the Mountain and Valley Folds indicated.
9. Enlarged view. Valley-fold the model in half.
10. Pull the Fisherman upright.
11. Valley-fold the flap on the man to the right.
12. The completed fold reveals the arm. Turn the model to point the other way.
13. Valley-fold the flap on the body. Watch the little Mountain Fold which forms the hand holding the tiller.
14. Push in the bottom corners of the Boat.
15. Mountain-fold into the Boat the two little corners indicated. These hold the Boat together (a weak point of the fold). Use tweezers.

    Finally, the completed Fisherman in Boat.

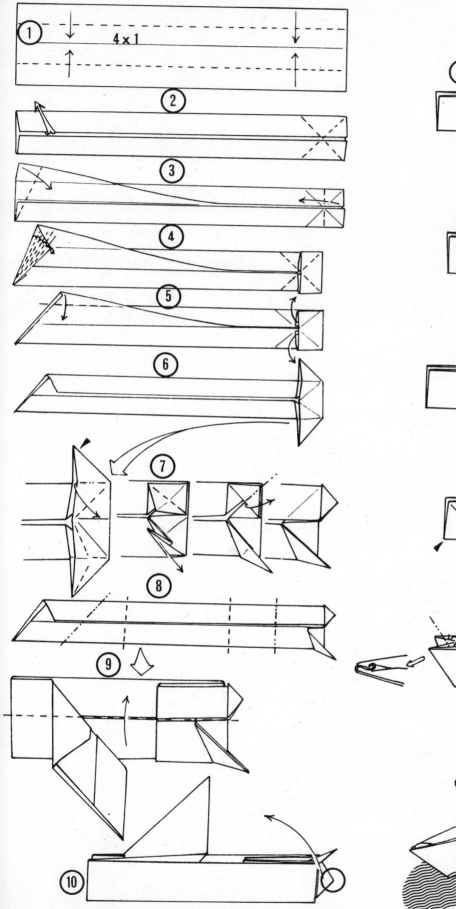

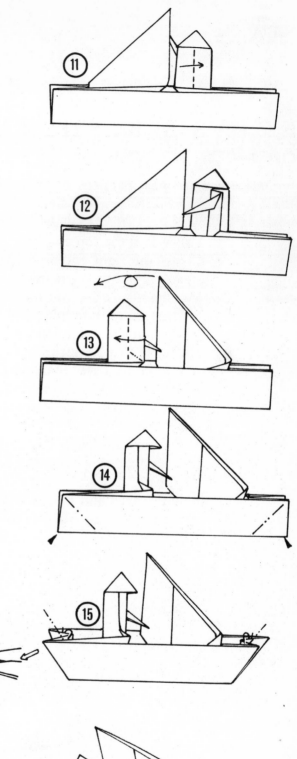

185

ELIAS'S FISHERMAN IN A BOAT

Origin: *America*. Neal Elias.

Here you see what happens when real genius takes a hand.

Use a rectangle of paper 6 × 1, creased along its length.

1. Valley-fold the top and bottom flaps to the centre crease.
2. Crease the right end as for the previous Boat, and pull the corners inwards in the creases. Fold the right-hand flap upwards.
3. Mountain-fold the two outside flaps on the left. Make two Rabbit's Ears of the two little triangles indicated.
4. Valley-fold the model in half.
5. Make the two Reverse Folds indicated.
6. Mountain-fold the Man on the left. He swings round to become parallel with the Boat. Squash-fold the sail.
7. Make a Rabbit's Ear of the Man and pull him in front of the Boat. Valley-fold the two flaps on the sail.
8. Valley-fold the Man into the Boat. The Man himself swings under and upwards, and his base goes into the Boat itself. Mountain-fold and Valley-fold the sail into the Boat. This also serves as an ingenious locking device. The extra drawings show how the head and hat are folded.
9. Almost complete. Valley-fold the hat back and front.
   Finally, the Fisherman in a Boat—in full sail.

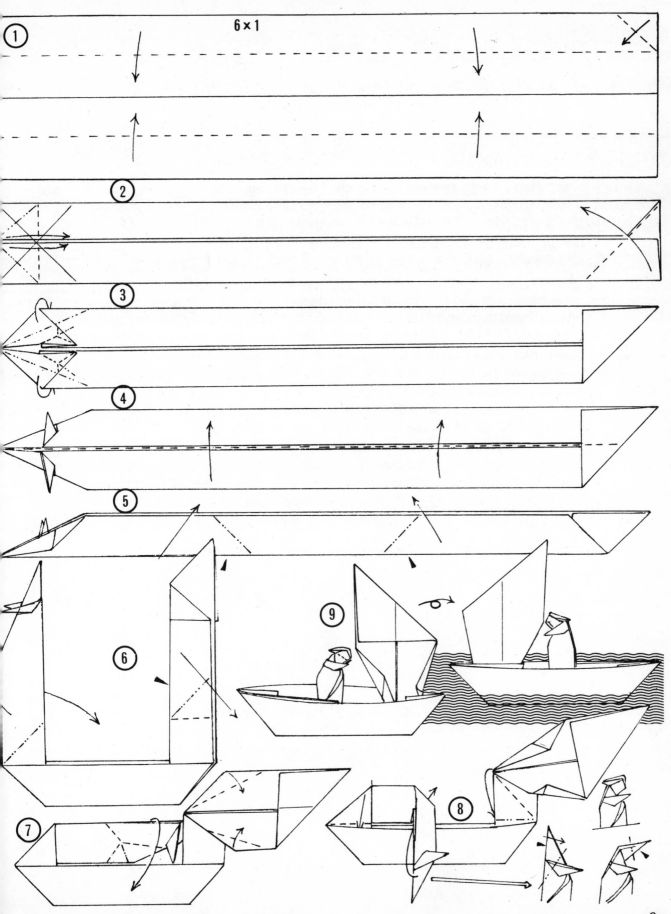

6 × 1

HIAWATHA

Origin: *America*. Neal Elias.

Another wonderful boat variation, but from a square this time.

Use a square of paper. Begin with the Bird Base, position 3 (*Page* 18).

1. Valley-fold the front flap over to the left.
2. Make a Rabbit's Ear of this flap.
3. Rabbit's Ear completed. Mountain-fold the model in half.
4. Enlarged view. Reverse-fold the upright.
5. With Mountain and Valley Folds in front and behind, Crimp the upright.
6. A group of folds. Crimp the head in front and behind. Mountain-fold inwards th two little flaps in the neck. Follow through these folds until the feathered head completed. Fold over and over the pointed flap on the right over to the left ar upright. This will form the paddle.
7. Another group of folds. These show how the paddle is formed.
8. Valley-fold the next flap on the right over to the left.
9. Mountain-fold the bottom of the boat.
10. Very carefully, turn the boat inside-out, so taking the front single thickness of th boat around to the back, and thus containing everything.
11. Mountain-fold the tips of the boat into the boat. Crimp the ends.
    Finally, the finished Indian in a canoe, with paddle and feather. A superb model.

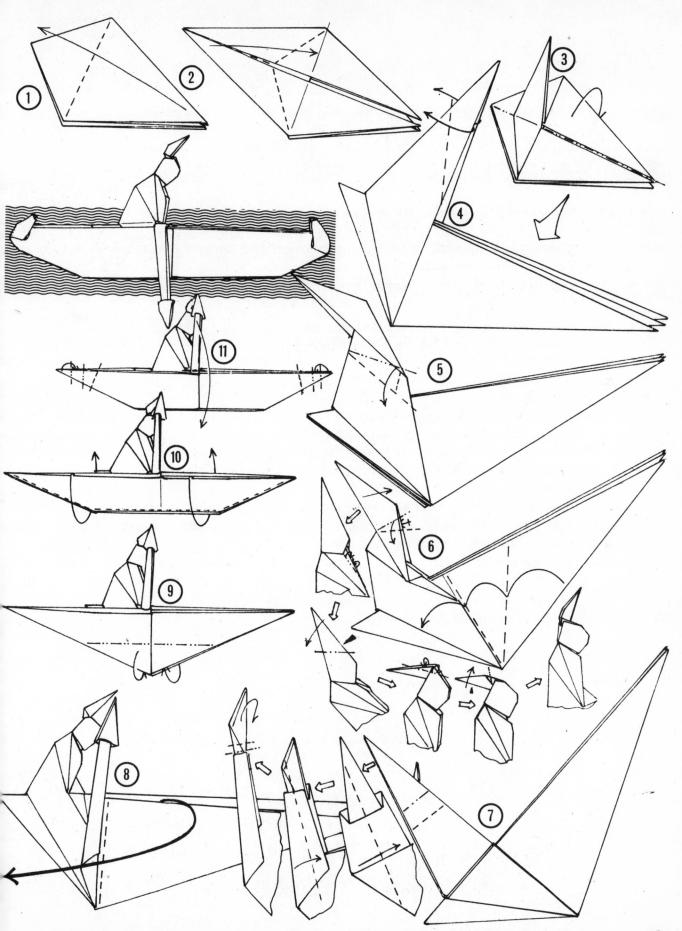

189

SITTING SCOTTIE DOG

Origin: *America*. Neal Elias.

Use a square of paper. Begin with a Bird Base, position 3 (*Page* 18). Fold to position 3 of Hiawat[ha] (*Page* 188).

1. This is the beginning. Turn the model over. The upright goes to one side.
2. Valley-fold the front flap upwards.
3. Open out as indicated. Watch the Xs. Bring top flap downwards.
4. Fold completed. Valley-fold the model in half.
5. Start forming the head with two Reverse Folds. Reverse-fold the half-hidden poi[nt] at the bottom.
6. Reverse-fold the leg in front, and repeat behind. Open out the flap inside the he[ad] (using tweezers if necessary). The extra drawing shows how. Two Reverse Fol[ds] are used again.
7. The head should look like this now. Turn in the nose tip, and with two Rever[se] Folds form the muzzle. Mountain-fold the flap at the back of the head, and t[he] flap next to it. Repeat in the opposite way with the flaps behind.
8. Flaps all folded. Mountain-fold the muzzle. Reverse-fold the leg in front and repe[at] with the leg behind.
9. Mountain-fold the flaps along the leg on both sides, and repeat with the leg behin[d]. With Mountain and Valley Folds, Crimp the body in front and behind. With [a] Mountain and Valley Fold push the ear in.
10. Mountain-fold the little flap to form hind legs in front and behind. Form the ta[il] with Mountain and Valley Push-in Folds. Crimp the ear backwards and inwards.
11. Valley-fold the bottom flap in front, and repeat behind.
    Finally, the completed Scottie.

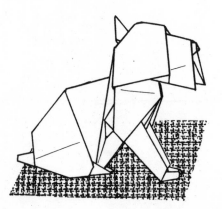

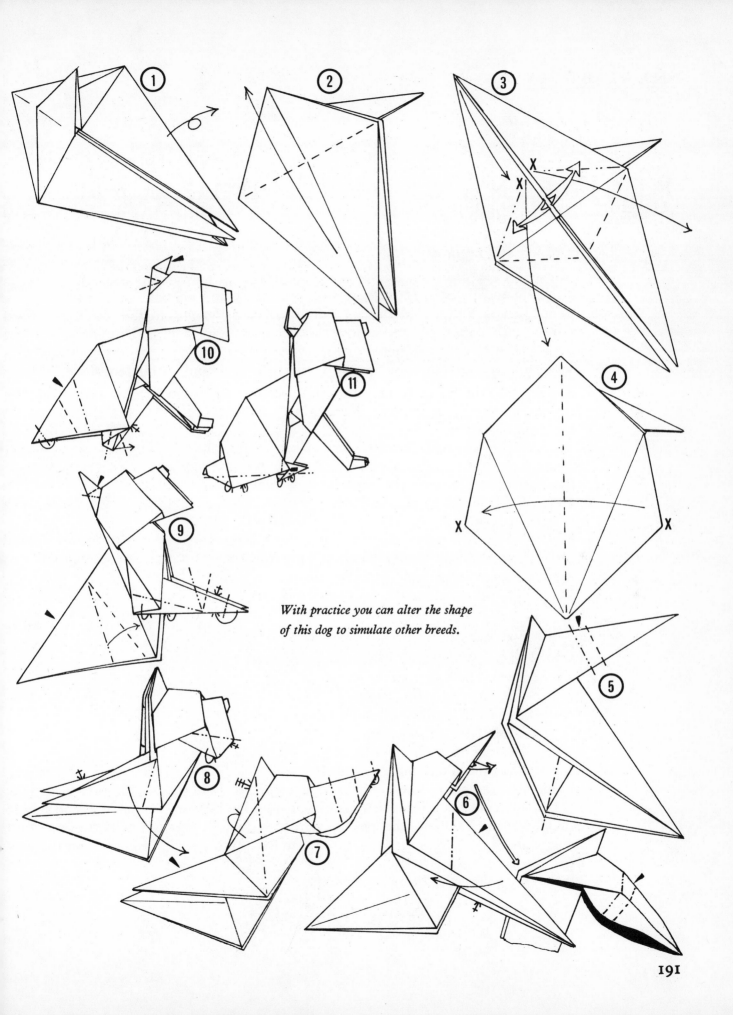

With practice you can alter the shape
of this dog to simulate other breeds.

RECLINING SCOTTIE DOG

Origin: *America*. Neal Elias.

Use a square of paper, and begin with Fold 8 on previous page.

8. Reverse-fold legs in front and behind. Sink ear.
9. Mountain and Valley-fold the rear portion in front and behind. Sink ears.
10. Mountain and Valley-fold the tail. Mountain and Valley-fold the rear leg forwar in front and behind. Mountain-fold the front elbow in front and behind. Form th front paws with Reverse Folds.
11. Mountain-fold the flaps on the tail in front and behind. Mountain-fold the bell in front and behind.
    Finally, the Reclining Scottie.

STORK WITH BABY

Origin: *America*. Neal Elias.

This is the traditional Japanese crane, ingeniously provided with the well-known bundle.

Use the two squares of paper illustrated in Fig. 1. They are joined together. The paper should b coloured on one side only.

1. Valley-fold the large square across its diagonal. Fold a Bird Base from this poin (*see Page* 18, *position* 2).
2. Large Bird Base completed. Turn the model over.
3. Valley-fold the small square across its diagonal.
4. From this point, fold a Bird Base.
5. This is how it will result. Valley-fold the two side flaps.
6. Mountain-fold the two side flaps.
7. Reverse-fold the partly-hidden points.
8. This is the result. Turn the model over.
9. Reverse-fold the head. The bundle is now enlarged. Fold the bundle as on Page 189 Fold 4. Open out the inside flaps. Mountain-fold the bottom flap in front, and repea behind. Reverse-fold legs and head. Again Reverse-fold legs and head. Reverse-fol the legs and feet. Reverse-fold the tip of the head into itself. Mountain-fold the tin flaps under the head.
    Finally, the completed Stork with Baby.

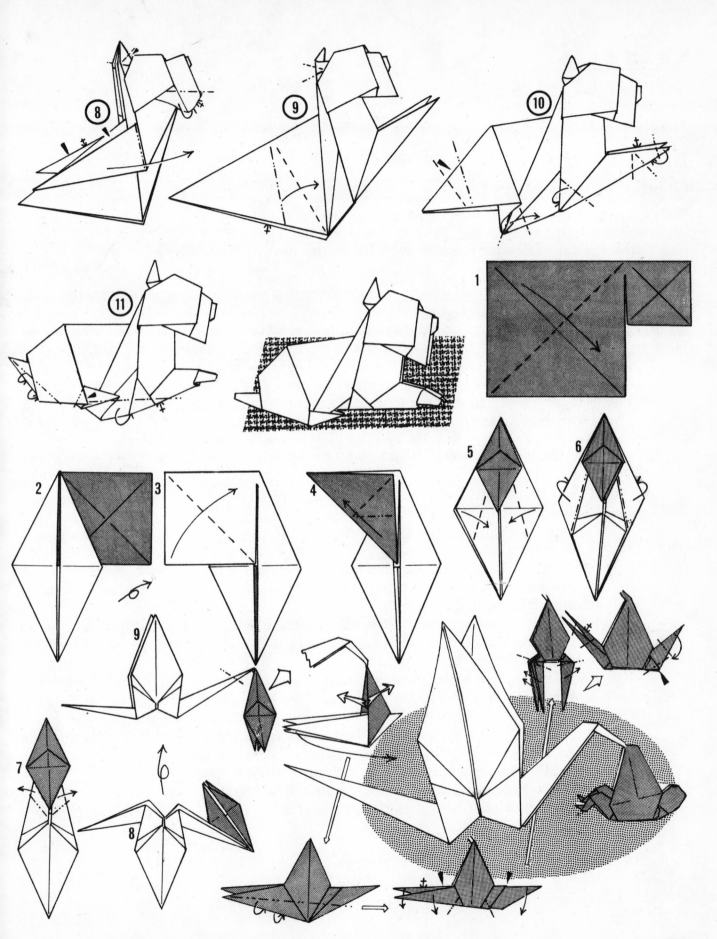

BIRD BATH

Origin: *America.* Neal Elias.

With great skill, Mr. Elias has contrived to make the Bird Bath one colour, and the Birds white.

Use a square of paper coloured one side only. Begin with Bird Base, position 2 (*Page* 21), and then unfold completely.

1. Valley-fold the bottom flap carefully. Note that the crease must only be made along the marked line.
2. With special crease made, Mountain-fold the bottom flap. The side pieces of the flap go into their Bird Base creases. Refold the Bird Base as for 3.
3. Bird Base partly re-formed. Carry on folding as for 4, and bring bottom flap up.
4. The fold completed. Study the markings carefully. Fold over and over the bottom half-concealed flap into the base. Push in, or Sink, the corners of the big flap, and Mountain-fold the narrow flap into the bottom. Push the rest of the big flap into the pocket behind it, with a Valley Fold first, and then a Mountain Fold.
5. This should be the result. Watch X. Valley-fold the flap at the back right down to the bottom, and turn the model over.
6. This is the result. Fold side flaps in (these are larger than shown, see 7) causing obtuse corners to sink and flatten.
7. Reverse-fold the two long pointed flaps at the top. Valley-fold the triangular flap at the bottom. Now follow through the extra drawings. Open out the hidden flaps. Mountain-fold the triangular flap into the pocket behind. Now Mountain-fold the bottom half so that it goes behind. Finally, Valley-fold inwards the two long flaps which will form the base (*see* 8).
8. Reverse-fold the left point, which will become a bird. Reverse-fold the right point, which makes the other bird. Mountain-fold the top triangular flaps into the model in front, and repeat behind.
9. Reverse-fold the left bird. Follow through extra drawings. Open out bird, and move X to the right. It is now half white and half coloured. Make the Mountain and Valley Fold, and then Mountain-fold the bird. Now Mountain- and Valley-fold the beak, as shown in Fig. 10. Book-fold the bird on the right, front and back. Follow through the extra drawings again. Make two Crimp Folds. Mountain- and Valley-fold the beak. Mountain-fold the breast flaps front and back.
10. The Bird Bath is complete. Turn it round, and reveal the two white birds. Finally, adjust your Bird Bath to look like this.

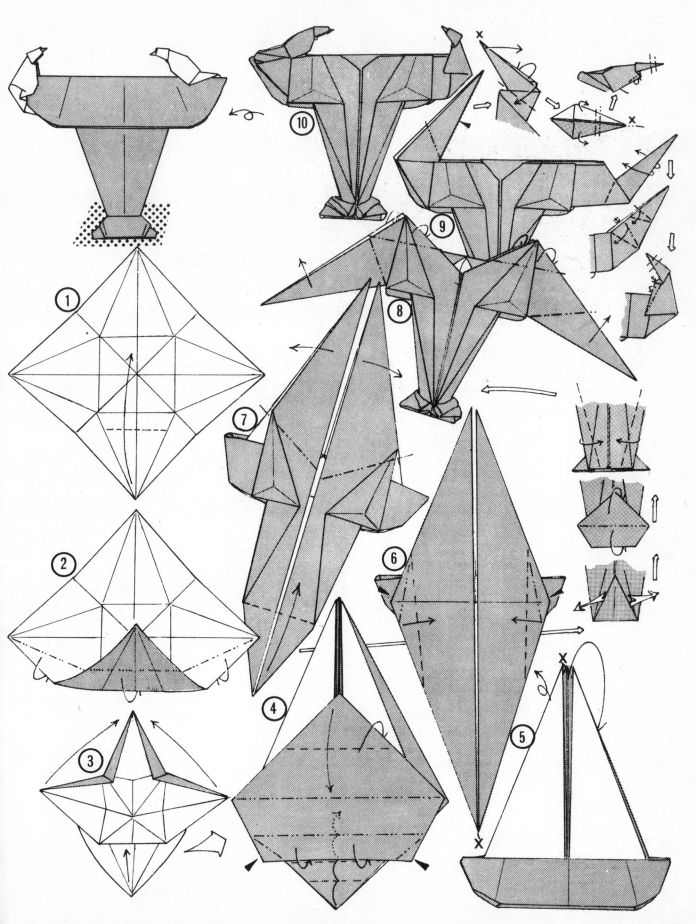

GOAT

Origin: *America*. Neal Elias.

A difficult model. Fold very carefully! Use a rectangle 2×1, creased down the middle both ways

1. Mountain- and Valley-fold the rectangle.
2. Crease the model as a whole along the Mountain Fold lines both ways. Now push in the four corners (one hidden).
3. This is the result. Fold flap C over to D.
4. Squash-fold flap A.
5. Petal-fold flap A.
6. Valley-fold flap C and the Petal Fold over to the **left**.
7. Treat flap B as for 4, 5 and 6. Valley-fold flap D over to right.
8. Squash-fold flap D.
9. Mountain-fold the flaps on flap D. Fold the three remaining flaps in the same way as flap D.
10. A and B should now be in the position shown. Reverse-fold all six points.
11. Valley-fold the front flap, A flap and B flap upwards.
12. Mountain-fold the whole model in half.
13. Hold as indicated, and pull the bottom middle point to a horizontal position. The folds underneath will move, and must be pressed flat.
14. The top is the head, which contains the two horns. Pull the horns out (*see extra drawing, and Fig.* 15). Valley-fold the front legs below. The whole side flattens (*see* 15). The horizontal part is the tail, which contains two legs. Reverse-fold the two hidden legs. The extra drawing shows how to do this.
15. Mountain-fold the flaps on both horns, as shown in the extra drawing. Reverse-fold the front legs. Reverse-fold the hind legs. See that the under-part resembles the circled X.
16. Reverse-fold the head between the horns. Mountain-fold the chest flaps. Reverse-fold the front legs. Reverse-fold the back legs. Watch the angles.
17. Mountain and Valley Reverse-fold the tail (*see extra drawing*). Shape the horns with Reverse Folds (*extra drawing*). Form the muzzle (*extra drawings*). Reverse-fold the front legs into shape (*extra drawing*).

    Finally, the finished Goat as it should look.

With careful folding, you should get a result first time.

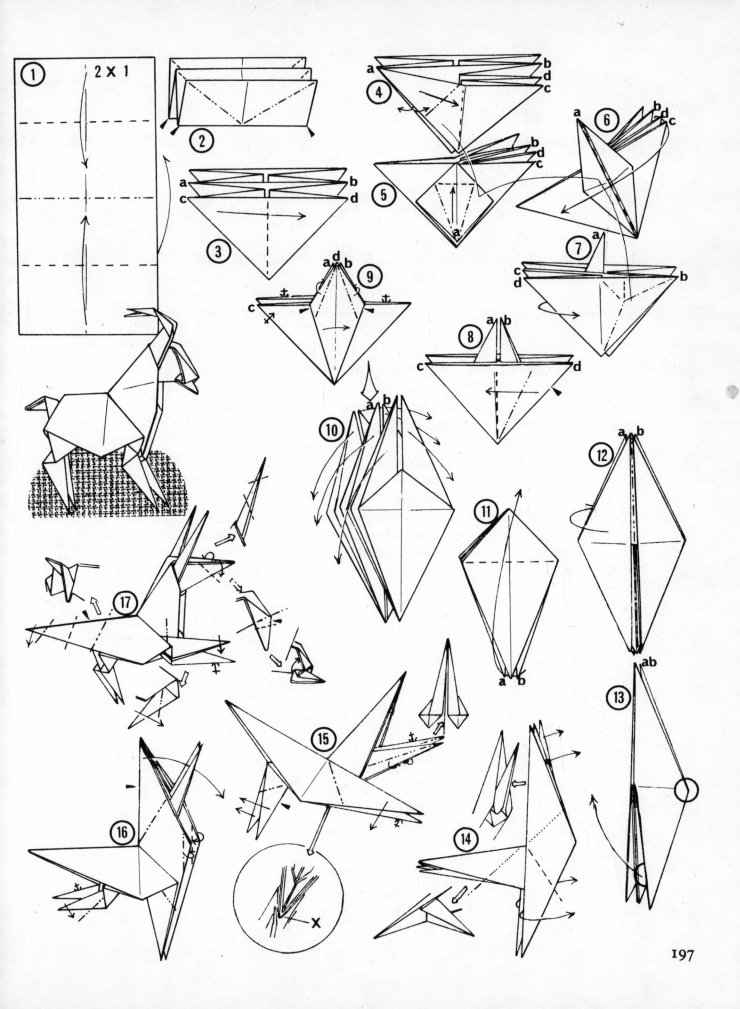

DOVE COTE

Origin: *America.* Neal Elias.

Use a square of paper, coloured on one side only. Begin with a Bird Base, position 3 (*Page* 18).

1. Open out the Bird Base completely, colour side down.
2. Valley-fold and Mountain-fold the two flaps top and bottom, along the markings.
3. Valley-fold the model in half.
4. Push in the arrowed corners. The Bird Base creases will help.
5. Push in the four corners indicated, so re-forming the Bird Base.
6. Enlarged view. The flaps left and right will become birds. Reverse-fold these flaps up and down, opening out to do so, as shown in Fig. 7.
7. Here is the left flap open, and the folding half done.
8. Both flaps folded. Note the difference between the two flaps or birds. Push in the corners indicated, and repeat behind.
9. Mountain-fold the two long flaps into the model in front and behind. Reverse-fold the right bird.
10. Reverse-fold the left hidden bird. Mountain-fold the bottom point of the Dove Cote, and tuck into itself (*see Page* 43 folds 12 and 13). Valley-fold the flaps of the right bird in front and behind.
11. Mountain and Valley Reverse-fold the left bird into shape, as shown in the extra drawings. Reverse-fold the right-hand bird, and follow through the extra drawings. Finally, the Dove Cote completed.

With this delightful Walt Disney type fold, we close the Neal Elias Section.

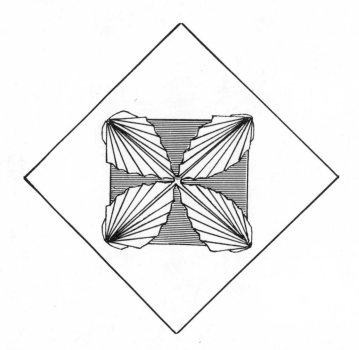

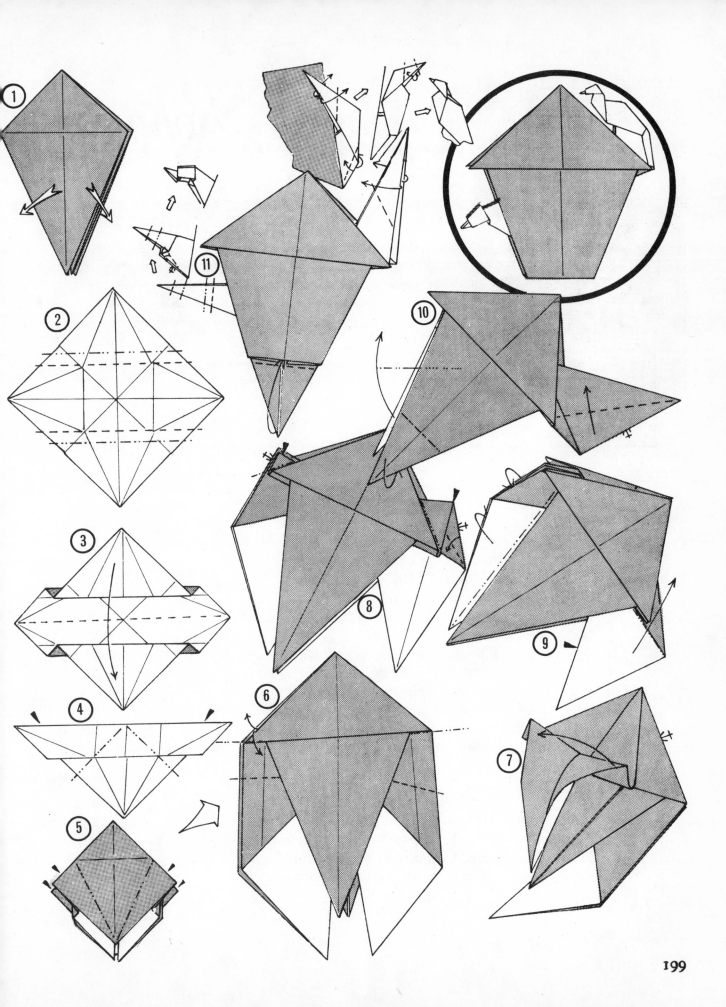

Fred G. Rohm

*Born 1907. Married, with two children and four grand-
children. Graduate of the University of Pennsylvania. Now
Chief Experimental Engineer, Lycoming Division, AVCO
Corporation. Was a professional musician, and is keen on
magic. Plays the Hammond Organ, and is an inveterate mathe-
matical puzzle fan.*

*Began paper-folding with The Lovers' Knot which was shown
to him by an aunt. Later came across the Water Bomb Base.
An enthusiastic reader of* Paper Magic.

SEE-SAW

Origin: *America*. Fred Rohm.

Use a square of paper. Begin with the Fish Base, position 3 (*Page* 20).

1. Squash-fold the centre flaps indicated.
2. Mountain-fold the flaps top and bottom.
3. Make Rabbit's Ears left and right.
4. Open out the right Rabbit's Ear, which will become the boy.
5. Enlarged view—the boy half open. Complete, and open out the girl on the left.
6. Both opened out. Mountain-fold the See-Saw in half.
7. Reverse-fold girl and boy. Fold Rabbit's Ears with centre flaps in front and behind.
8. Both girl and boy are marked for eccentric Rabbit's Ear folds in front and behind. Fold these carefully, to form arms and hands. Squash-fold the centre Rabbit's Ears in front and behind.
9. Sink the girl's back. Squash-fold the hand. Reverse-fold the head. Squash-fold the boy's hand. Reverse-fold tip of the head. Crimp the neck. Mountain-fold the small centre flaps. This will be the fulcrum.
10. Reverse-fold the girl's hat to form a brim. Crimp her neck. Valley-fold the hand. Mountain-fold the flap below in front and behind. Valley-fold the boy's hand. Valley-fold the flap below, in front and behind.

Continued overleaf

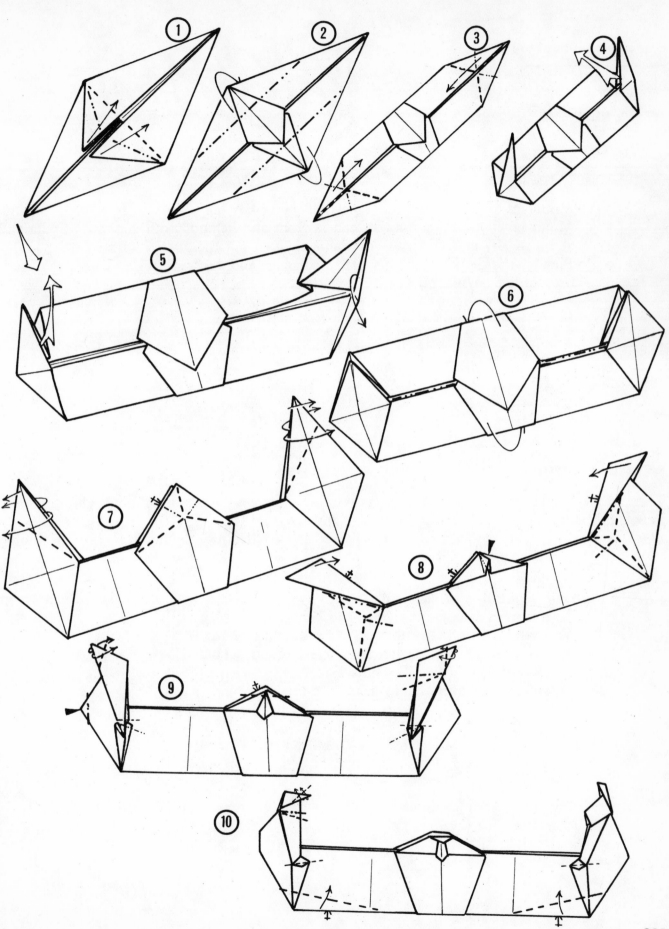

See-Saw (*continued*)

11. Mountain-fold inwards the lapels of both boy and girl in front and behind. Mountain-fold the See-Saw in half in front and behind. Both flaps tuck under and automatically pull down the fulcrums. Flatten out the gussets formed.
Finally, the See-Saw, which really balances and rocks. The boy, incidentally, is dressed like an Indian, wearing a feather.

CIRCUS PONY
Origin: *America*. Fred Rohm.

This remarkable model contains two cuts, but the result justifies the means. At first sight, this seems to be a formidable fold, but you will find it straightforward if you follow the illustrations carefully. Use a square of paper, of black or other suitable colour. Begin with the Bird Base, position 3 (*Page* 18). The top is sunk, as shown here.

1. Sink the top.
2. Top sunk this way. Compare it with Page 21. This is a close-up view. Cut through both flaps as indicated, in front and behind.
3. Valley-fold all cut flaps upwards in front and behind.
4. Squash-fold the two top left flaps in front and behind. Cut lower flap as indicated, and Reverse-fold ends. The cuts make the ears.
5. Petal-fold the centre flap in front, and repeat behind. Turn the model over.

Continued overleaf

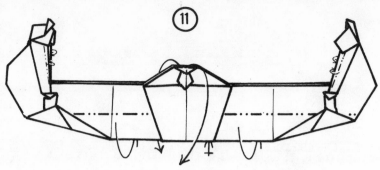

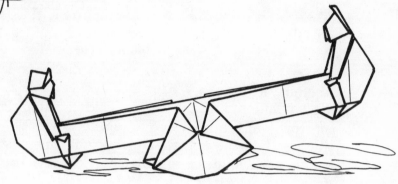

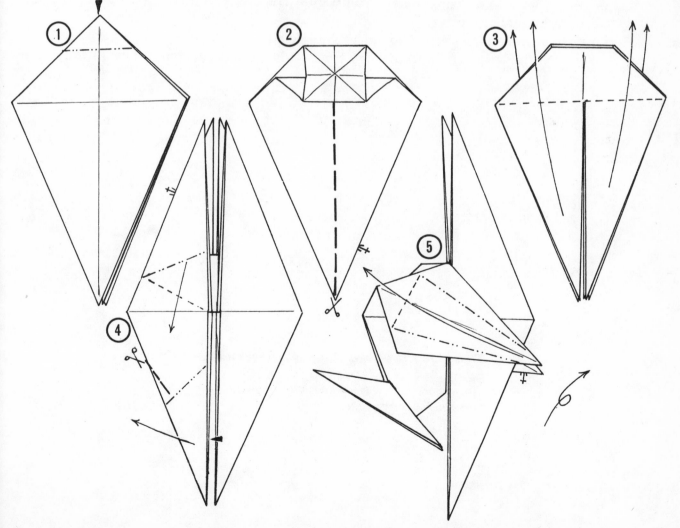

Circus Pony (*continued*)

6. Valley-fold neck flaps together in front, thus making the mane. Reverse-fold top of tail. Reverse-fold back legs, setting the leg behind at a slightly different angle. Valley-fold the front legs downwards.

7. Reverse-fold the tail. Reverse-fold the front legs at different angles. Reverse-fold the hind legs as marked.

8. Valley and Mountain Reverse-fold the muzzle. Mountain-fold the tail into itself in front and behind. Reverse-fold four hooves.

9. Reverse-fold the tail. Crimp the rump into itself. Mountain-fold the neck flaps in front and behind. Crimp the chest over itself. Mountain-fold the hind leg flaps in front and behind.

10. Mountain- and Valley-fold the ears into the head (*see arrowed result*). Mountain-fold the lower chest inwards in front and behind. Mountain-fold and belly under in front and behind. Mountain-fold the rump into tail pocket. The arrows show the results for belly and rump.

11. This drawing shows the Folds in 10 completed.
    Finally, the wonderful Circus Pony from both sides. This pony stands firmly on its feet.

These rearing ponies were chosen to illustrate the title-page of this book. This design is an example where two cuts have been used to produce a result so wonderful that the means have been justified.

CIRCUS ELEPHANT

Origin: *America*. Fred Rohm.

In this model, the creator has managed to find legs, tail and trunk "from nowhere." There are no cuts.

Use a square of paper creased as for the Fish Base (*Page* 20).

1. Mountain-fold across the diagonal.
2. Valley-fold the corner flaps upwards in front and behind.
3. Fold Rabbit's Ears in front and behind.
4. Valley-fold the flaps left and right upwards. The Rabbit's Ear moves up automatically. Repeat behind. Note that you form another Rabbit's Ear.
5. Squash-fold this double Rabbit's Ear (underneath portion only). Repeat behind.
6. Squash-fold the top portion and flatten, as in 7. Watch this!
7. Hold as indicated, and pull down the arrowed flap to the original position as in 4. Repeat behind.
8. Make the two creases on the lower half. Open up this half, and fold as in the follow-through drawings to produce a tail. Close up model.
9. Crimp the trunk end inwards. Crimp the neck outwards. Trunk and ears will begin to form. Crimp the rear portion inwards to form rear legs. Repeat behind. Make Valley Fold creases on all the markings before folding.
10. Push in ear at front, and repeat behind. Push in ear on the right edge in front and behind. Mountain-fold the leg flaps in front and behind. Reverse-fold the tail portion.

Continued overleaf

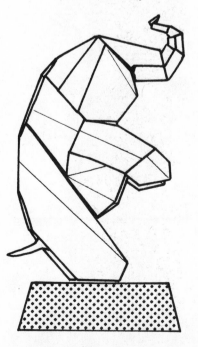

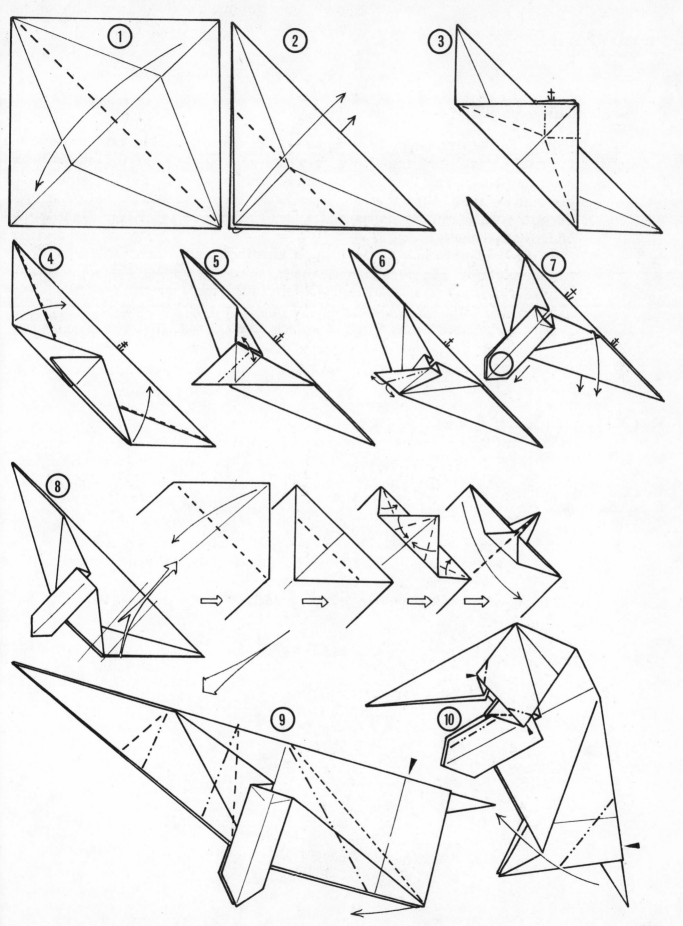

Circus Elephant (*continued*)

11. Valley-fold the trunk flaps upwards and under the ears (lift the ears) in front and behind. The extra drawing shows this clearly. Crimp the front feet outwards and Mountain-fold the leg flaps in front and behind (*see extra drawings*). Form the rear legs with a Valley Fold and a Crimp (*see* 12).

12. Form the trunk with Mountain and Valley Crimps (*see* 13). Reverse-fold the tail underneath (*extra drawing*).

13. Sink the head, and Sink the back. Note how the trunk is first pleated before the Crimping begins. The extra drawing shows the correct results. Watch X. Portion X is lifted, revealing crease underneath. Crimp inwards the whole rear portion, as shown in the extra drawing. Sink the rump, and squeeze the tail into shape.

Finally, the finished Circus Elephant, which stands.

ROHM'S PIG

Origin: *America*. Fred Rohm.

This pig is made in one piece, with no cuts. The base was used to make the traditional pig in *Paper Magic*, and is also the base for the Crib (*Page* 136). Use a square of paper creased as indicated in Fig. 1.

1. Valley-fold the flaps downwards and upwards to meet at the centre crease.

2. Crease along the Valley Fold markings. Fold inwards the arrowed points below. The flaps will move in the creases made above.

3. The base completed. Mountain-fold the model.

Continued overleaf

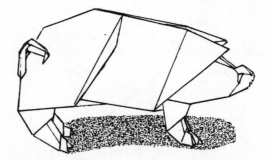

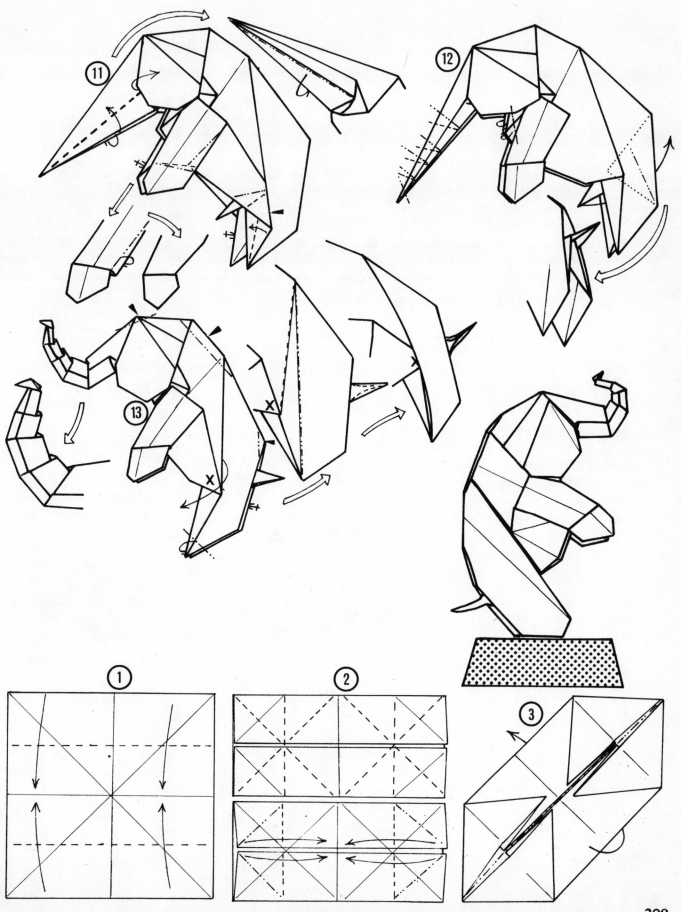

Rohm's Pig (*continued*)

4. Squash the two flaps indicated. Repeat behind.
5. Sink the corners indicated. Repeat behind.
6. Crimp the belly over. Repeat behind. Crease first. Valley-fold the legs to the left. Repeat behind.
7. Folds completed on both sides. Straighten out the body. The creases are used later.
8. Mountain-fold the flaps on the tail left. Mountain-fold the belly flap and push in the leg flap. Mountain-fold the belly right. Mountain-fold the head portion right and push in the leg flap. Repeat all folds behind.
9. Reverse-fold the tail portion and belly. Reverse-fold the head portion and belly. Repeat all folds behind. Now Crimp the body in the old creases from postion 7, but in the opposite way.
10. Valley-fold the tail in front and behind, and push arrowed flap into rump. Crimp the hind leg and repeat behind. Reverse-fold the front leg and repeat behind.
11. Valley-fold the tail flaps in front and behind. Push in the ham flap. Repeat behind. Form the trotters with Mountain and Valley Reverse Folds, and repeat behind. Reverse-fold the front legs and repeat behind. Fold a Rabbit's Ear to provide the ear, and repeat behind. Push in the snout. Repeat behind.
12. Mountain and Valley Reverse Folds form the curly tail. Mountain-fold the rump flaps in front and behind. Mountain-fold the back flaps in front and behind. Mountain-fold the flap in the middle and repeat behind. When the snout flap is pushed right in, Mountain and Valley Reverse-fold the snout. Complete the front trotters in the same way as the rear ones.
Finally, the completed Pig.

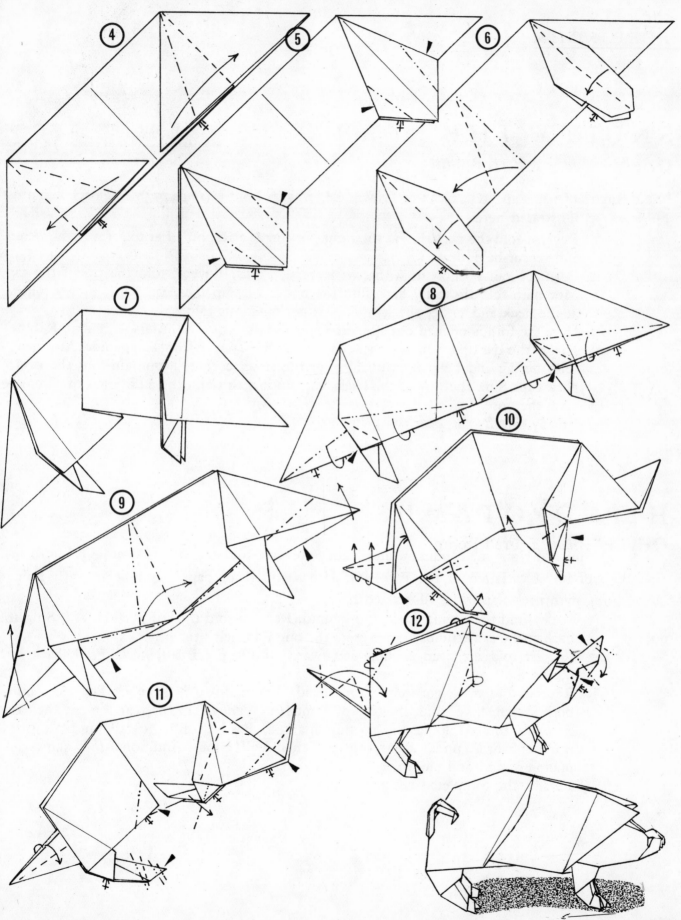

SNUFFY THE BEAR

Origin: *America.* Fred Rohm.

Use a square of paper in grey, black or brown. Begin with Fold 9 (*Page* 207). The neck flap must be down, as illustrated here.

1. Reverse-fold the neck. Treat the right portion as a Rabbit's Ear to form legs in front, and repeat behind.
2. Push the tail portion in with two Reverse Folds. Reverse-fold the tip of the tail. Mountain-fold the belly flaps into the body. Lift up the head flaps, Valley-folding at the neck and under the leg. This is an ingenious fold.
3. Here the fold is opened out. Reverse-fold the nose portion. Make eccentric Rabbit's Ears of the Ear tips. Sink the back. Crimp the front feet in front and behind. Mountain-fold the leg and belly flap, pushing in the small corner. Mountain-fold the centre neck flap. Sink the tips of the back feet. Follow through the additional drawings to form the nose.
Finally, Snuffy the Bear completed.

HIPPOPOTAMUS

Origin: *America.* Fred Rohm.

Another wonderful variation of the Elephant. Use a square of paper, and begin with Fold 9 (*Page* 207), with neck flap up as illustrated here.

1. Valley-fold the legs in front and behind. Reverse-fold the tail portion, and Sink the back at the same time. Crease first; the one fold helps the other.
2. Reverse-fold the head portion downwards. Pull tail, in a Reverse Fold, back into position.
3. Reverse-fold nose portion. Crimp head. Mountain-fold the neck flap, or Sink—both are effective. Sink the toes of front feet. Valley-fold the rear legs, at the same time Mountain-folding the portion marked. Rabbit's-ear the tail on both sides; in other words, pinch it together and then Valley-fold. Additional fold shows formation of ears and mouth.
Finally, the completed Hippopotamus.

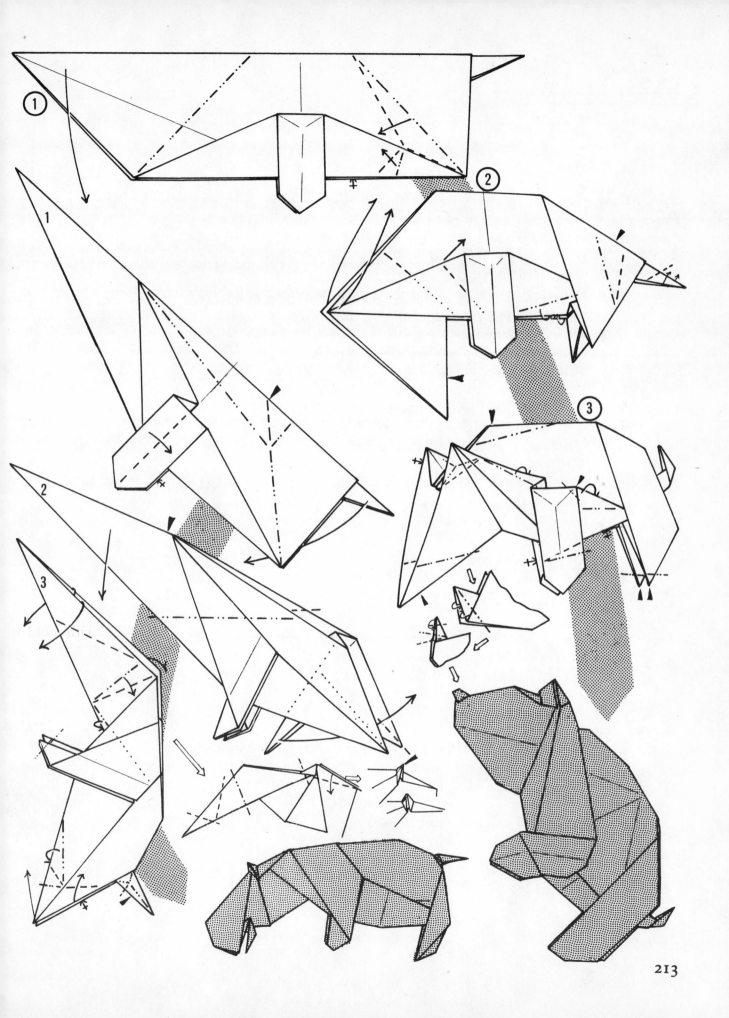

IT'S MAGIC

Origin: *America*. Fred Rohm.

Fred Rohm made this model especially for me because he feels that my first paper-folding book, *Paper Magic*, gave him such a good lift with his paper-folding. Use a rectangle of paper 2 × 1, coloured on side, and creased across the middle both ways.

1. Fold a Water Bomb Base on the left flap. Valley-fold inward the two flaps on the right.
2. Valley-fold the flaps indicated. This is the Water Bomb (*Page* 50) but with a difference, so follow these folds carefully.
3. Valley-fold the two flaps.
4. Enlarged view. Valley-fold the two flaps.
5. Valley-fold the two flaps.
6. Open out the flap indicated.
7. Refold the flap, reversing nearly all the creases.
8. This shows the result.
9. Mountain-fold the little flap under. Repeat all folds with the portion above.
10. The completed Bomb.
11. This is how the model should look now. Turn the model over towards you.
12. Fold a large Rabbit's Ear.
13. Squash-fold the Rabbit's Ear. *Come back and look at this position when you reach Fold* 18.
14. Petal-fold the Squash Fold.
15. Watch the spot **X** as you make the next folds top and bottom.
16. Here is the result.

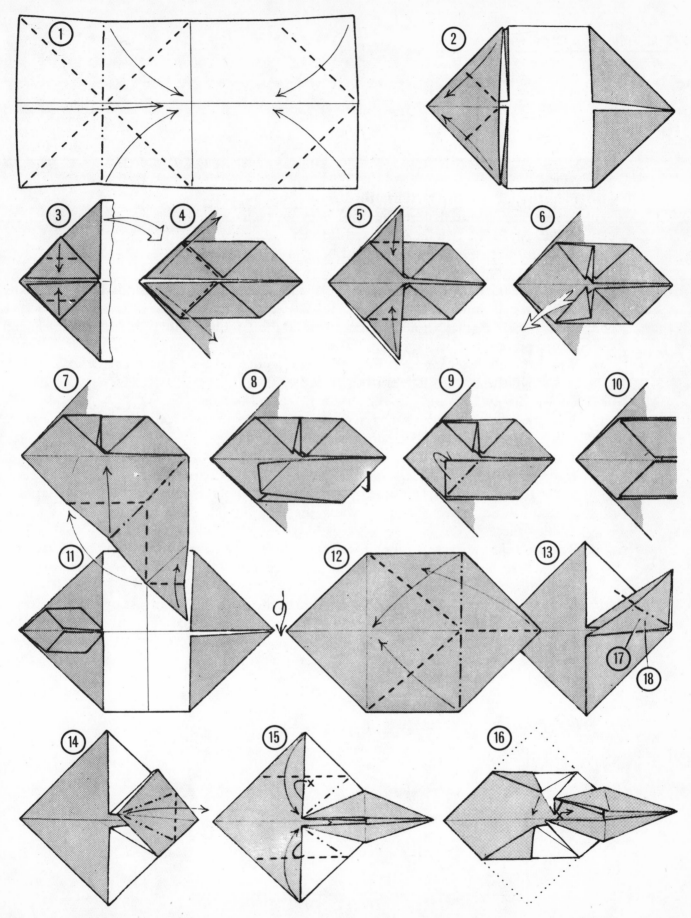

It's Magic (*continued*)

17. Open out the flaps behind the Petal Fold. Refer back to position 13 on the previous page.
18. Flap opened out like a Blintz Bird Base (*Page* 24).
19. Mountain-fold the flap on the right over to the left.
20. Reverse-fold the two flaps marked into the model.
21. Push in the two corners above and below.
22. With the front flap lifted, push in the two corners behind.
23. Book-fold the flap indicated on the dotted axis, so that it goes behind. Turn the model over towards you.
24. Model turned over. Fold the eccentric Rabbit's Ear. Valley-fold the kite-shaped centre piece.
25. Watch carefully! Mountain-fold the two pointed flaps behind to the base point, and move the bottom halves to the middle.
26. Enlarged view. Push in the corners in front and behind.
27. Mountain-fold a Rabbit's Ear as indicated (*see position* 28, *which is the underneath view*). Turn the model over towards you.
28. This is difficult to explain, but a look at position 29 will help. Valley-fold flaps top and bottom inwards. Mountain-fold the other two flaps forward. This fold automatically Valley-folds the base of the rabbit. Mountain-fold the little belly flap and repeat behind. Reverse-fold forward the flap between the ears, which makes the rabbit's face.
29. Reverse-fold the ears. Mountain-fold the chest flaps in front and behind. Mountain-fold the front leg behind itself and repeat behind. Crimp the body in two places (*see position* 30).
30. Mountain-fold the little flaps along the back. Form the paws shown in the extra drawing. Details of the formation of the face are enlarged for you. Pull down the first layer of the triangle (*see sideways view*). Form the nose (*see front view of nose*). Valley-fold the little flap inwards. Fold up face. Crimp the nose.
    Finally, It's Magic! completed.

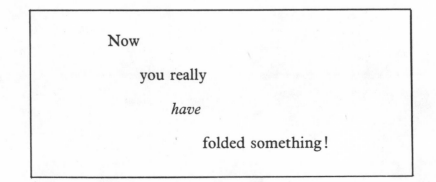

Now

    you really

        have

           folded something!

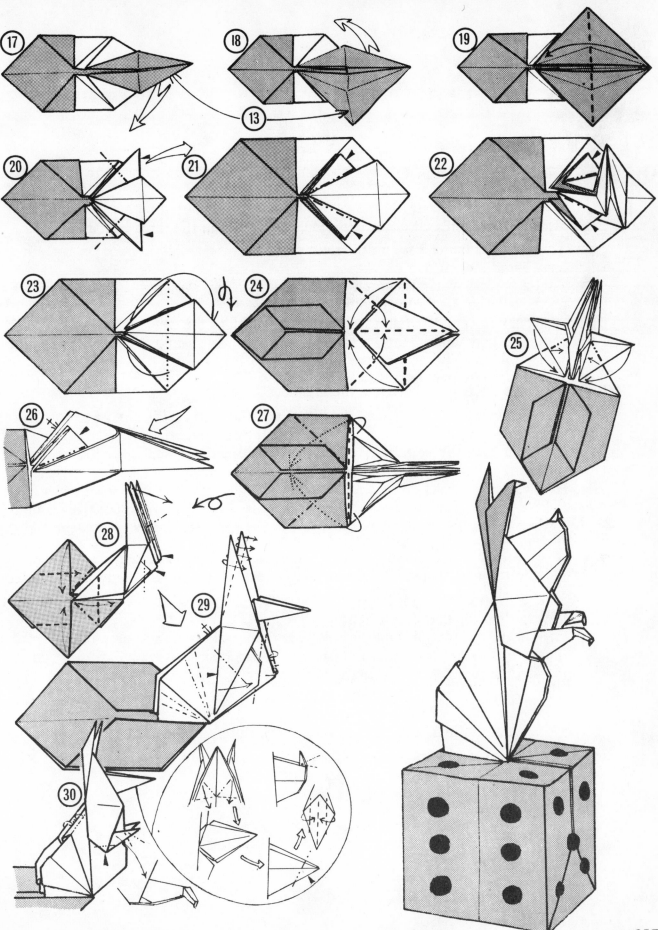

PERFORMING SEAL

Origin: *America*. Fred Rohm.

An inverted follow-up to It's Magic! Use a rectangle of paper, coloured on one side, proportion 3 to 1. Begin with rectangle creased down the middle and between the three sections.

1. Fold a Water Bomb Base on the right portion.
2. Valley-fold the left flap.
3. Fold a normal Water Bomb on the right portion (*see Page* 50). Fold a Rabbit's Ear on the left flap (half a Fish Fold).
4. Water Bomb completed on the right. Mountain-fold the whole right flap under.
5. Model is now shifted to a horizontal position. Valley-fold the flap on the right. Valley-fold the large flap on the left.
6. Valley-fold the same large flap back again.
7. Fold a Rabbit's Ear, and lift the large flap into a vertical position.
8. Enlarged view of the eccentric Rabbit's Ear. The next fold is similar to that in the base of It's Magic! position 28. Reverse-fold the two bottom flaps inward. Valley-fold front and back the vertical side flaps, one small and one sail-shaped. The arrowed corners then move in (*see position* 9).
9. Here you see that the sail-like flap has turned on its axis in this enlarged view. Fold a Rabbit's Ear on the sail-like flap (the other half of the Fish Fold, positions 3 and 4).
10. Reverse-fold the top point, which will become the tail flippers. Mountain-fold the Fish Base flap on its axis.
11. Valley-fold the flipper flaps down in front and behind. Open out the tail flipper hidden flaps.
12. Sink the top of the tail flippers. Reverse-fold the tip of the same flap into itself. Reverse-fold the bottom portion.
13. Push in the tail rear, making two flippers. Crimp the front and back of the neck, as shown in the extra drawings. Blow up the Water Bomb.
    Finally, the completed Performing Seal.

VERA CRUZ

Origin: *America*. Fred Rohm.

Use a rectangle of paper, 3 × 1, coloured black on one side. Begin with paper creased down the middle and between the sections.

1. Mountain-fold the narrow top flap. When this is done, Valley-fold the larger flap, as shown in the extra drawings. Mountain-fold the corner flaps. Mountain-fold the long side flaps as in position 2.
2. Mountain-fold the long inside flaps outwards to the edge.
3. Fold a tall Rabbit's Ear.
4. Enlarged view. Mountain-fold the two long double flaps under. Mountain-fold the two breast flaps inwards in front and behind. Mountain- and Valley-fold the arms upwards (*see position* 5).
5. Mountain-fold the arms and hands under front and repeat behind. Crimp the body outside. Repeat behind. Crease first.
6. Mountain-fold the front of the robe into the body, and repeat behind.
7. Here is an opened-up view of the interior.
8. Fold a Rabbit's Ear with the long flap on the right.
9. Open out the pleated top.
10. Mountain-fold the flap marked, with the result shown above. Follow through the extra drawings, which show clearly how the cross is formed. You may have a little trouble with this, but persevere.

Finally, the finished Vera Cruz.

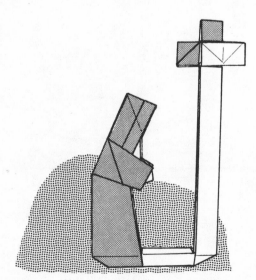

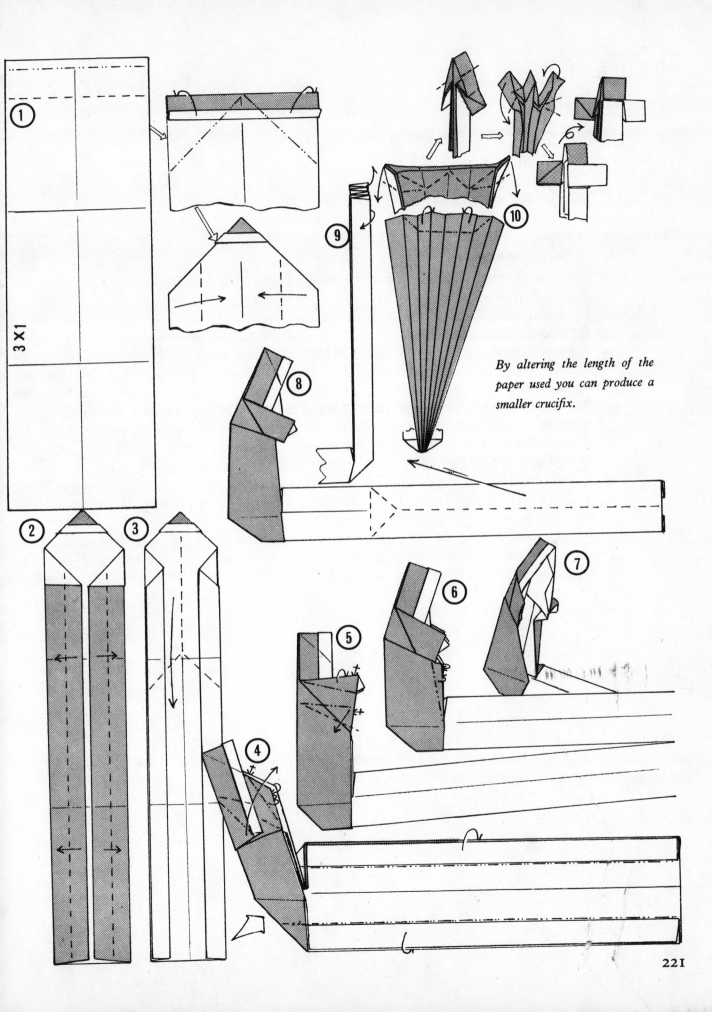

3 X1

By altering the length of the
paper used you can produce a
smaller crucifix.

SANTA CLAUS

Origin: *America*. Fred Rohm.

Use a square of paper, coloured red on one side, and begin with the stretched Bird Base (*Page* 175).

1. Valley-fold the middle back flap upwards.
2. The flap is up in position. Turn the model over.
3. Fold a Rabbit's Ear on the top flap.
4. Mountain-fold the model in half.
5. Open out the upright from the inside. Reverse-fold the two legs.
6. Reverse-fold the opened out flap. This becomes hat, head, body and arms. Reverse-fold the right-hand pointed flap, which becomes the bag of toys. Book-fold the legs on their own axis to the right, i.e., from the front inside to the back (*see position* 7).
7. Reverse-fold the hat. Mountain-fold the front flaps back and front to form the coat edge, as in the additional drawings. Valley-fold the little flaps on the right to form the posterior (*see position* 8). Look underneath the leg flap, and fold back a little flap (*see additional drawing*). This will make a white top to the boot.
8. Crimp the head and body portion in front and behind. Valley-fold the legs in front and behind. Watch X. Open out the upright flap as for position 5, but this time by pushing X out to the front (*see position* 9).
9. Reverse-fold the top of the bag, and follow through the additional drawings, which show how the toy elephant is folded. The extra drawings to the left show how the head and chest are crimped and folded. Watch the formation of the hands. You will notice that similar folds appear throughout Fred Rohm's models.
Finally, the completed Santa Claus.

This splendid model arrived just two days before the completion of this book, in reply to my suggestion that Mr. Rohm should try to produce this figure. An incredibly clever piece of paper-folding, it makes an admirable climax to the Fred Rohm Section.

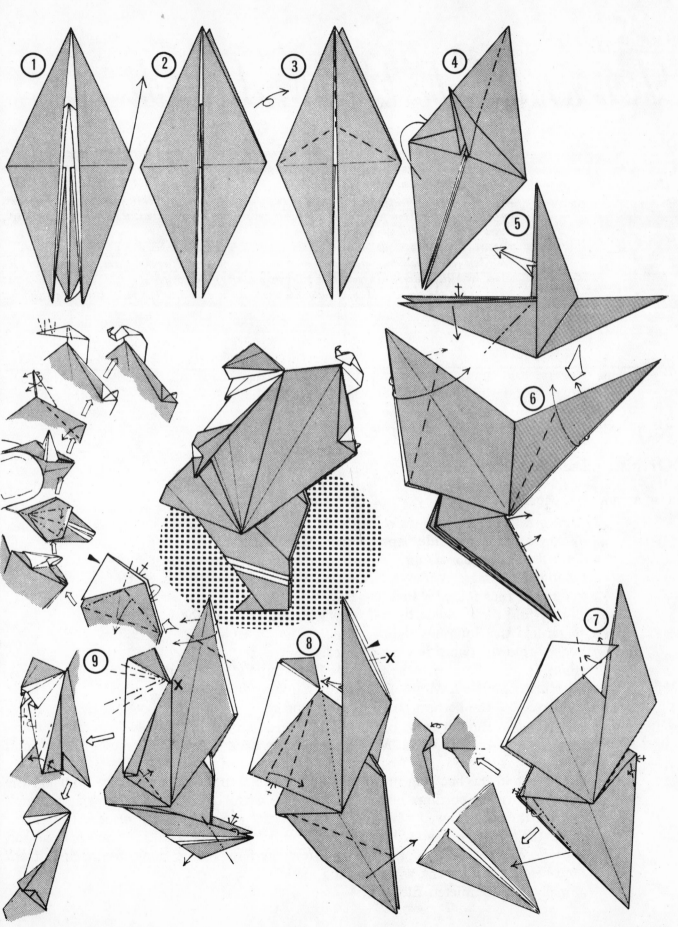

Reverend Robert Edward Neale

Protestant Minister. Instructor in the Program in Psychiatry and Religion, Union Theological Seminary, New York City. Aged 33. Current professional interest: the psychology of play, and the role of play in religion.

Married, with two daughters. Advocation: magic (especially card tricks), string games, tangrams, and Origami. Has been paper-folding for four years, and started with a Bow Tie and the Barge, described by Gershon Legman in The Phoenix.

Acquired Paper Magic, *and became acquainted with Lillian Oppenheimer.*

"My best folds," he says, "are those formed from a single sheet of square paper, are simple to construct, with clean lines, and require no pasting or cutting. The complicated folds may be clever and realistic, but the simple folds may possess a style that is true art. The latter is my objective and occasional joy."

NEALE'S ELEPHANT

Origin: *America.* Robert Neale.

Use a square of paper in brown, grey, or black, creased as shown.

1. Valley-fold the top flap downwards.
2. Valley-fold the two side flaps inwards. Watch X.
3. Pull X out into position 4.
4. Mountain-fold and Valley-fold the two marked flaps on either side of the vertical X. You have thus folded a Fish Base.
5. Valley-fold the two side flaps downwards. Squash-fold the vertical flap.
6. Petal-fold the Squashed flap.
7. Valley-fold the two side flaps upwards.
8. Fold Rabbit's Ears with the two side flaps, but Valley-fold the tips first.
9. Folding completed. Mountain-fold the model in half.
10. Reverse-fold the bottom portion (trunk end).
11. Reverse-fold the tail end.
12. Reverse-fold the tail again. Mountain-fold the back flaps into the body in front and behind.
13. Reverse-fold the back leg into itself. Reverse-fold the hidden tail. Open out flat the head and trunk portion. Follow through the extra drawings. Pull down the trunk so that the two arrowed edges meet exactly, and press them into place. At the same time, the top of the head will sink. When pressed flat, Valley-fold the ears to the right, and Reverse-fold the trunk. Mountain-fold the flaps in the trunk into itself in front and behind. Fold trunk as in finished model.

Finally, the completed Elephant.

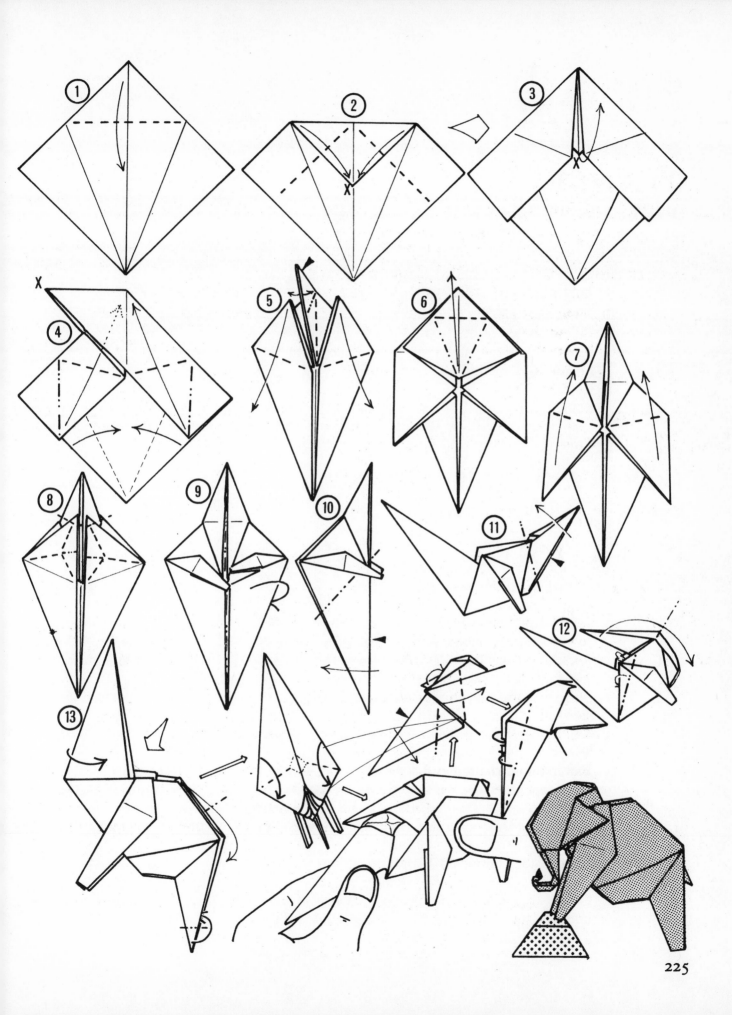

GIRAFFE

Origin: *America*. Robert Neale.

It is essential, in this model, to get the ears right. The secret lies in those extra folds.

Use a square of yellow paper, folded to position 7 on previous page.

7. Fold Rabbit's Ears on the flaps left and right.
8. Mountain-fold the model in half.
9. Enlarged view. Reverse-fold the lower portion.
10. Reverse-fold the upper portion. Valley-fold the two bottom flaps into the model in front and behind.
11. Reverse-fold the hind leg into its own crease. Reverse-fold the head. Complete the head, as shown in the extra drawings. If you wish to form a little tail, there is a hidden triangle which can be Reverse-folded, but this is not shown in the original model. Finally, the completed Giraffe.

FLAMINGO

Origin: *America*. Robert Neale.

Use an equilateral triangle of paper, cut to shape as described on Page 101.

1. Mountain- and Valley-fold the triangle. Follow through the extra drawings. Squash-fold the vertical flap. Petal-fold the vertical flap. Valley-fold the two side flaps, which will form legs. Mountain-fold the two long legs under and outwards.
2. Book-fold the legs one thickness, and bring up the arrowed flap. Repeat on the other side.
3. Valley-fold the legs downwards at the root. Valley-fold the neck flaps in to the centre line.
4. Valley-fold the leg flaps inwards to the centre line. Valley-fold the model in half.
5. Form the back leg with two Reverse Folds, the front leg with one Reverse Fold. Push in, or Reverse-fold, the tail. Form the neck with Reverse Folds. Open out the head and form beak and head with Reverse Folds. Crimp the neck in front and behind.
Finally, the completed Flamingo.

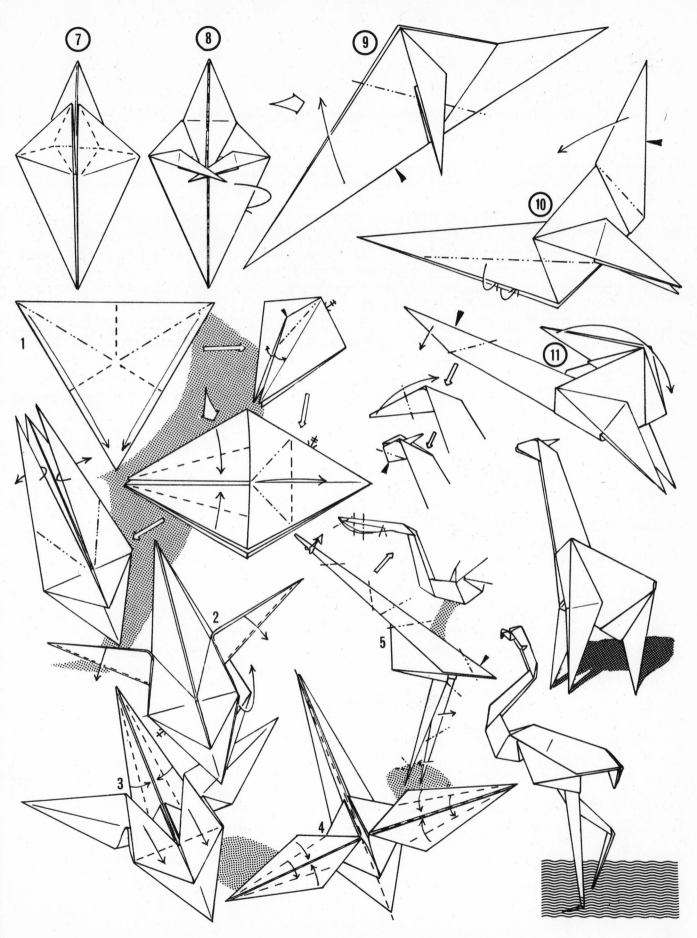

227

BULL

Origin: *America*. Robert Neale.

Use a square of paper folded to position 5 (*Page 225*).

5. Mountain-fold the model in half.
6. Squash-fold the triangular flap and repeat behind.
7. Petal-fold the Squash Fold and repeat behind.
8. Squash-fold the flap on the left.
9. Enlarged view. Petal-fold the Squash Fold. Reverse-fold the lower portion.
10. Valley-fold the large Petal Fold upwards. Valley-fold the small Petal Fold to the right. Reverse-fold the lower portion, which will become head and horns.
11. Reverse-fold the horns. Reverse-fold the hind leg.
    Finally, the completed Bull.

MATADOR

Origin: *America*. Robert Neale.

Use a square of paper, and begin with a Bird Base which has been "Sunk" (*Page 21*).

1. Mountain-fold the little flaps in front and behind. Valley-fold the two large flaps over to the left in front and behind.
2. Reverse-fold at different angles the two long flaps on the left. Mountain- and Valley-fold the end of the flap on the left, and repeat behind.
3. Fold a Rabbit's Ear on the big flap, and repeat behind. These are the arms and hands. Reverse-fold the lower pointed flap.
4. Reverse-fold the top tip twice. This will be the pigtail. Mountain-fold the flap just below under. Repeat behind. Fold a Rabbit's Ear with the arm and repeat behind. Mountain-fold the next flap down the Matador's posterior under. Repeat behind. Reverse-fold the leg three times.
5. Mountain-fold narrow flaps. Form head, hat and pigtail (see additional drawings). Finally, the Matador.

Display this model with the Bull. They look well when mounted on a strip to form a base-board. In the photograph I have managed to make them stand together.

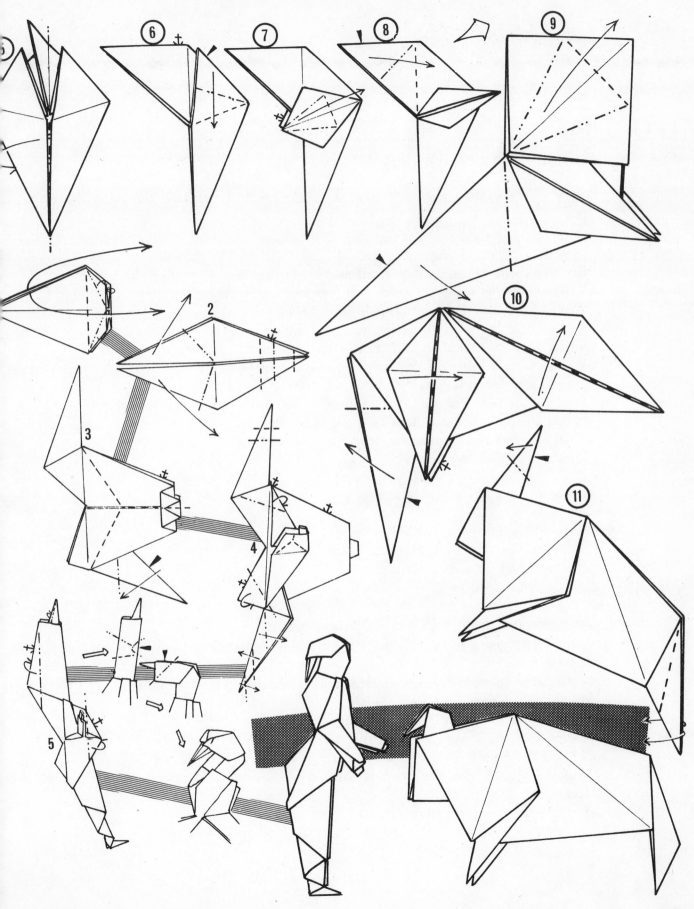

GOOSE

Origin: *America*. Robert Neale.

Use an equilateral triangle, constructed as shown (*Page* 101). Begin with the paper folded as at Fig. 1 (*Page* 227).

1. Valley-fold the small triangular flap at the bottom middle. Mountain-fold the model in half.
2. Book-fold the outside wings front and back, under and to the right.
3. Valley-fold the wings in their own creases to the right in front and behind—but watch the Valley Fold which is hidden below.
4. Treat both wings in the same way, as shown in extra drawings. Open out wing. Valley-fold into itself. Fold over and over under the flap opposite.
5. Valley- and Mountain-fold the tail portion two thicknesses downwards. The bottom goes in and the sides come down.
6. Fold completed. The foot can be eased into position. Reverse-fold the neck.
7. Mountain-fold the neck flaps in front and behind.
8. With Reverse Folds form the head.
   Finally, the flapping Goose.

GORILLA

Origin: *America*. Robert Neale.

Use a square of paper and begin with the Water Bomb Base.

1. Valley-fold the left flap to the right. Mountain-fold the right flap under. Repeat behind.
2. Valley-fold the left flap downwards, and repeat behind. Mountain-fold the right flap under, and repeat behind.
3. Mountain-fold the long side flap under and repeat behind.
4. Valley-fold the lower flap upwards. Valley-fold the rear arrowed flap downwards.
5. This is the result. Valley-fold the head downwards and fold in the sides. The extra drawing shows how the head is formed. Mountain-fold and Valley-fold legs and feet.
   Finally, the completed Gorilla, which stands up.

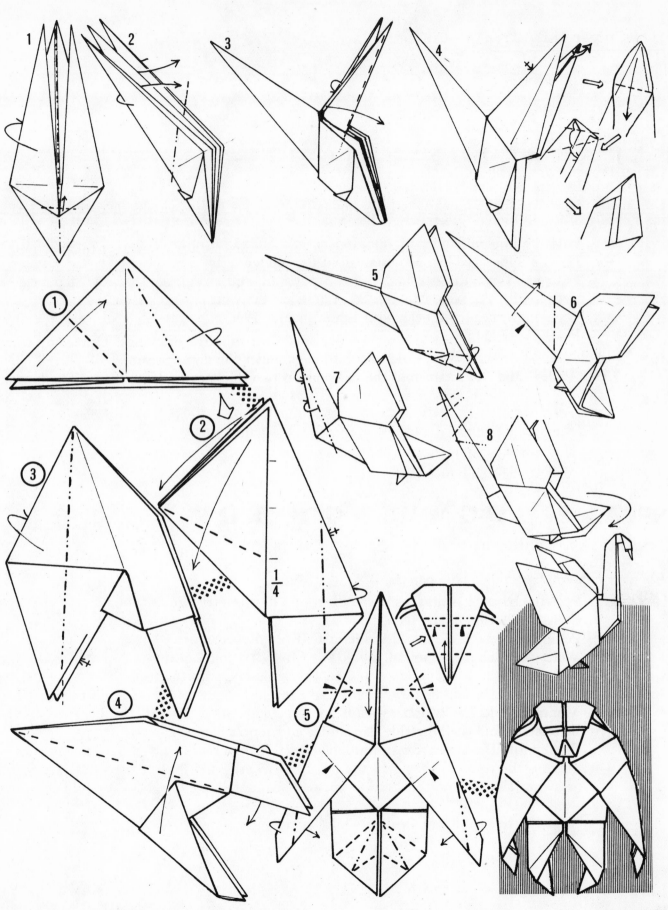

PARAKEET IN FLIGHT

Origin: *America*. Robert Neale.

Use a square of bright blue or green paper. Begin with the stretched Bird Base (*Page* 175).

1. Fold the hidden flap into a double Rabbit's Ear to form the leg.
2. Having folded the leg, Mountain-fold the model in half.
3. Enlarged view. Reverse-fold the top portion. Squash-fold the narrow flap below. Repeat with the same flap behind. These are the wings.
4. Form neck, head and beak with three Reverse Folds.
   Finally, the Parakeet.

Held by the tail and chest, the bird will flap its wings when the tail is pulled. Paper models that work are very hard to invent.

NEALE'S HUMMING BIRD

Origin: *America*. Robert Neale.

Use an equilateral triangle of blue paper.

1. Fold the triangle as notated in the diagram. This is a triangular Water Bomb Base.
2. Squash-fold the middle flap.
3. Petal-fold the middle flap. Mountain-fold the flap X under.
4. Valley-fold the model in half.
5. Valley-fold the wings in front and repeat behind. Crimp the neck. Sink the head as the Crimp is made.
6. Mountain-fold the two body flaps in front and behind. Form the beak with two Reverse Folds.
   Finally, the Humming Bird complete.

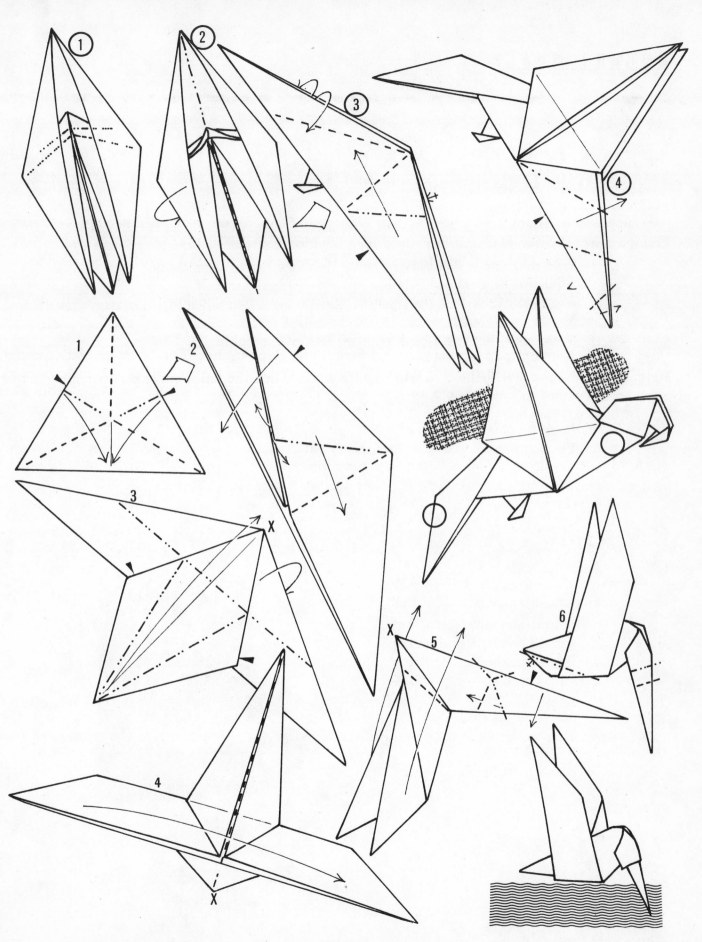

NEALE'S COBRA

Origin: *America*. Robert Neale.

Use an isosceles triangle of paper 28 cm. high, and 6 cm. at the base. Begin with the triangle creased down the middle.

1. Fold a Water Bomb Base on the wide end.
2. Fold two Rabbits' Ears.
3. Mountain-fold the two side flaps under. Turn the model over.
4. Valley-fold the two long flaps to the centre line.
5. Valley-fold the two marked flaps outwards.
6. Where the tail meets the head fold a long Rabbit's Ear. The body becomes the Ear, but do not flatten it. Make Valley Fold creases in the middle of the hood portion. Fold a Water Bomb Base in the neck. The follow-through sign shows you what should have happened.
7. Back view.
   Finally, the completed Cobra, ready for action.

Both Robert Neale and Samuel Randlett have produced a snake, and both models are most realistic. This fine model makes a fitting close to the Robert Neale Section.

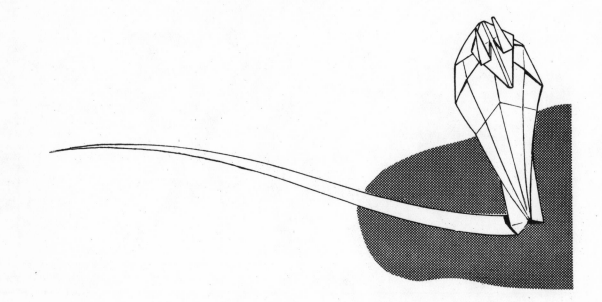

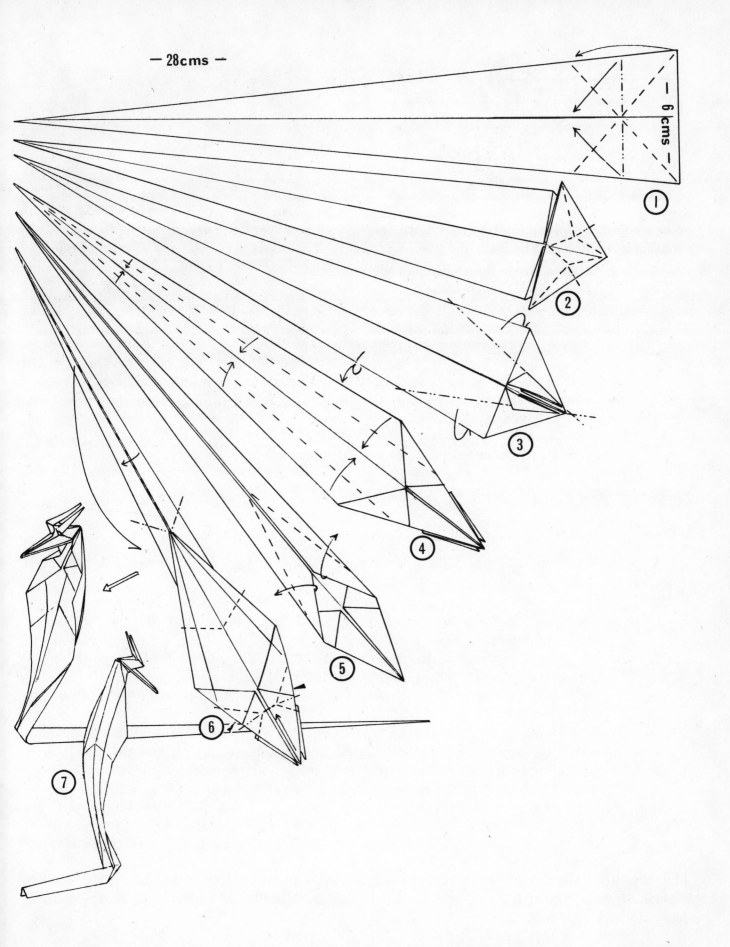

— 28cms —

6 cms

①

②

③

④

⑤

⑥

⑦

235

George Rhoads

Born 1926, in Chicago. Graduate of the University of Chicago. An artist, who has exhibited paintings in Paris and New York. Was introduced to Origami by Gershon Legman, in Paris. Was shown the works of Akira Yoshizawa, and acquired a copy of Paper Magic. *George Rhoads earns his living by house painting, carpentry, illustrating, and by painting pictures in the* Trompe l'oeil *technique, executed with great realism. Married, with two children. Is also an astrologer and graphologist.*

RHOADS'S ORNAMENT

Origin: *America*. George Rhoads.

Use 24 squares of paper, of any colour. Begin with each piece folded into Bird Base, position 2 (*Page* 18).

1. Let us assume that you have decided on a two-colour layout. Paste together the two sides of a blue Bird Base, as shown by the shaded portions. Paste together similar sides of all the Bird Bases.
2. and 3. Here you see two bases ready to assemble. The pasted portions are shown by dotted lines. Paste together the two shaded areas.
4. This show two pairs of Bird Bases being pasted together to make a group of four alternate colours.
5. This is the group ready for the final fixing. Put paste on one of the two shaded areas and bring together the two shaded areas as shown by the arrow. The lettering is there to help you to follow the new positions each time the model is folded.
6. This shows a completed section. There are six of these.
7. Here, two sections are being brought together. The shaded areas are pasted to the corresponding areas. Now fix together the other four sections. When you come to the last two sections you will have to press the pasted parts together from the outside. Finally, Rhoads's Ornament completed.

This delightful display of colour provides a fitting note on which to introduce the George Rhoads Section. You will find that Rhoads's Ornament is well worth making up as a permanent decoration for your room.

236

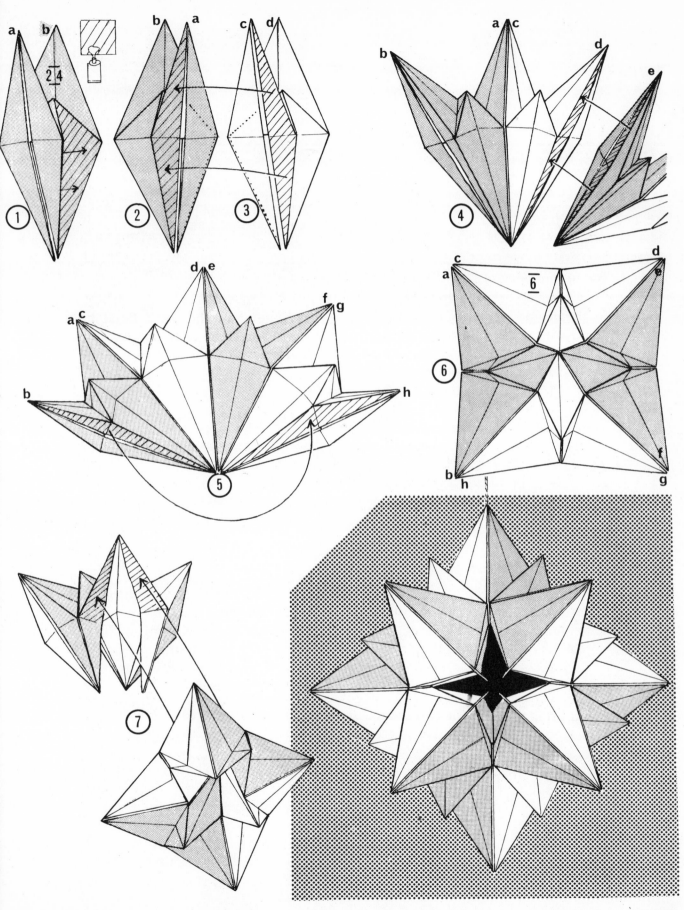

237

RHOADS'S BAT

Origin: *America*. George Rhoads.

This bat is a fine piece of paper-folding, and the result is most awe-inspiring.

Use a square of paper, black or brown on one side. Ideally, if the paper were black or brown on one side, and red on the other, the ears of the finished model would be red inside. Begin with the square creased down the middle.

1. Mountain-fold the two corners indicated.
2. Crease as marked, and the paper will fall into shape 3.
3. Petal-fold the flap.
4. Open out the outer flaps from the back (*see Blintz Bird Base, Page 24*).
5. Fold corners marked X down to the arrowed positions.
6. Squash-fold the upright flap.
7. Push in the flaps left and right. Now Valley-fold the middle flap upwards.
8. Push in the two flaps indicated. Now Mountain-fold the top half of the model, leaving the front flap where it is.
9. This is the result. Turn the model over in the direction indicated.
10. Make a Water Bomb Base out of the flap indicated.
11. This is the result. Turn the model over in the direction indicated.
12. Valley-fold the two pointed flaps upwards, to make the ears. Open out the flaps on the head and Valley-fold the head flap towards you. The head should lock behind the ears.
13. Here is the result. Valley-fold the flaps at the bottom of the ears (*see additional drawing*). With a sharp knife or razor blade, cut loose the double flaps indicated. When the cutting is done, lift up one by one the "Hold" flaps, and put the cut flaps in front, with the tips Reverse-folded. These will form the feet.
14. First of all, make creases on all marked lines except the curved bottom one. Mountain-fold the ends of each flap left and right. Valley-fold and Mountain-fold the shoulders. These folds will cause the lower long flap to turn inwards. Valley-fold the long flap, which will cause little gussets to be formed left and right.
15. This is the result. Valley-fold the tips of the wings. Turn the model over in the direction indicated.
16. Mountain-fold under the two body flaps. Valley-fold the cheeks to form little gussets which look like eyes. Open out the ears.
   Finally, the completed Bat.

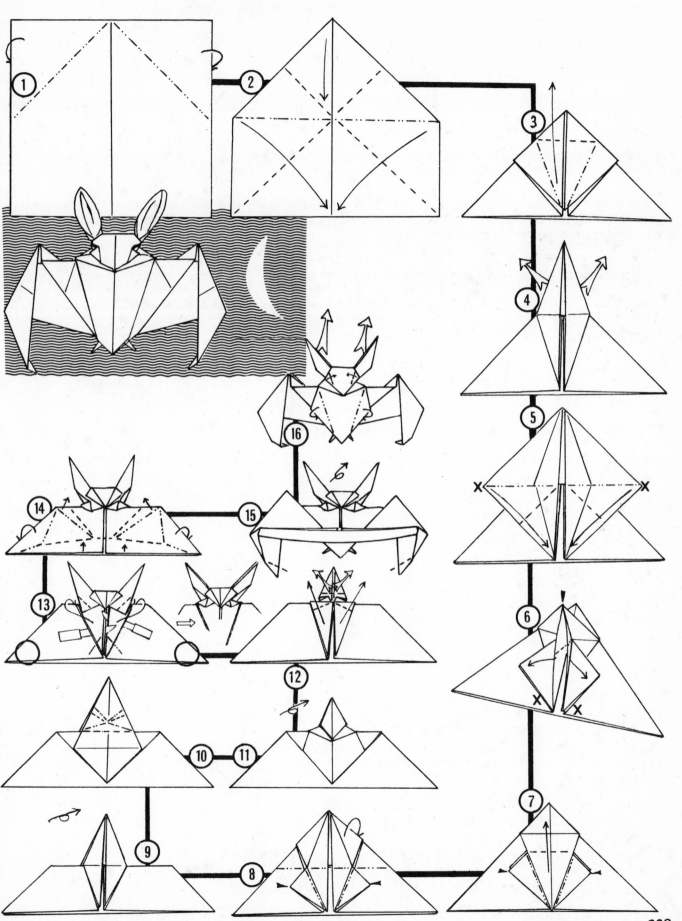

239

RHOADS'S LLAMA

Origin: *America*. George Rhoads.

Here we make use of a very unusual base, which is, in fact, two-and-a-half Bird Bases. Once you have mastered the art of making this base, you will realise that it has all sorts of possibilities.
Use a piece of paper cut in the shape illustrated—two squares, joined by an equilateral triangle. Use ruler, pencil and scissors.

1. Mountain-fold and Valley-fold the triangle in the middle.
2. Squash-fold the upright flap.
3. Petal-fold the Squash Fold.
4. Valley-fold the model in half over to the left.
5. Valley-fold the flap to the right.
6. Squash-fold the flap indicated.
7. Petal-fold the Squash Fold.
8. Repeat these folds with the other square.
9. Enlarged view of the result. Squash-fold the large flap marked. The arrows indicate how you divide up the flaps in equal numbers on each side.
10. The Squash Fold in progress.
11. The result. Squash-fold the large portion indicated.
12. You should now have a base like this (even if you have had a great struggle to arrive at it!). Valley-fold the front and back flaps upwards.
13. Valley-fold the top flap over to the left. Fold a Rabbit's Ear with the lower flap. Repeat top and bottom with the similar flaps behind.
14. Reverse-fold the head portion at the top. Fold a Rabbit's Ear with Mountain Folds with the lower flap, and repeat behind.

Continued overleaf

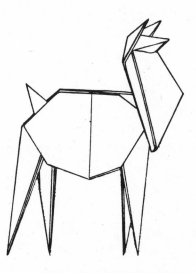

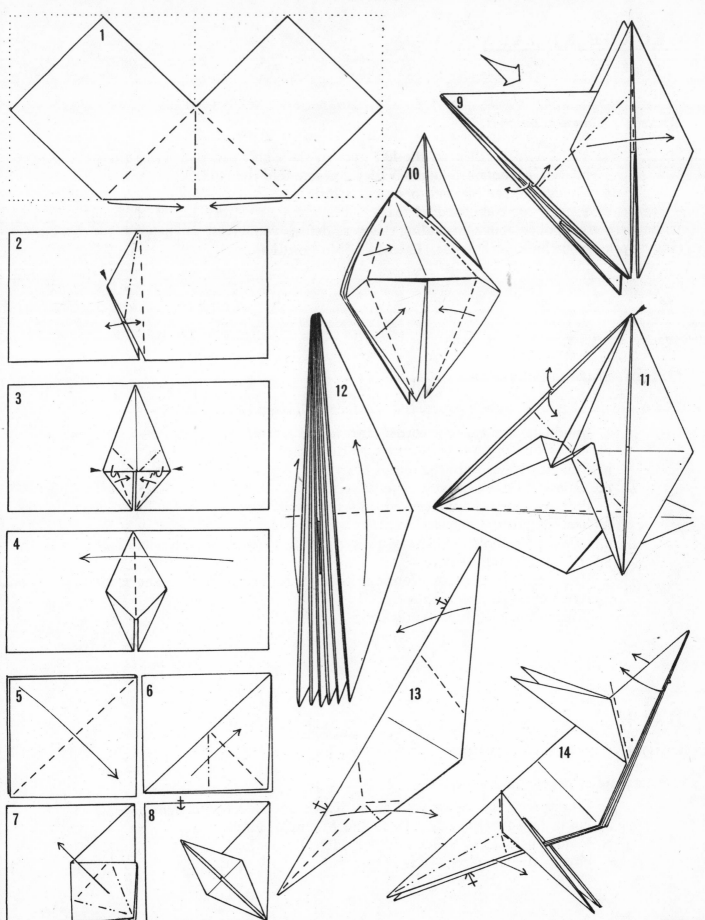

Rhoads's Llama (*continued*)

15. Valley-fold the flap on the left over to the right, and tuck in to the neck. Repeat behind. Mountain-fold and Valley Reverse-fold the tail.
16. Valley-fold the ears and open out a little.
    Finally, the completed Llama.

If the method described above for folding this base defeats you, crease the paper as for the Turkey (*Page* 244), but include the triangle. Then fold into position.

WATER LILY

Origin: *Japan*. Traditional.

Use a square of pink or yellow paper, that has been Blintzed (*Page* 19).

1. Mountain-fold the four corner flaps to the centre.
2. Valley-fold the four corner flaps to the centre.
3. Enlarged view. Turn the model over.
4. Valley-fold the four corners to the centre.
5. Pull the flaps from underneath to form petals. You will have to open up to do this. See Fig. 6 for the result.
6. One petal complete. Shape by pressing your fingers into each petal. Repeat with the other flaps, and turn over.
7. View from underneath. Continue folding the flaps round to the front until three layers of petals are complete.
    Finally, the completed Water Lily.

BOX

Origin: *Japan*. Traditional.

Use a square of paper that has been Blintzed.

1. Crease along the Valley Fold marks. Open out the left and right flaps.
2. Form the box with Valley Folds and Mountain Folds.
3. Mountain-fold and Valley-fold the sides into the box.
    Finally, the completed Box.

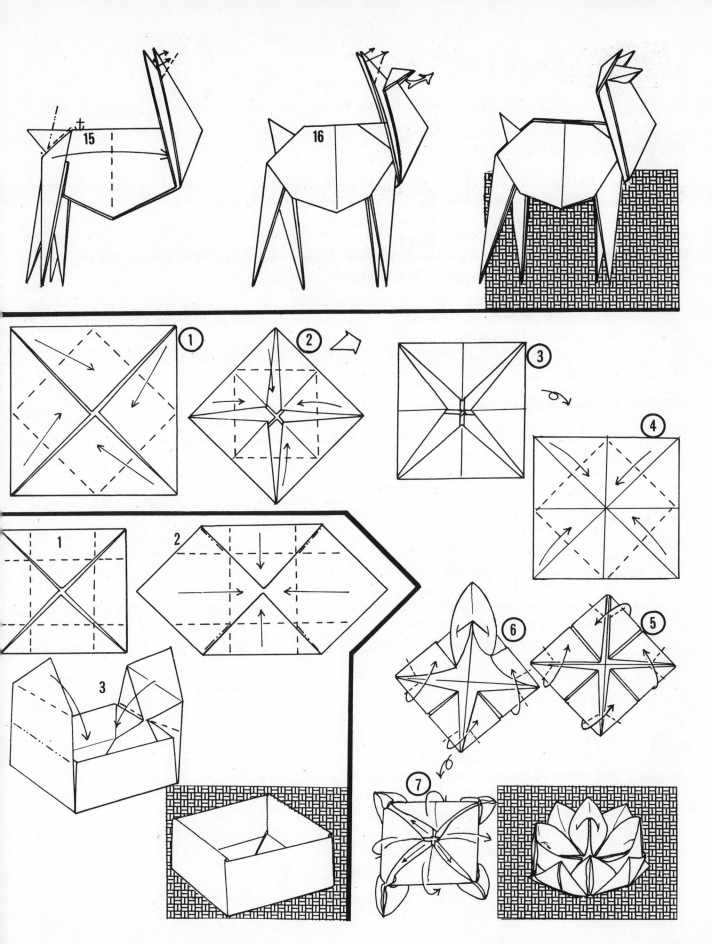

15

16

SLEEPING BAT

Origin: *America*. George Rhoads.

An effective variation of Rhoads's Bat (*Page* 238). In this model, it is not necessary to cut the legs.

Use a square of paper, black or brown on one side. Begin with Fold 14 of Rhoad's Bat. If the legs are left uncut, a flap will occupy the area inside the dotted lines.

14. Valley-fold centre flaps to left and right.
15. Mountain-fold the two corner flaps. Now Mountain-fold the two large flaps (*left and right*) under.
16. Petal-fold the back as marked. Tuck the resulting top of the flap into the neck.
17. Valley-fold the tips of the wings and then the little side flaps. Turn the model over in the direction indicated.
    Finally, the completed Sleeping Bat.

TURKEY

Origin: *America*. George Rhoads.

This is made from a double Bird Base.

Use a rectangle of paper in the proportions of 2 to 1. Begin by folding a Bird Base on each half of the rectangle and then unfold.

1. Crease carefully along the marked lines and then refold to arrive at the base illustrated in 2. The letters are for your convenience.
2. The base almost flattened. When flat, turn over to the left.
3. Mountain-fold front and back the two flaps indicated. Swing the model into position 4.
4. Reverse-fold legs A and C. Squash-fold wing, front right. Repeat with the similar flap behind. Note the eccentric angles.
5. Reverse-fold the neck. Mountain-fold the flaps on the leg and repeat behind.
6. Reverse-fold the head. Reverse-fold the legs in front and behind. Reverse-fold the tail. Watch the middle part of this flap.
7. Reverse-fold the beak. Reverse-fold legs in front and behind.
   Finally, the completed Turkey.

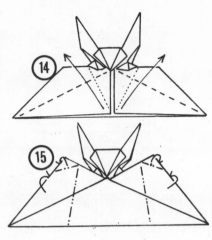

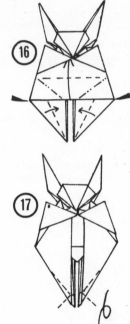

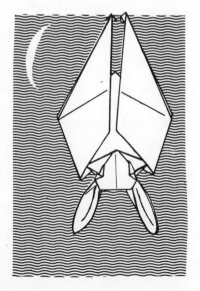

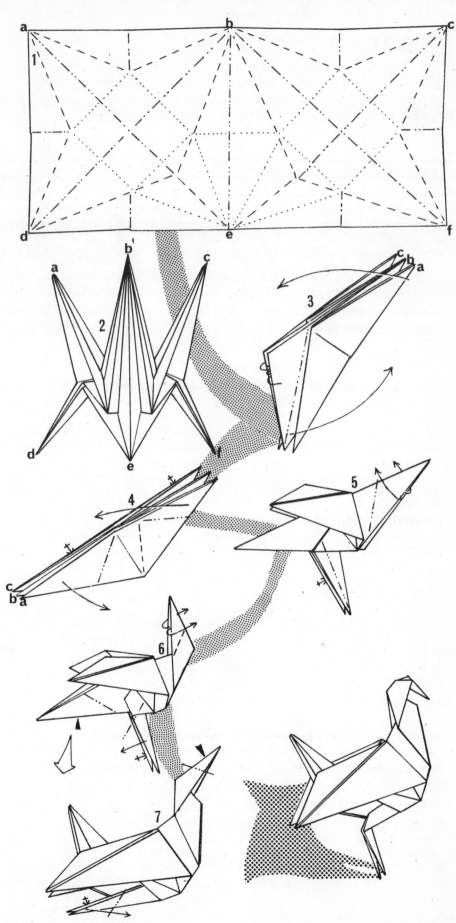

BIBLIOGRAPHY

The best Western publications on origami are those of Harbin, Kenneway, and Randlett; the best Japanese works are those of Nakano, Uchiyama and Yoshizawa.

Harbin, Robert

Paper Magic 1971 impression, John Maxfield Limited, 9 The Broadway, Mill Hill, London, NW7 3LN. American edition: Charles Brandford, Newton Center, Massachusetts. This book, illustrated by Rolf Harris, contains more than one hundred folds and is ideal for the beginner.

Origami: The Art of Paper Folding 1968, The English Universities Press Ltd, London. American edition: 1969 (paperback) Funk and Wagnalls, New York. Models old and new in pocket format.

More Origami 1971, Hodder Paperbacks, London. This sequel to *Origami* presents distinguished contributions by contemporary folders along with traditional models.

Kenneway, Eric

Simple Origami 1970, Dryad Press, Leicester. Splendid models by the author, with fine contributions by Mooser and Yoshizawa.

Randlett, Samuel

The Art of Origami: Paper Folding, Traditional and Modern 1961, E. P. Dutton & Co., Inc., New York. British edition: 1963, Faber and Faber, London. Fifty-seven models, many of them by the author, along with essays on origami history, teaching and creation. Jean Randlett's illustrations are superb.

The Best of Origami: New Models by Contemporary Folders 1963, E. P. Dutton & Co., Inc., New York. Sixty-seven models by fourteen of the world's leading folders, with illustrations by Jean Randlett. This book is an absolute must. The figures are quite outstanding, and the material cannot be found elsewhere. Highly recommended.

Folding Money, Volume 2 1968, Magic, Inc., 5082 N. Lincoln Ave., Chicago, Illinois 60625. Victor Frenkil's alphabet from dollar bills, with examples of words and linked initials from bills, and origami by Robert Neale, Neal Elias and John Nordquist.

Bunny Bill 1964, Magic, Inc., 5082 N. Lincoln Avenue, Chicago, Illinois 60625. Robert Neale's brilliant action model—a bill folded into a rabbit that pops out of a hat—illustrated by Jean Randlett.

The Flapping Bird: An Origami Monthly Published at $6.00 a year by Jay Marshall, 5082 N. Lincoln Ave., Chicago, Illinois 60625. New works by the finest creative folders.

Nakano, Dokuohtei

Correspondence Course of Origami 1970, Dokuohtei Nakano Origami Institute, 32-6, Kamikitazawa 3-chome, Setagaya-ku, Tokyo, 156, Japan. The twelve lessons of this course comprise a monumental textbook of the author's advanced approach to origami; some 250 original animals, birds, insects, reptiles, and human figures of high quality are developed with great technical power from his system of basic folds. The course is in English and is beautifully drawn; finished models, photographs and paper are included. Most impressive, and strongly recommended as a worthwhile investment.

Uchiyama, Koshio

Origami 1962, Kokudosha, Takata Toyokawa Cho, Bunkyo-ku, Tokyo, Japan. A major work, concerned in part with cut-and-fold origami; there are many fine uncut models. Mr Uchiyama's chart of the fundamental crease-patterns in basic folds repays study.

Origami Asobi (Origami Play) 1967, Kokudosha, Takata Toyokawa Cho, Bunkyo-ku, Tokyo, Japan. Twenty-seven imaginative figures by the author.

Yoshizawa, Akira

Origami Dokuhon I (Creative Origami) 1967, Kamakura Shobo Co., Ltd., 21 Ichigaya-Sanaicho, Shinjuku-ku, Tokyo, Japan. This masterpiece is now published in a larger format, with an English translation included. There are over sixty superlative models, each of which shows the author's genius. Mr Yoshizawa has produced several other beautiful origami books, including *Origami Ahon* and *Origami Tanoshi*, which may be ordered directly from Akira Yoshizawa, International Origami Center, P. O. Box 3, Ogikubo, Tokyo, Japan.

The following books are also worth investigating:

Arnstein, Bennett

Origami Polyhedra: How to Make Three-Dimensional Geometric Models 1968, Exposition Press, 386 Park Avenue South, New York, N. Y. 10016. Origami bases taped together to produce decorative three-dimensional solids.

Cerceda, Adolfo

Folding Money (Volume 1) 1963, Magic, Inc., 5082 N. Lincoln Ave., Chicago, Illinois 60625. Eight dollar-bill folds explained by the eminent Argentine folder.

Honda, Isao

The World of Origami 1965, Japan Publications Trading Co., 1255 Howard Street, San Francisco, California 94103. In this general summary of the editor's previous compilations, the Japanese tradition is presented along with coarsened versions of models by Akira Yoshizawa.

Kasahara, Kunihiko

Creative Origami 1968, Japan Publications Inc., Tokyo; distributed by Japan Publications Trading Co., 1255 Howard Street, San Francisco, California 94103. Over one hundred figures, mostly in close imitation of Yoshizawa.

Kawai, Toyoaki

Origami 1970, Hoikusha Publishing Co., Ltd., 20, 1-chome, Uchikyuhoji-machi, Higashi-ku, Osaka 540, Japan. A small book notable for its color photographs of models.

Lewis, Shari, and Oppenheimer, Lillian

Folding Paper Puppets 1962, Stein and Day, New York. Fourteen simple action models, and a transcript of an origami lesson given by Lillian Oppenheimer.

Folding Paper Toys 1963, Stein and Day, New York. Twenty-one models: boats, gliders, puppets, action toys, furniture.

Folding Paper Masks 1965, E. P. Dutton & Co., Inc., New York. Twenty-one masks by Giuseppe Baggi.

Mander, Jerry; Dippel, George; and Gossage, Howard

The Great International Paper Airplane Book 1967, Simon and Schuster, New York. A basic reference book on the subject.

Sakade, Florence

Origami, volumes 1, 2 and 3 1957, 1958, 1959, Charles E. Tuttle Company, Rutland, Vermont. Each volume contains about sixteen models from the Japanese tradition.

Sakoda, James Minoru

Modern Origami 1969, Simon and Schuster, New York. Over fifty new models in the author's highly individual style.

Soong, Maying

The Art of Chinese Paper Folding for Young and Old 1948, Harcourt, Brace and Co., New York. A clear explanation of the Chinese tradition.

Takahama, Toshie

Creative Life With Creative Origami Makō-sha Publishing Co., Ltd., 14-6, Hongo 4-chome, Bunkyo-ku, Tokyo, Japan. Worthwhile figures of medium difficulty, beautifully illustrated. (Toshie Takahama is the leader of a group of folders in Tokyo. Her address is 24-1, Matsunoki 3-chome, Suginami-ku, Tokyo.)

van Breda, Aart

Paper Folding and Modelling 1965, Faber and Faber, London. Good simple models.

These and other books on origami can be obtained from

The Origami Center, 71 West 11th Street, New York 10011.

John Maxfield Ltd., 9 The Broadway, Mill Hill, London NW7 3LN.

INDEX